# THE LEARNING HABIT

A Groundbreaking Approach to
Homework and Parenting That Helps Our Children
Succeed in School and Life

**Stephanie Donaldson-Pressman**

**Rebecca Jackson**

**Dr. Robert M. Pressman**

A PERIGEE BOOK

A PERIGEE BOOK
Published by the Penguin Group
Penguin Group (USA) LLC
375 Hudson Street, New York, New York 10014

USA • Canada • UK • Ireland • Australia • New Zealand • India • South Africa • China

penguin.com

A Penguin Random House Company

Library of Congress Cataloging-in-Publication Data

Donaldson-Pressman, Stephanie.
The learning habit : a groundbreaking approach to homework and parenting that
helps our children succeed in school and life / Stephanie Donaldson-Pressman,
Rebecca Jackson, Robert Pressman.
p. cm.
ISBN 978-0-399-16711-9 (paperback)
1. Homework. 2. Study skills. 3. Parenting. 4. Families.
I. Jackson, Rebecca (Rebecca P.) II. Pressman, Robert M. III. Title.
LB1048.D66 2014
371.30281—dc23 2014011124

First edition: September 2014

PRINTED IN THE UNITED STATES OF AMERICA

10 9 8 7 6 5 4 3 2 1

Text design by Laura K. Corless

For our dear friend, Richard

# CONTENTS

# INTRODUCTION

This book is written by three researchers who are also parents. The impetus for our work and our research is our unwavering belief that parenting is our most important job. While being parents provided the motivation for this book, our other jobs provided the material. We are all clinicians who work with children and families.

There is something else about this book that makes it unique: It is based on the largest survey of family routines ever conducted. The Learning Habit Studies were a 3-year project, which involved both traditional paper research studies, interviews, and a groundbreaking online research study that surveyed nearly 50,000 parents in all 50 U.S. states. Conducted in the fall of 2013, the findings are both conclusive and provocative. The recommendations we make are rooted in science, clinical experience, and parent and teacher interviews.

Stephanie Donaldson-Pressman is the clinical director of the New England Center for Pediatric Psychology (NECPP) and a bestselling author; she works with parents and children, both independently and in groups. Rebecca Jackson's work as a psychometrist involves testing children for learning disabilities, cognitive deficits, and psychological disorders. Because her overstuffed suitcase on wheels is brimming with all kinds of fascinating tests and gadgets, her children refer to her as "the kid detective." Dr. Robert M. Pressman is the research director of the NECPP. He was the lead researcher for our three collaborative studies, conducted with NECPP, Brown University's Alpert Medical School, and Children's National Medical Center; Rhode Island College's Psychology Department also participated in the first two studies. The findings from these studies provided significant new data about the habits, routines, and challenges of families living in this digital age. As a clinical psychologist, Dr. Pressman also works with children and their families.

We are all trained observers, whose jobs and habits are to write about what we see. This book is the result of not only research studies but hundreds of interviews and thousands of hours of clinical observation.

## WHAT'S HAPPENING IN OUR HOUSE?

Over the last few years, we have seen dramatic changes in the educational landscape. Homework, once considered an adjunct to classroom teaching, has become a central piece of the educational process—and an important component of students' grades. The integration of technology and homework, via online teaching tools and textbooks, has further complicated the process, as the line between *educational* and *recreational* media consumption becomes increasingly blurred. More and more "nonessential" school programs are being cut. The very activities that enriched our lives and provided us with opportunities in athletics and the arts are being eliminated. Teachers are being forced to teach to the (mandated) tests rather than challenging their students, stimulating their thinking, or creating pride in simply learning something new. Brightly colored textbooks and teaching manuals filled with illustrations have become digitalized; while this sounds exciting in theory, it often translates into nondescript black-and-white photocopies of the material being used in classrooms and sent home in the form of worksheets—so that all students can participate. Despite the focus on mandated tests, we are graduating children who lack the skills to survive, much less thrive, in college. Once first in the world in college-graduated students, the United States is now 10th.[1] Almost *half* of our students who enter college do not graduate.[2] They simply do not have the confidence, study skills, or learning habits necessary to handle the work and challenges independent collegiate living entails.

Technology has also become an ever-present influence on our lives. Our children have the benefit of instant communication and easy access to information. That is a wonderful thing—except when it's not. What we observe are children who can relate to screens with ease, but have few social or communication skills; kids who can play video games for hours, but can't read a book for longer than 10 minutes; kids who can text and tweet, but can't focus on a challenging math problem or make sense of a few paragraphs in a history book. "It's boring!" they cry. And compared to the instant gratification of video games, texting, and social media, it probably is.

Homework used to take 30 minutes—at most—to create special projects, finish up a few math problems, or prepare for a spelling test. Kids would simply scan the chapters and answer the assigned questions during study hall or before class—fiendishly scribbling before the teacher walked in! Not anymore. Today, homework can take several (stressful) hours a day.[3] Digital homework assignments and online research and tutorials are now the norm; yet parents are given little to no guidance on how to help their children integrate these tools into their homework routines for maximum benefit. Love it or hate it, technology-based homework is here to stay.

The focus on test scores has also made *achievement* the most important thing. As a result, we are producing a nation of kids who are afraid to make mistakes, try new things, and even ask questions in class—because they may be perceived as stupid. If you can't be an achiever, if you can't be the best, then it's better not to try—because you might fail.

# ARE WE THE ONLY ONES?

We wanted to find out if what *we* were seeing was universal. We wanted to study families who have met these challenges and produced children who graduated from college in four years—rather than five or six or never. Why were their kids academically successful? What did they do to give their children such terrific social skills, emotional health, and the confidence that allowed them to communicate so clearly and assertively? We joined forces with other scientists, and conducted three separate learning habit research studies to find out.

In one of the most comprehensive psychosocial research studies of all time on this topic, nearly 50,000 parents from 4,600 cities across the nation took time out of their busy lives to offer us a candid look at their daily habits and routines. Since this study was offered online and participants were guaranteed anonymity, something interesting happened: Moms and dads felt comfortable being completely honest about their children's grades, social interactions with peers, discipline and behavioral issues at home and at school, and, yes, about their media use.

Of course, collaborating, analyzing, and cross-correlating such a massive amount of data was a daunting task. We had to compare a multitude of diverse topics, to see if there were links between factors like sports and communication skills, grades and social involvement, bedtimes and personality traits, and parenting style and independence. Eventually, however, we were able to find the links—connect the dots—and identify habits used by those families whose children were experiencing academic, emotional, and social success. Once identified, these habits were then combined with parenting techniques that can incorporate these *best practices*.

# A NEW CONCEPT OF HOMEWORK

The goal of this book is to help parents understand and facilitate the habits and routines that help children learn. This can often mean synthesizing seemingly unrelated tasks. For example, you might not think that communication skills are part of the homework process, but you will after reading this book. So are sports and social skills. Sleep is of the highest importance. What about cell phone use, video games, and computers? You guessed it—media use is an important part of homework and building successful learning habits.

Prepare to think of homework from an *entirely* new perspective. Welcome to homework for Generation M².

"Generation M²," that's how our school-age children were described at a forum attended by the chairman of the Federal Communications Commission (FCC), media executives, and child development experts. In their report, "Generation M²: Media in the Lives of 8- to 18-Year-Olds,"[4] the Kaiser Family Foundation presented their findings and concerns relative to entertainment media overuse by 8- to 18-year-olds. Our own findings concur with theirs: This generation's media use is, indeed, exponential. It has an impact on virtually all aspects of family life and *homework*.

This book neither promotes nor condemns either media use or academic homework; both are here to stay. However, the parents we interviewed said they were confused, angry, and overwhelmed by the stresses their children have to manage—especially those presented by homework. Karen, one of the parents we interviewed, said it took her eight-year-old, third-grade daughter *more than one hour*, every night, to do her online math homework—frequently resulting in tears of frustration. Even more upsetting to Karen was her concern that her child wasn't really learning or understanding the *process* of doing theoretically based math problems—a concern voiced by numerous parents with children in that class.

"It feels wrong," Karen declared. "It feels crazy! But where do you draw the line?"

Parents want answers. They want to know where to draw the line to restore sanity to their everyday lives. In this culture of rapid technological advancement, educational changes, and social instability, parents feel a disturbing lack of balance. There's a little voice in the back of their minds whispering, "Something's not right." And it isn't. That's why we want to start the conversation about *learning habits* for Generation M$^2$ and how we, as parents, can reboot our parenting style to help our children succeed.

Our overarching purpose is to provide answers and techniques that parents can use—right now, today—to make their families run more smoothly and increase their children's chances of success, regardless of the current curriculum used at their children's school. To do that, we have taken a lot of literary license. For example, we use the words *I*, *we*, and *the therapist* interchangeably, for readability and interest. We also know the rules about pronouns (one of us was an English teacher), and we frequently ignore them, using the plural pronoun *they* in place of the phrase *he or she* or the awkward *s/he* because the latter are annoying to read. We sincerely beg your indulgence and forgiveness—we'd rather be readable than rigidly correct.

We also use many stories. People like stories, they relate to stories, they learn from stories. These are true stories; we have altered names and other identifying information to preserve the confidentiality of our patients and interviewees. You will likely see yourself and your kids within these pages; no worries—we haven't been secretly spying on you. There is a universality of parental experience that transcends socioeconomic status, gender, educational level, and job description. Some of these stories are our own, from our personal parenting experiences. Whether shared to illustrate a positive or a negative technique or experience, we use them without apology.

Finally, we urge you to take the series of family challenges outlined in Chapter Eleven. These are fun, interesting techniques and games that your family can do, and they take *just 24 hours per challenge*. Use them to enhance your parenting skills and create some learning habits for your kids—and, perhaps, for you. They're thought provoking, often highly amusing, and a great way to involve everyone in the family.

Watch other parents; notice if they're learners or if they're stuck. The learners will be the (quietly) successful and interesting ones, the ones with nothing to prove, the ones who are excited about what they do; they are the ones who not only listen—but hear. It's that openness to learning that draws others to them. That's the *best* thing you can do for your children: give them enduring learning habits. The ability to learn is what will help them succeed in life.

# PART I

Lifelong Learning Starts at Home

# CHAPTER ONE

# Connecting the Disconnect: The Learning Habit Studies

*When you know better, you do better.*
—Maya Angelou, author, poet, and recipient
of the Presidential Medal of Freedom

Growing up, I always enjoyed shopping for back-to-school supplies. Although my mother took us shopping for clothing, the official role of "Trapper Keeper and pencil purchaser" was delegated to my father. I remember sharpening all of my newly purchased pencils before the first day of school, as if at any moment I might suddenly need 24 sharpened pencils. To this day, a row of neatly sharpened pencils evokes nostalgic back-to-school memories; memories my youngest child may not share. Within the next few years, asking a child to sharpen their pencil will be as obsolete as rolling down the car window. According to the Common Core State Standards Initiative, keyboards will soon replace pencils.[1]

The fact is, the world in which our children are being educated and socialized and will eventually become employed and self-sufficient is vastly different from our own. We need to understand and appreciate those differences, so we can adapt the way we think about learning. We need to prepare our children for academic and financial success by instilling *in our homes* a series of habits they can carry with them for the rest of their lives. To accomplish this, we'll be placing a very different spin on the word *homework*.

It's a challenge, as school assignments continue to morph every year. My eleventh grader has a manual textbook that is similar to the ones I had in school. His report card still comes home on a piece of paper in his backpack. My kindergartner has digital homework assignments, and I'm required to have a login and password to check her online report card. Yet they both attend school in the same school district. Many of these homework habits and tools are linked to various forms of media consumption that, if not properly managed, can work against our children. Too much information from too many sources can result in more confusion than clarity. But we can't ignore it: This is how Generation $M^2$ is being taught—through media and online educational tools. This book will teach you how to successfully synthesize all this wondrous new technology into our children's lives, so it helps—rather than hinders—learning.

> *It's a new dawn, it's a new day, it's a new life for me, and I'm feeling good.*
>
> —Nina Simone, singer, songwriter, pianist, arranger, and civil rights activist

Although Nina Simone's lyrics embody the spirit we hope our children will take with them into adulthood, optimism may not be enough. Our children live in a world of changing educational opportunities, dwindling enrichment programs, world economic volatility, and the specter of unemployment. There is a growing gulf between the life a child has in their parent's home and the life they can expect as adults. Although few of us would consider ourselves wealthy, most were able to get decent jobs after we graduated from college, some without even going to college. Others went on to graduate school, which further increased their job opportunities and potential income. Our generation was able to achieve a modicum of success through a combination of hard work and a decent economy.

For Generation $M^2$, success is going to be much harder to achieve.

Being accepted to, paying for, and graduating from college is a daunting task. According to Zinch, a website designed to help colleges and students connect, financial factors are the primary focus for parents of college-bound teens.[2] In a recent survey, the #1 concern of parents was "University Fees/Student Debt," a true sign of our changing economy.[3]

These aren't the only new challenges our children will encounter. When we were teenagers, our parents' primary concerns were teen pregnancy, smoking, drinking, and recreational drugs. Today's parents are faced with all of that, plus random acts of violence, media addiction, Internet-enabled sexual contact, and few to no extracurricular activities. If your child has a cell phone, computer, or tablet, their friends (or anyone else) can reach them at any time, day or night. It's not surprising that since 2012, *bullying* and *sexting* have topped the list of parental concerns for school-age children.[4]

Despite all these new challenges, our goals have remained consistent. We want to raise happy, successful, confident children. We want them to grow up, go to college, and support themselves. We want them to own a home and raise a family. It's called the American Dream!

Unfortunately, there seems to be little correlation between our goals and what we're doing to help our children achieve those goals. Parents and educators are in agreement that children need to attend college to compete in the workforce. Parents are also keenly aware of the inflated cost of a higher education. If it's so expensive to *attend* college, it makes sense that we, as parents, intensify our efforts to ensure our children graduate from high school with the skills and learning habits they need to *complete* college. The problem, we discovered, is that parents aren't taught what habits and skills to focus on.

In 2013, we surveyed parents of high school seniors and asked this seemingly innocuous question: "What have you done to prepare your child to graduate from college in four years?" Most parents couldn't come up with a clear answer. A few chuckled and replied, "I told them I'd stop paying for it." (We laughed, until we imagined adding a fifth year's tuition to the bill.) Only one in twenty parents connected college completion with ensuring their children had the skills to balance the academic demands and distracting social pressures of collegiate life.

Nearly 60% of Americans have attended *some* college; they just can't seem to *complete* college.[5] Yet, there has been a startling lack of information regarding the skills children need to do so. One theory put forward was that students who don't have the necessary learning habits panic, then quit, because the experience is too threatening.[6]

These are *smart* kids we're talking about. Kids with high IQs. For years, psychologists believed IQ was the ultimate predictor of academic success, so it stands to reason that a child with a higher IQ will be successful in college, doesn't it? Not necessarily. We now know that *goal setting (motivation)* and *self-worth (emotional integrity)* are far better predictors of success.[7] Our children don't lack intelligence; they simply haven't acquired the habits they need to successfully deal with the pressures, demands, and relative freedom, of college.

## THE HUDSON FAMILY

Take, for example, my childhood neighbors, the Hudsons. Susie was one of four Hudson children. We were best friends—and fierce competitors. When we were younger, I would regularly get better grades than she did, a fact that pleased me immensely. Susie was not a gifted child, but she was a damned hard worker. Susie had an older brother, Adam. Even Susie couldn't deny that Adam wasn't the brightest bulb in the socket. In case you think I'm being mean, I saw Adam eat a scratch-and-sniff trading card when he was 14 years old, because he thought it would, and I quote, "Taste like it smelled."

Unlike Susie, Adam was in remedial classes and remained there throughout high school. But both Susie and Adam were accepted to state universities, worked diligently, and graduated in four years.

They studied for months to prepare for the MCATs and LSATs, respectively, and scored high enough to get into graduate schools. Where are they now? Susie is Dr. Susan Spargo, a pediatrician, which came as no surprise to me, as she had stated her intention to go to medical school our senior year of high school.

Here's the shocker: Adam is now a lawyer at one of the top law firms in Boston. Does it get under my skin to think that "scratch-and-sniff" Adam makes a hefty six-figure salary?

You betcha!

## The Secret Behind His Success

As researchers and trained observers, we have spent our careers watching children like Adam flourish, while supposedly smarter children failed. Did his parents know something we don't know? Did his parents do something we're not doing? In both our clinical practice and research, we have encountered highly motivated parents who genuinely want to do the right things to help their children; they just aren't sure what those *right things* are. Here are some of the concerns expressed by parents in our practice:

> I just feel like he could do more. I know parents always say that, but it's true.

> There's so much competitive pressure—from the school and from other parents. It infuriates me! I wish I didn't care, but I do.

> Math used to take my third grader 10 minutes, and then her school started using an online program for math homework. Now, I have to sit with her at the computer for 70 minutes! Is that normal?

Parents are frustrated by their inability to get clear information about the *right things* the Hudson family has apparently figured out. What learning habits and behaviors contribute to a child's educational success or failure? Why do some children succeed, despite enormous obstacles, while others (from seemingly more advantaged backgrounds) quit at the drop of a hat? Was it genes, parenting style, learning habits, or all of the above? These are questions that have baffled educational experts and research psychologists for decades—until now.

## THE LEARNING HABIT STUDIES

The initial purpose of the Learning Habit Studies, which took place over three years, was to clarify which learning habits led to a child's educational success or failure, and focused primarily on homework routines. It was conducted by the collaborative team of Brown University's Alpert Medical School, Children's National Medical Center, Rhode Island College's Psychology Department, and NECPP, for which Dr. Robert M. Pressman was the lead researcher.

The first study was a traditional survey of more than 1,000 participants in 12 pediatric offices. The survey forms were available in both English and Spanish for parents of children in grades K–12. The survey focused on the relationship of homework to family habits and stress. Surprisingly, the data showed most parents didn't object to homework at all; they accepted it as a necessary part of their children's education. The results also exposed a strong correlation between a child's media use and their grades.

The research team then replicated the study to see if the results were consistent. The first study was conducted in the spring of 2011. The same study was repeated in the fall of 2011. The results were practically identical. For the first time, researchers now had *proof* that media habits in children had a clear impact on their academic success. The importance of homework, and how both parents and children dealt with it, was proven to have a pervasive influence, not only on children's grades, but also on their achievement in nonacademic areas as well.

But the research team needed more information to identify the *specific* habits that promoted a child's ability to learn. We didn't want to focus exclusively on learning as it related to academic success. As clinicians and researchers, we wanted to find out if the learning process affected a child's emotional development and social adjustment—and vice versa. We wanted to discover how children learn to make friends, communicate clearly, set and achieve goals, and develop emotional and psychological balance. Are the habits that build social adjustment, for instance, the same habits that promote academic success? It seemed obvious that learning habits were affected by a plethora of factors, but which ones in particular? The most significant, we hypothesized, was family environment and parenting style, but we didn't know for sure.

In the summer of 2012, Dr. Pressman proposed that the research team develop an *online* study of family habits that would explore these topics. Then on December 14, 2012, a 20-year-old man fatally shot twenty children and six adult staff members at Sandy Hook Elementary School in Newtown, Connecticut. Not since the attacks on the Twin Towers had our nation been so traumatized. This mass murder was no terrorist plot; it was the singular act of a young man who lived in that town and had attended those schools. While frightened parents searched for answers, portraits of the brave adults who tried to shield the children from harm began to emerge. We mourned their loss and wept for their families. We wanted answers. How could this happen?

Slowly but surely, a portrait emerged of a loner, an awkward kid who never talked, who wore the same clothes day after day, who was a wiz at computers, and who spent his time in the basement playing single-shooter video games.[8] Suddenly, an entire nation was focused on media use and mental health. Should certain things have been noticed? Were there actions that could have been taken to prevent this horrific event? The decision to incorporate emotional and social adjustment into the Learning Habit Study was now becoming more important than ever. We needed unimpeachable evidence about the specific habits that parents could incorporate into their daily lives to help their children develop emotionally, socially, *and* academically.

Thus, the third Learning Habit Study was conceived. The gestation was, in itself, a learning process.

Developing the online survey, however, was a challenge. We needed a large database of questions if so many variables were to be included, but the survey had to be short enough that people would answer it.

Home schooling needed to be incorporated as well, which necessitated design changes; home schooling vocabulary, the way comprehension and mastery are measured, and even the concept of grade levels are completely different from traditional schools.

Question content was another obstacle. This was not a one-size-fits-all survey. The information relevant to parents of first graders was often irrelevant to parents of middle or high schoolers. Finally, the study needed to cast a pretty wide net to glean the most powerful and useful information.

A study this large could not be accomplished through traditional means. We have all seen online surveys (including those annoying ones that pop-up randomly on our screens), but the efficacy of running a scientific research study online had yet to be tested. The task was simply so complex that no other research team had attempted it. Parents looking to connect the dots and gain answers to questions on media use, for example, have come up empty-handed. The research model needed to cross-correlate data on a significantly wide range of topics and to use unimpeachable statistical analysis was not available. The team forged ahead, anyway.

We needed to be certain of three things:

✓ The information we were seeking addressed genuine concerns.

✓ We were asking the right questions, the right way.

✓ We could get the word out to enough parents willing to take the survey.

The development of the research study model and the statistical model was a huge hurdle. The research team was undertaking a unique project and it took not only out-of-the-box thinking but also the involvement of some extremely creative minds to ultimately give birth to this baby.

Some incredible media partners signed on to help promote the survey: the *Huffington Post*, WebMD, *Parents* magazine, the National PTA, AOL, and influential bloggers such as Lisa Belkin (*Parentry*) and *5 Minutes for Mom*. These organizations and bloggers reviewed the survey and gave their feedback during its beta testing. They wrote articles to introduce the survey to their audiences, to make it easily available, and then to publish the results. Without them, it simply would not have been possible to attract such an impressive number of respondents.

During the fall of 2013, nearly 50,000 families took part in the groundbreaking online study called the Learning Habit Study. This study has given parents and researchers alike valuable insights into the family routines that help a child learn and grow. When the largest study on family routines in the history of the United States is conducted, you unearth some interesting findings.

The way academic homework is handled, for example, is as essential as the family dinner. In fact, several other evening and after-school activities had the exact same impact on academic grades as schoolwork. These activities—skills—are essential in preparing our students for the rigorous standardized testing they will experience in school, and for helping them achieve a well-balanced life. According to our findings, those children whose parents balanced all of these activities equally scored highest in academic performance and emotional well-being. One discovery of the Learning Habit Study was the development of an unusual personality profile dubbed the Loner Profile. Information about this is included in Chapter Three. Our conclusive findings show a disturbing trend about which parents should be aware.

Other results were equally astounding, yet so fundamentally sensible, that they pointed to the universality of a new habit, the *Learning Habit*.

*The Learning Habit* is a combination of parenting style and habit creation. In all of the research, this combination of Empowerment Parenting and Habit Building proved the most effective.

## KNOWLEDGE IS POWER

The material we present in this book is the product not only of our own studies, but of several hundred studies dealing with the merits of homework, learning theory, and family dynamics. In general, we've learned that parents can influence their children's learning habits in two ways:

✓ It all begins with how we interact with our children on a daily basis. Use of a parenting technique known as Empowerment Parenting is the single most effective way to help our children build effective habits. Chapter Two illustrates the Empowerment Parenting technique and provides real-life examples.

✓ The second method involves *creating opportunities* for our children to develop the eight essential learning habits, described in Part II of the book:
  • Media management
  • Academic homework and reading
  • Time management
  • Goal-setting
  • Effective communication
  • Responsible decision-making
  • Concentrated focus
  • Self-reliance

Part III, the final section of the book, includes guidance and games designed for parents ready to take immediate action. The 21

Family Challenges (outlined in Chapter Eleven) break down the eight essential skills into *one-day experiments* that relate to each of those skills. Each challenge requires only a 24-hour commitment! Families are encouraged to take the challenge and then incorporate incremental lifestyle changes, based on what they learned. Families may choose to tackle any of the 24-hour challenges, in any order, to uncover some intriguing information about their habits and discover which of their family's routines may need a tune-up.

## THE POWER TO EMPOWER

Learning Habits are the way children master the skills essential for academic, social, and emotional success. Carefully structured changes in family routines, reward systems, and expectations can result in higher grades, increased self-esteem, and organizational skills that enable children to take on new challenges and persevere. These skills are the backbone of a successful life.

While writing and researching this book, I contacted my old neighbor Susie Hudson. I was so excited to tell her all about our research and the importance of "habits" and "parenting styles." Susie, of course, was nonplussed. "That's exactly what my parents did," she replied.

Oh, well. For the rest of us who weren't so lucky, continue reading. *The Learning Habit* is the end product of three research studies, hundreds of interviews, and thousands of hours of therapeutic experience. We know that the combination of Empowerment Parenting and the building of Learning Habits works, and we want you to know it, too. So, buckle up—we're going to take you on an amazing journey.

# CHAPTER TWO

# How Learning Habits Start: Empowerment Parenting

**A Parenting System Allowing Children to Develop Productive Habits That Continue in the Absence of Parental Cuing, Assistance, or Input**

---

Sow a thought, and you reap an act;
Sow an act, and you reap a habit;
Sow a habit, and you reap a character;
Sow a character, and you reap a destiny.
—*Samuel Smiles, Scottish author and reformer*

## Keys to Empowerment Parenting

» Build habits through rules.
» Empower children through choices.
» Encourage children through effort-based praise.

If you're reading this book, you're probably a parent. You may also be an educator, pediatrician, or child advocate. You understand how difficult life can be for children who are experiencing school-related challenges. Whether the problems are academic, behavioral, or social, children who are not doing well can feel powerless and alone. A huge component of a child's self-esteem depends on what happens in school and in school-related matters, such as homework comprehension and completion, peer relations, and the ability to read. Just as adults need to feel some sense of control over their lives, so do children. Yet, the avenues available for children to exercise control are too often limited to refusal, acting out, or other unhappy behavior. Empowerment Parenting does what the name implies—it gives children the power to make choices about their behavior and to gain control over the direction of their lives. This can help them develop learning habits that will last forever.

## ENCOURAGING HABIT CHANGE

During the winter of 2013, Boston had one of the most severe flu outbreaks in U.S. history. To complicate matters, several strains of stomach virus and whooping cough were also spreading throughout the school system.

In an effort to curb the epidemic, teachers were constantly reminding students to wash their hands. Parents also received several notices about the importance of hand washing. By January 2013, Mayor Thomas M. Menino had declared a public health emergency.

One of the two kindergarten teachers in a Massachusetts elementary school had the most absences that year. "It was awful," she told us. "The stomach flu ripped through my classroom like a tidal wave."

She tried to remind students to wash their hands, and when she did, they would usually comply. However, on the days she didn't ask, the students didn't wash their hands. "They're a group of five- and six-year-olds," she explained. "Hygiene isn't exactly their top priority."

In behavioral terms, the children required their teacher's reminder to "cue" them to wash their hands; if there was no reminder ("cue"), there was no hand washing (behavior/routine).

Cue → Routine

Meanwhile, as pandemonium spread, another kindergarten class-room in the same school maintained nearly perfect attendance. Without realizing it, Mrs. Janet Evans was giving the school administration and scientists around the world valuable information on how to instill lasting habits in children.

Mrs. Evans is a 16-year teaching veteran. Every morning, she begins the day with a classroom meeting. She reviews the day's calendar of events and revises the classroom rules, when necessary.

"How many of your students were absent during the epidemic?" one researcher inquired.

"I think we only had three flu-related absences," she replied. "Two children were on family vacations—luckily for them."

The average classroom absentee total during the 2013 winter was 37 days. Did classroom size have anything to do with it? No. Mrs. Evans had 21 students, the school average. What about length of day? Massachusetts schools have a full day of kindergarten, state-wide.

## THE MILK EXPERIMENT

Mrs. Evans described what would later be dubbed the Milk Experiment. Several years ago when schools and pediatricians started stressing the importance of hand washing for germ prevention, Mrs. Evans implemented a classroom rule that she explained to her students on the first day of school. First, she asked her students to hum the tune "Happy Birthday" out loud. Then, she asked them to hum the tune inside their heads. Next, Mrs. Evans took the class over to the classroom sink and showed them how to lather their hands while humming the tune "Happy Birthday" inside their heads. "Each day, when you return from recess, you will wash your hands," she told them. "Once your hands are washed, you may have your milk. Our classroom rule is 'We wash our hands after recess and then we get milk.'"

Mrs. Evans then described what happened later that day. Only two of her students came in from recess and went straight to the sink and washed their hands. When those students were at the sink washing, Mrs. Evans placed a carton of milk at their assigned seats. Some of the children rushed in from recess and immediately took a seat. They found no milk waiting for them.

"May I have my milk?" one of the students asked.

Mrs. Evans smiled, pointed at the sink, and in a kind voice asked, "What's our milk rule?"

"Oh yeah!" the boy replied, and immediately hopped out of his seat, walked over to the sink, and vigorously washed his hands. When he returned to his desk, he found his milk waiting for him.

Notice that Mrs. Evans did not ask the boy to wash his hands. She did not remind him, nag him, or yell at him. In fact, she never even mentioned the words *wash your hands*. All she did was direct him back to his cue (his empty desk with no milk on it).

Cue → Routine → Reward

This went on for two days, and then something else happened. The children no longer needed the cue. They would walk immediately to the sink after recess without asking for milk. Undoubtedly, the health of everyone in the class benefited from this one simple instruction.

Routine → Reward

Without knowing it, Mrs. Evans's Milk Experiment was a perfect example of *Empowerment Parenting*—teaching her students how to make their *own* choices. The students could choose *not* to wash their hands; that was the *no-milk* choice. They weren't punished if they didn't wash their hands. If they wanted milk, however, they had to *choose* to wash their hands. Mrs. Evans's milk rule and clear, explicit instructions gave her students the freedom to make their own choices.

She empowered her students to create a particular learning habit, by the children's internalizing her instructions and connecting them to their own wants and needs. Because they wanted milk (the reward), they taught themselves to wash their hands (behavior/routine). That's a self-reinforcing system—performing the desired behavior first and then getting the reward; no external cuing required!

In the other classroom, students received milk regardless of whether or not they washed their hands. They were never given a choice, with the opportunity to experience both the responsibility and the reward of their choice. So, they never formed a learning habit. It's that simple.

The researchers also noticed an additional benefit to Mrs. Evans's Milk Experiment: the length of time the students washed their hands, which further contributed to her students' health. Although every student in the school was instructed to wash their hands, Mrs. Evans's students washed their hands 10 seconds longer than the other kindergarten students; an average of 22 seconds—two seconds longer than the Centers for Disease Control and Prevention's (CDC's) guidelines for killing germs.

Did Mrs. Evans tell her students to wash their hands for 20 seconds? No. But apparently children who make a choice to do something out of intrinsic motivation, as opposed to being reminded, do it with more gusto and genuine enjoyment. As Mrs. Evans's students hummed while they washed their hands, the other students rushed through the task, if they did it at all. Two students from the other class actually simulated hand washing (turning on the faucet and placing their hands near the water, but never actually washing them).

At the NECPP, clinicians and researchers have spent decades gathering information on habit formation in children. Dr. Pressman explains why the Milk Experiment was so successful in establishing hand-washing habits:

> Janet Evans used an important behavioral technique. She created a rule that allowed her students to make choices and kept them motivated. Her rule was simple, clear, and, most important, it was self-reinforceable: "First you wash your hands, and then you have your milk." The clearer the choice, the more successful the rule will be.

## EMPOWERING CHILDREN THROUGH HABIT FORMATION

The establishment of sensible household rules is one of the backbones of Empowerment Parenting. It encourages habit formation.

In 2010, researchers at NECPP began studying the impact of household rules on habit formation. They began by examining current patients' charts and looking for patterns. One researcher noted that 20 of the families had children between the ages of 5 and 10 years, with similar bedtime and sleep issues.

"Bedtime issues were a challenge for many families," commented Dr. Pressman. "In some households it took parents several hours to get their children to go to sleep. This was a source of nightly stress for parents, who often found themselves sleep deprived. These children were often observed to be hyperactive and have increased irritability during the daytime."

Upon further review of the patients' charts, all 20 families appeared to have another common characteristic: Their bedtime rule was vague and inconsistent.

**Group A.** This group was not given any specific instructions regarding bedtime. Each family in Group A already had a bedtime rule. The rule for the children was, "Bedtime means I go to bed when I am told to." They were asked to be as consistent as possible with bedtime, and report their results.

It was not surprising that the parents in Group A showed no improvement in getting their children to go to bed. Researchers explained this was because the rule was non-specific, inconsistent, and dependent on the parents' involvement to instruct/cue their child. The parents in Group A couldn't resist engaging in conversation and giving directives to their kids. The parents in Group A remained the *cue*.

**Group B.** The parents in Group B were shown how to make a bedtime rule that would become a learned habit. They were told it would take a few days, but after it was learned, there would be no more bedtime chaos. As a bonus, many of them would likely see a decrease in daytime behavioral problems. The parents in Group B were excited to see results. They were highly motivated!

The rule for Group B had five requirements; it must be:

- ✓ *Clear:* "Bedtime means that you are in your own bed at 7:30 every night."

- ✓ *Realistic:* Ask yourself if the rule can really be followed. The rule must take into consideration the steps that precede bedtime, like bathing and story time. The activities will move from more active (dinner, playing) to less active (bath, story time). If bedtime is set either too early or too late, it's not realistic.

- ✓ *Time oriented:* An exact time is used, for example, "7:30 every night."

✓ *Reinforceable:* All caregivers in the house must agree to stick to the rule. If one parent doesn't abide by the bedtime rule, it will not be reinforceable. After the first few days, it will become self-reinforcing.

✓ *Consistent:* It has to be done exactly the same way every night, so that children know what is going to happen; this is what builds the bedtime habit. To be on the safe side, parents agreed beforehand to be present, in their home, at bedtime for two weeks. However, after four nights the habit was stabilized in all Group B families.

**Group B Statement.** Bedtime means I am in my bed for the night at 7:30.

The parents were instructed to use a *family meeting* to introduce the new rule to their child. Many parents are already familiar with family meetings. For those who aren't, family meetings are where you'll decide on, introduce, and evaluate rules.

## Family Meeting Best Practices

Here are a few tips to keep family meetings short and focused:

» Have an agenda that all caregivers have decided on in advance.

» Be topic specific; one topic is discussed, not several. If a family member brings up another topic of importance to them, it can be scheduled to be addressed at a different family meeting.

» Keep the meeting short, clear, and respectful.

» Family meetings work best when they are regularly scheduled events, usually early in the day and on weekends, when everyone feels relaxed.

*continued . . .*

In a family meeting, parents:

» Talk with their children about the problem or situation that has arisen.
» Introduce the rule designed to resolve it.
» Encourage discussion about how the rules are working.

///////////////////////////////////////////////////////////////////////////////////////////////

As expected, the children in Group B struggled with the new routine the first evening. However, their parents were extremely well prepared and felt empowered to help their children learn this important routine.

When children got out of bed, parents were taught to do the following:

✓ The first time a child gets out of bed and exits their room, ask, "What's our rule?" If they do not respond or if they answer with anything other than the rule, simply state the rule, very pleasantly. "The rule is in bed for the night at 7:30." Gesture toward the darkened bedroom (palm up, pleasant expression on the face).

✓ If the child comes out again, ask, "What's our rule?" If the child does not respond correctly (saying the rule and going back to bed), restate the rule and gesture toward the bedroom (palm up, pleasant expression on the face).

✓ The parents were instructed to move toward the bedroom so the action conveys to the child, "Come with me" not "Go away!" The action includes the child rather than excluding (rejecting) them. If the child correctly says the rule, the parents nod, smile, and gesture toward the bedroom.

✓ If the child comes out of their bedroom *again*, parents were instructed to ask, "What's our rule?" If the child didn't answer the question correctly, the rule was restated: "The rule is in bed for the night at 7:30." Parents were also permitted to gesture toward the child's bedroom but were not permitted to say anything else.

The parents in Group B were not worn down by the bedtime routine. They did not need to negotiate anything with their children. They just asked a question and then used non-verbal prompts. Their children knew exactly what was going to happen every night; they knew what was expected of them, and they did it.

By night four, all 10 Group B children went to bed without any problems.

The routine (the same activities in the same order, repeated every night) and the time (7:30) became the cue, not the parents.

The clearer the choice, the easier the choice is to maintain. Consistency and repetition are the keys to establishing habits.

## EMPOWERING CHILDREN THROUGH CHOICES

Children often feel like they have very few choices in life and are being "ordered around" throughout the day. One of the best ways parents can promote independence in children is through rules. Children are *free to choose* whether or not they want to follow the rule. This is a strange concept for many parents to conceptualize. Think about the children in the bedtime experiment who were in Group B. They were certainly free *not* to follow the bedtime rule. They wouldn't get yelled at or spanked for not doing it. They wouldn't even lose any privileges for not doing it.

They could *choose* to have a temper tantrum, sleep on the floor, or even play with a toy in bed. Yet, after a few nights they all *chose* to go to bed at 7:30 without a fight. Why?

This illustrates an important part of Empowerment Parenting: the power of choice. Empowerment parents use choices—within predetermined parameters—instead of commands. The children in Group B *could not choose* to get attention from their parents or watch television; those were *not available choices*.

In the Learning Habit Studies, researchers found that parents who lashed out at their children had the fewest rules or habits in place. These parents used commands to remind their children. Most of us don't like to be *ordered* to do something. It is not surprising, therefore, that when we use commands with children, we tend to get resistance. The problem with commands is that the only correct answer a child can give is, *yes*.

Commands—no matter how sweetly expressed, for example, "Honey, would you please turn the TV off and start your home-work?"—are inconsistent, unpredictable, and often erratic. Parents rarely enjoy giving them, and children rarely enjoy receiving them; they lead to dissention and resentment.

Rules, on the other hand, are guides for conduct and actions. They are, as parents learned through the bedtime experiment, an accepted procedure that leads to a habit. Children ultimately inter-nalize their choice to follow the rule, and that's how a new habit is created!

I have a friend whose response to her children's unreason-able requests or demands is, "That's not our policy." It struck me as funny—and smart. Policy, rule, or principle, it's all the same thing.

## ENABLING VERSUS EMPOWERING

In our model, we use the word *enable* to mean making it possible for our children to continue unproductive behaviors. For instance, making excuses for them, doing their jobs for them, bending or breaking rules with the "just this once won't hurt" rationalization.

The choice to use empowerment as your parenting style means that you want your child to develop the habits that create independence and self-reliance. Enabling Parenting (also referred to as Traditional or Authoritarian Parenting) is the polar opposite; it encourages *dependency* and inhibits a child's ability to learn productive habits; it focuses on *outcome* (the grade, the award) rather than on skill development, responsibility, and effort. Regrettably, although these parents are trying to help their children, they may actually be encouraging them to *maintain unproductive behaviors*. These kids may continue to be irresponsible, disorganized, or unfocused because they know Mom or Dad will always be there to get them out of a jam. Parents who enable often do so out of fear; unrealistic fears about their child's safety, fear of letting their child fail, or fear about not looking like a good parent. Enabling a child does not permit that child to feel or internalize the impact of their choices. This parenting style inhibits learning.

Empowerment Parenting offers children opportunities to learn by:

✓ Allowing them to experience the consequences of their actions.

✓ Giving children choices within reasonable parameters.

✓ Encouraging children to take responsibility for things they control—because the parents refuse to take on the responsibility.

✓ Helping them to think in terms of options and consequences, causes and likely effects.

✓ Building habits that will allow them to reach their goals.

Within this model, parents are not afraid to let their children make mistakes, because they understand that that is how we learn. Children are neither rescued from their errors in judgment nor condemned for them; they are supported in learning from them. They are establishing the learning habit.

## FOSTERING LEARNING IN CHILDREN

In 2010, as researchers were embarking on some of the first Learning Habit Studies, an interesting parenting phenomenon was occurring in the United States. A parenting style referred to in pop culture as "helicopter parenting" was rapidly making headlines. The phrase was actually coined as early as 1969, in a book by psychologist Haim G. Ginot, to describe an "over-parented teenager."[1]

One of the characteristics associated with these hovering parents was an inability to let their children experience options and consequences. Children are not permitted to feel the impact of their choices; they are rescued. Holly Andrews, a self-described helicopter parent, fiercely defended her decision to leave work in the middle of the day to deliver a homework assignment that her daughter had left in the car. "I'm *not* going to let my daughter fail!" she said.

That seemed to be the common theme among this growing cohort of hovering parents: fear of failure. "Failure" is an interesting description; it seems to justify all manner of sins. As the first few generations of helicopter-parented children began to graduate from college, employers across the country noticed a common trend: an inability to cope with setbacks and other challenges. Since then, employers have complained that these latest recruits seem overly narcissistic and unable to take responsibility for their mistakes.

## Case Study: The Lost and Found Money

Kenny (age 7) was given $5 by his father for helping him clean out the garage. Kenny wanted to go to Walmart to buy a toy with his money. His father told him to keep the money in his pocket and not play with it so that he wouldn't lose it. When the family, including Kenny's aunt, got to Walmart, Kenny's father noticed that Kenny was playing with his money and showing it to some children. His father cautioned him that if the money was lost, it would not be replaced. The family finished their shopping, went to check out, and Kenny no longer had his $5. After searching the store with no success, his parents told him that was a shame, but that he wouldn't be able to buy the toy. Kenny tried to grab the toy away from his father, then started to cry, threw himself on the floor, and had a full-blown tantrum. The parents told him they were leaving the store and no one was buying anything. At that point, Kenny's aunt pulled out her wallet and gave him $5, telling him that she wanted to buy the toy for him.

Auntie may have thought she was doing a kind thing or she may simply have taken the path of least resistance to end an embarrassing experience. Whatever the intent, the effect was to enable Kenny to act irresponsibly and engage in socially unacceptable behavior.

Kenny has now learned that:

- ✓ If he loses something, there will be someone there to replace it, and/or

- ✓ If he makes a big enough scene, he'll get his way.

### Remember: Replace the Word *Fail* with the Word *Learn*

When Holly said, "I'm not going to let my child fail," she was really saying, "I'm not going to let my child learn."

## Case Study: Sasha's Choice, Mom's Decision

**Sasha (age 12):** In Sasha's home, there is a rule: Before bedtime, the children are to consult their planners, gather all their school supplies and whatever equipment (musical instruments, gym clothes, etc.) is needed for the next day, pack their backpacks, and have the backpacks and equipment placed by the back door. On Wednesday evening, Sasha neglected to consult her planner and forgot to pack the book report due on Thursday; it counted for 30% of her midterm grade.

During lunch, her friend Emery asked if Sasha was worried about her book report; Emery said she'd stayed up very late to finish hers, because it was such a big part of the grade. Sasha realized her mistake, asked for permission to go to the office, and called her mother in a panic. She explained that she needed her book report, which was probably still in the printer. She apologized to her mother, begging her to bring it right over, as English class was starting in 15 minutes.

**Option One:** Against her better judgment, Mom drops everything, finds the book report, and takes it to school. Sasha is very grateful and promises to never do this again.

*Goal:* To keep Sasha from getting a low midterm grade; to protect her image as a responsible and caring mom. To be a hero to her daughter.

*Lesson:* Sasha learns that, when push comes to shove, her mother will bend the rules to protect Sasha's grade and to keep Sasha (and maybe Mom) from looking bad to the teacher.

**Option Two:** Mom refuses to bring the book report to the school.

*Goal*: To teach Sasha that she is the one responsible for her work; that there are natural consequences that occur from not following rules.

*Lesson*: If you don't take responsibility for things within your control, no one else will either.

## THE REAL ENDING

Her mother said, "What's our rule, sweetie? I really am sorry about your predicament, but I'm not going to stop what I'm doing to bring you your book report." She didn't lecture or make statements like, "Maybe next time you'll remember to check your planner." She simply said that there was a rule in place, and she was not going to change it. Sasha was furious with her mother and hung up on her, in tears. She told her teacher what had happened; the teacher told her to bring it the next day, but that she would have to deduct one letter grade for submitting the report late. Sasha didn't talk to her mother for two days—but she never forgot to check her planner again.

Sasha thought her mother was being really mean; however, she learned to take responsibility for something that was well within her control. Why? Because her mother refused to assume that responsibility.

Had her mom said, "Oh, all right, but you'd better not do this again!" and taken the book report to school, Sasha's behavior (not checking her planner) would have been reinforced. When we reinforce an inappropriate behavior, we are creating a habit—an unproductive one. What her mother did was to help Sasha build a learning habit—a habit (checking her planner and being ready for the next day) that became self-reinforcing. Sasha does her job—she maximizes her chances of doing well. Because her mother refused to help her, Sasha now assumes responsibility for being prepared for school. She doesn't need or rely on her mother to take part in this task. She is learning both responsibility and independence.

When we reinforce an inappropriate behavior, we are creating a habit—an unproductive one.

## LEARNING HABIT SURVEY RESULTS

To the question of what a parent will do "When my child leaves something at school," 37% of parents of six-year-old children answered, "I will often or always go to school to help her/him get it."

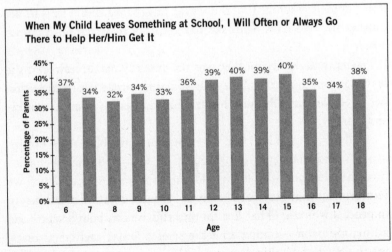

FIGURE 2.1

Of interest is that exactly the same proportion, 37% of parents of 18-year-old children, answered, "I will often or always go to school to help her/him get it." When parents use enabling techniques with young children, they continue them throughout their children's school career; they think they need to—because their kids have never been allowed to develop learning habits.

When Sasha's mother told her *no*, she recounted, "I could just hear the gossip in the teacher's lounge. 'Poor Sasha. I had to grade her down, of course, but my heart just went out to her. She was so upset! I can't believe her mom couldn't bring that report—it's not like Sasha's a bad kid.' And the other mothers—the ones whose kids brought their homework—what would they think? It was one of the hardest things I ever had to do."

Let's be honest, we've all been guilty of sharing opinions at the bus stop about the *poor kids* whose moms send them to school in mismatched clothes or wearing shorts on a cold fall day, or without their backpacks. What if those "bad mommies" were really allowing their children to learn by experience and build a learning habit?

No one wants to be thought of as a bad parent, and no parent enjoys feeling guilty. Maybe, after reading this book, you'll think differently about some of the judgments you've made about other parents—because we all do that! And then we think, "Phew! I'm so glad it wasn't me who . . ." let her child go to school with no lunch money—or without an umbrella—or with a mismatched outfit, as we bask, however briefly, in our own parental superiority.

## Case Study: Jen and Sara

**Sara (age 13):** Sara's mother, Jennifer, came into my office absolutely fuming. It was one of those unpredictable weather days; starts out sunny, then rains so hard that the streets flood, then gets sunny again, then starts hailing—a typical New England day. It was obviously going to rain that morning, so Jen told her three daughters to wear their slickers and rain boots. Sara, age 13, refused, stating, "They're weird. I won't wear them." An argument ensued, and then escalated until Jen and Sara were yelling at each other. Sara finally put on the rain gear, crying and cursing her mother, and ran out to the bus—in the rain.

"I can't believe how stubborn she is!" Jen exclaimed. "She has to turn everything into a fight, just to try and get her way. Like she's always right and I'm always wrong. I can't understand why she does that! Where is this coming from?"

"Have you looked in the mirror lately?" I said laughing. "Not for nothing, but it seems like she's mirroring you."

"What are you talking about? I was right; it was raining!" Jen asserted.

"About that 'being right' thing, did you feel good when Sara left, crying?" I asked.

Jen made a face. "No, of course not. But I didn't want her to get rained on and spend the whole day wet. For heaven's sake, what would her teachers think?"

"Okay. Let's look at a worst-case scenario. Sara gets soaked, spends all day wet, develops pneumonia, and dies a terrible death, gasping for breath, knowing that it's all her own fault, and if she'd only listened to her dear, loving, always right mother . . . ," I said, smiling.

Jen gave a little laugh, and said, "Well, when you put it that way, it sounds ridiculous. I didn't think she'd die!"

"Really? You didn't think she'd die? Hmmm . . . did you think she'd get . . . seriously ill?"

"N-no," Jen replied, a bit uncertainly.

"Okay. I want to make sure I understand. You didn't think she would die, or even get sick. What was the *really awful thing* that you thought would happen, then, if she didn't wear her rain stuff?" I asked.

"You don't have to be so dramatic! I just knew she'd be wet and miserable all day, and there was no need for that! I knew that her teachers would think I'd lost my mind letting her go to school soaking wet. And the other mothers? Forget it! All she had to do was wear her slicker and boots."

"Jen, let's just pretend that this is what happened today," I said. "You checked the weather online, you saw the forecast, you saw the big, black cloud rolling in, and you suggested to the girls that it would be a good day to wear their rain gear because there was going to be a downpour within minutes. Sara said, 'I don't want to wear it; it's weird.' And you said, 'Okay, it's your choice, honey. Weird or wet, it's up to you.' And she left with no slicker, no rain boots, and she's soaked before she even gets on the bus. What do you think might happen the next time it's raining before school?"

"She'd probably realize that I was right, and she should wear her rain stuff!" Jen retorted.

"Maybe," I replied. "She would probably have learned from her experience, and might make a different choice. Or she might decide that wet is better, for her, than looking weird. Either way, it would be her decision, and she would be the one to live with the consequences. And there would be no fighting, no tears, and no everyone starting their day upset. Was the scene this morning really worth it? What do you think Sara had the opportunity to learn?"

"Probably that her mother is a total bitch," Jen said. "I get it. But it's so hard to watch your kid make a bad choice!"

And it's really hard to know that other people are watching, too, and wondering what they're thinking about you. Keep thinking: *short-term pain, but long-term gain.*

## PARENTAL CHOICES

Most of us engage in a new activity with a goal in mind. That goal might change, become clearer, or even be discarded as we gain more information. So it is with parenting. We start out with a mass of insecurities, "She's so small—is she breathing?" and then, as we gather a measure of confidence, we start to frame some big goals for our parenting, such as: being the best parent—just like/not like my parents, giving her opportunities, lessons, the best of everything. As the child enters school, most of us focus on achievement. We want our child to be educationally successful, socially adept, and emotionally healthy, centered, and happy. Achievement: that becomes our goal for our children.

We often try different strategies to help our children achieve. Helping with homework or insisting on suitable clothing, we believe, will make their lives easier and protect them from discomfort, pain, embarrassment, or failure. In essence, we are making their choices for them.

When we are choosing for our kids, we are making some interesting choices for and about ourselves also. The first choice we are making is to believe that we are right, that we absolutely know what is best for our child. In the case of Jen and Sara, Jen knew that wearing a slicker and boots was best, and it probably was—for Jen. But maybe it wasn't, for Sara. Perhaps, rather than concentrating on the outcome (incomplete homework, wet child), we need to change our perspective and focus, instead, on the habit that we are facilitating. When we open our minds—when we decide that maybe we can sit back and see what choices *they* make and what lessons *they* learn—then we become learners right along with our children. And learners are the most interesting people!

It helps to understand that when we are focused on the end of a discrete situation (staying dry) or when we are trying to help our children to achieve (getting a good grade), we are aiming at the wrong target. When we are fixed on their *achievement*, we are making *ourselves* responsible for it. In that scenario, our kids may indeed achieve—but only as long as we stay involved. At some point, we have to cut the cord, and our children will not have acquired the habits they need to be able to depend on themselves—to be successful without our intervention.

Establishing a learning environment means encouraging the behaviors that, over time, become habitual. The earlier we start, the easier the task.

## Case Study: Daisy

**Daisy (age 8):** It was the first day of school for Daisy and Dylan, twin third graders. The night before, the twins' mother had told them to lay out their clothes for the next day and to consider that it was going to be a very hot day and that their school had no air-conditioning.

Dylan came to breakfast in a collared short-sleeved shirt and khaki shorts. Daisy had gone into the closet where their mother kept holiday items, including their Halloween costumes from previous years. She appeared for breakfast wearing a full-length blue Aquaman outfit, to which she had added a piece from her brother's cowboy costume—leather sheepskin chaps that belted around her waist and hung down almost to her knees. On her head was a "Ron Burgundy" wig her father had worn the year before, for Halloween.

Daisy stomped aggressively to the table, never taking her eyes off her mother. Her brother started to laugh. Mom sent him "the look," poured Daisy's juice, and set out the cereal bowls, a carton of milk, and three boxes of cereal.

Daisy said, "So—how do you like my outfit? Isn't it super?"

Her mother sat down with her coffee, thought a minute, and then said, "Daisy, it's your choice. If that's what you want to wear all day, in 90-degree heat, then wear it."

Daisy's older brother and father came in, sat down, and ate breakfast. Nobody said a thing about Daisy's wardrobe choice.

When she was finished eating, Daisy took her dishes to the sink, ran back upstairs, and came down in a T-shirt and shorts.

## PRAISE FOR EFFORT

The last component of an Empowerment Parenting approach is praising children for their effort, rather than for their intelligence, abilities, and achievements. Recently, several news stories have been reported on the negative effects of *unearned praise* or *too much praise* on a child's ego. These reports are somewhat confusing, and leave parents wondering if they should praise children at all or what type of praise to offer.

Many years ago we developed a praising-for-effort system. This involved praising children for specific things that required effort or hard work. An integral part of our therapeutic model includes praise for trying hard, keeping a positive attitude, and continuing to work at solving problems. We watched for incremental changes in patients; we noticed small but measurable changes in a children's behavior.

Johnny, a nine-year-old boy in group therapy with ADHD, constantly interrupted other kids who were trying to talk. After we used the praising-for-effort system, he started listening more and interrupted only three or four times during a session. This was tremendous progress, as he had previously interrupted any time someone else spoke. We praised him, saying things like, "Nice listening today; I could see how hard you were working," and "Hey, we noticed that you've really been trying hard to wait your turn. That's very cool!" Our results were extremely encouraging.

Research on the same topic was also being done on the West Coast. At Stanford University, Carol Dweck was conducting experiments with children to determine the effects of praise on their desire to be challenged.

First a group of children were given easy puzzles to solve. After solving them, half of the children were praised for their intelligence—for example, "You did so well; you must be very smart." The other half was praised for their effort—such as, "You did so well; you must have tried very hard."

The same children were then given the opportunity to try much harder puzzles. The group who had been praised for their intelligence, when given the choice to try harder or easier puzzles, chose to be given easier puzzles. The children who had been praised for trying hard elected to work on harder puzzles, "that I can learn from."

Therapists across the country now had conclusive proof: Praising for effort encourages children to believe that they can learn and improve; praising for ability has a stultifying effort on children—it makes them afraid to tackle hard challenges because they might fail. Ability itself isn't any guarantee of success; it's whether you look at ability as something inherent or as something that can be applied and developed.

## TRYING NEW THINGS

In our work with children at the Center (NECPP), we have noticed a single type of praise that is almost magical in its positive, lifelong effects on children: praise for trying something new. The method is simple but strategic. Children are encouraged to take a reasonable risk and try something new; they are then *praised only for trying* the new task. We have seen tremendous changes in behavior, self-esteem, and the development of respect and empathy in children who are praised for trying new things; not for the outcome of the new task. It doesn't matter if the task, game, or concept is perfectly executed; it matters that the child feels good about trying. That way, they'll continue to participate. Almost always, they'll achieve a degree of mastery because they believe that, by continuing to work at something, they can "get it." Dweck has used the term *open mind-set* to explain why people who believe that they can realize their *potential* do so, while others with the same attributes do not.

We know that we can actually grow our brain through challenging it; that we can continually work on developing cognitive ability, athletic prowess, and other skills.[2] Parents of the children we see are often shocked by the positive changes and growth they observe in their kids after only a few weeks of praise for effort rather than achievement. The children are happier, more energetic, more positive in their outlook, and much better behaved. The right kind of praise is almost magical in its ability to change behavior.

## Case Study: The Foosball Wizard

At the Center, we do a lot of small-group interactive play therapy. It's great for teaching skills and behaviors and also for uncovering feelings, belief systems, and hidden agendas.

In a group of four 10-year-old boys, one boy was the acknowledged "best" at foosball. The other boys always wanted to be his partner. (The way we play, we are constantly rotating positions, so it doesn't matter who you start out with or which side wins; each child plays each position and is briefly partnered with every other child.) Nonetheless, Robby was the self-proclaimed King of Foosball. After every group, he would brag to his mother about how good he was, and she would agree, saying, "You're my best boy. You are so good at everything!"

As often happens, one of the boys graduated from the group, at which time a new boy joined. This child, George, was a sweet, very shy boy, who didn't say much; when he did talk, he was extremely self-deprecating.

An interesting thing happened. When it was Robby's turn to pick the game we played, he, of course, chose foosball. Unbeknownst to Robby, George had a foosball table in his basement and had been playing against his older brothers for years. Robby got quite a shock, when George blocked all offensive shots and scored 10 of the 10 points that were earned. After another game, Robby completely retreated. Suddenly, he couldn't draw, couldn't think of anything to say when we did mutual storytelling, and just stood there, motionless, when we played charades.

He shut down.

So much of his identity was tied into being praised for his foosball skill that when that skill was challenged, he doubted his ability in all other areas. It was a classic example of what happens when a child is overpraised for achievement, and underpraised for effort.

The other boys weren't at all diminished by George's skill; they were complimentary to him, and were very curious about how he got so good. Blushing ferociously, he told them that, at home, he wasn't that good; he got beaten by his brothers on a regular basis. One of the boys said, "Doesn't that make you mad?" George replied, "Maybe a little, but mostly it makes me determined to practice more. I know that one day, I'll beat them."

## Remember

A big part of praising for effort means that we parents don't over-react when our child makes a mistake. We understand that mistakes are how we learn. If you're always in your comfort zone, if you never try anything new, you'll never grow.

The following case studies clearly show the difference that Empowerment Parenting can make in creating habits of self-reliance and responsibility. Effort-based praise is the key to helping children power through difficult tasks. If they fear they are either not good enough or not intelligent enough, they will give up.

## Case Study: The Chase Family

**Madison (age 8) and Megan (age 12):** Heather and Matt are working parents who have always tried to arrange their schedules so that one of them is home when their two daughters—Madison and

Megan—get home from school. Matt is the cook in the family ("Did I luck out or what?" says Heather, laughing), so Heather takes charge of the girls' after-school activities and schedules.

Much of Matt's business involves telephone conferences with Asian corporations, so he frequently goes into his home office after dinner and is occupied for several hours. Both girls are active in sports and dance, so Heather is busy being the chauffeur until suppertime. She is also the one who is around during homework time. She works from home and is able to arrange her time according to her family's schedule.

"We've never had any problems with Megan doing her homework. She's always loved school, loved reading. She's consistently on the honor roll. She never has to be reminded about homework," Heather reported. "She just goes into the den and does it."

"This problem with Maddie," Matt said, "came as a shock. I knew that math wasn't her favorite subject, but I had no idea that things had gotten so out of hand."

As the story unfolded, Heather said that Maddie liked to do her homework at the kitchen table, with Heather. "Until this year, homework really wasn't an issue. First grade, second grade—no big deal. It was mostly reading, and I did that with her. Maddie is a slow reader, and she sometimes gets discouraged, so I sit with her and help her out if she needs it. She likes having me there. This year, however, there is more homework, and a lot of emphasis on math. Often, she has reading to do and then has to answer questions. That's a pretty long process for Maddie; she needed help, sometimes, with how to frame the answer, so, I'd . . . give her ideas. Then the math. Oh my God! It got to the point where she would just hide the book and say she didn't have any math homework. I started out by helping her. Then she'd get tired and discouraged, so I'd walk her through the problem . . . suggest the answer . . . I was . . . helping too much."

"So, here's this kid," Matt interjects, "who's getting 90's and 95's on her homework—and then barely passing or even failing her tests. I couldn't understand it. I thought maybe she had test anxiety or something. Then last week, Heather had to go into New York for a two-day conference, and it really hit the fan. Madison was in the kitchen with me, and she kept asking me how to answer questions. It was a handout about the Pilgrims and she had three questions to answer. She kept asking me what the answers were, so I told her to just read the paragraph. She said that wasn't how Mommy did it, but I pointed out that it was a very short paragraph and she was a very smart little girl, so I knew she could do it. And she did, but she was really obsessing over the answers—erasing, redoing. It was kind of a mess when she finished, but at least it was done.

"Then came the math. Ten problems. She kept looking at me and down at the paper. I asked her what the problem was, and she said, 'You have to help me.' I told her I was right there; if she had a problem, just ask. And then she got teary and said, 'No! You have to *help* me—like Mommy does!' When I asked her what Mommy did, she really started to cry. She finally said, 'She explains what I have to do and says the answer . . . so I can understand how to do it.'

"So I sat down with her, and I looked at the first problem, and I told her to do it and I'd check it. She started screaming and crying, 'That's not what Mommy does!' She tore up the paper and said I was a bad daddy and she only wanted her mommy. She was inconsolable. I had no idea what to do."

"You can imagine how I felt when Matt called," Heather said, with tears in her eyes. "I wanted to help her. Talk about the road to Hell being paved with good intentions. I've been . . . essentially . . . doing her homework for her. Now she thinks she's 'stupid' and can't do anything right."

Did you cringe when you read that story? I can't think of a parent I know who hasn't had an experience like this; wanting to help, but having it backfire. Now compare that story to the next one.

## Case Study: The Ryan Family

**Ava (age 5):** Christina Ryan genuinely enjoyed the peaceful moments after dinner when she and her oldest daughter, Ava, would sit and color. One night Ava looked at Christina's drawing and began complaining that it was "better than mine." Christina told her that wasn't true, but Ava began to cry. "It's not fair, mine is so bad compared to yours!" she sobbed.

"The next day, we were coloring in her Fancy Nancy coloring book. So, Ava looks at my coloring and says, 'How come yours looks so good? Mine is bad!'

"I leafed through the coloring book and found the first picture she'd colored. I showed her the comparison between that one and the one she'd just colored. 'Can you see the difference? The one you did today is so much neater and more colorful than the other one,' I pointed out. She agreed, and then said, in a whiney voice, 'But yours is better.'

"I said, 'You know what? You're right!' The look on Ava's face was pure shock! Something about that statement snapped her right out of it. 'But Ava, Mommy's good at coloring because I practiced coloring. When I was your age, I colored with my mommy almost every day. She did the dark lines around the pictures and then filled them in—just like I do. Her pictures looked so beautiful to me, so I decided that I was going to practice coloring so I could improve—and I did.'

" 'I had to work really hard, but I loved to color, so I just kept at it.' I could see the wheels turning, so I figured I'd just go for it. 'You know how we do our exercises? And we run and ride our bikes. Why do we do that, Ava?'

"She thought for a minute, then said, 'We like to. It makes our muscles strong.'

" 'Right! And we get stronger the more we exercise our muscles. Well, guess what? Our brain is a muscle. We need to exercise it to make it stronger and stronger.'

"Ava's response was, 'No way!' So I explained about how the more we practice things the stronger the muscles in our brain get. Every picture she colored showed how hard she was trying to do the outlines and keep the coloring within them. I told her that I could really see the effort she was making, and I was so proud of her for trying her hardest.

"She said, 'Well, I have to practice a lot, just like you did, Mommy.' She hasn't cried over coloring again."

Christina reports that she uses the same technique to help Ava with schoolwork. She encourages her with praise for effort; she uses stickers as *effort rewards* for Ava's reading, practicing her handwriting, and other skills. Whenever Ava expresses a desire to give up, Christina praises her for growing her *brain muscle* by trying something hard. Every day, she gets a sticker—not for getting it right, but for staying with the task at hand.

Showing our children, as Christina did, that there is joy in learning, that we all are learning new things all the time, and that it takes a lot of practice for us to acquire a new skill—those are the empowering attitudes that help learning habits take hold.

# PART II

The Eight Essential Skill Sets

# CHAPTER THREE

# Media Matters: Managing Our Kids' Media Use

*"We all need water to live;*
*but if we get too much of it, we drown."*
—Herbert Spiegel, MD, Clinical Professor of Psychiatry,
Columbia University

**Ciara (age 12)** believes that she must stay on her iPad, "talking" to a stranger with whom she believes she has a "relationship," in order to stop this "close friend" from harming herself. Ciara's mother finds her—weeping, exhausted, and frantic—at 3:30 a.m.

**Simon (age 13)** is failing almost every subject and has few friends; his life revolves around his gaming. He's no longer interested in family activities; he's moody and, when not in school, stays in his basement hideaway and games.

**Sampson (age 11)** has his own business. An entrepreneur, he has studied Java, basic HTML, and web design in school. Currently, although a high honors student, he is allowed to spend only one hour per day on his computer; during this time, he designs websites, for which he gets paid.

**Kelly (age 8)** got her own TV for her birthday, a wall-mounted flat screen that her dad installed in her bedroom. Recently, her parents have noticed that Kelly seems tired, cranky, and unhappy during the day. They wonder if she is sick, and take her to their pediatrician for a physical exam and blood work.

## WHAT IS MEDIA USE, ANYWAY?

The term *media use* has previously been defined as interacting with anything that has a screen. Savvy parents know there are *different uses* for media, and bundling them into one category is senseless. Digital learning and testing is now an important part of children's academic experience. The ability to combine math or spelling curriculum with game play is an exciting interactive experience for both teachers and students.

However, this serves to further blur the lines of media use, as educational learning games vie for acceptance.[1]

## A MORE USEFUL DEFINITION

To help parents understand the ways that our Generation M[2] children are interacting with media, we have identified three discrete media categories for *The Learning Habit*. We call them the three C's:

**Media consumption:** To take in or use media passively, without contributing.

**Media creation:** To produce and distribute something in a way that requires active engagement, acquired skills, and complex problem solving.

**Media communication:** To use media to connect with another person.

## Case Study: Colleen's Cognitive Disconnect

**Nelson (age 5):** Colleen is a Connecticut mother who participated in the Learning Habit Studies interviews; she is the mother of one child, Nelson, and newly pregnant with her second. She had to be interviewed in the morning, while her son was in kindergarten. Colleen believed that she had Nelson's media usage well under control. During the interview, Colleen was asked how many hours a day her child used media.

She answered, "Two hours. I know that's probably not ideal, but sometimes it's the only way I can get stuff done."

The interviewer was standing in front of a white board holding a black marker. On the board she had already transcribed a list of the media devices Colleen's family owned:

2 televisions
2 iPads
2 early learning tablets
1 Xbox
2 cell phones
1 laptop computer
1 desktop computer
1 digital camera

"Do you have any screens built into your car?" asked the interviewer.

"Oh, yes," Colleen replied. "There's a built-in TV and DVD player in my SUV."

The interviewer changed the television total from 2 to 3. She then asked Colleen to reconstruct her previous day, and asked specific questions designed to build an accurate, almost minute-by-minute picture of how Nelson's non-school time was spent in relation to each media device. The researcher stepped away from the chart and showed Colleen the total. It was 5 hours, 55 minutes—essentially 6 hours.

| | |
|---|---|
| Upstairs TV | 30 minutes |
| Downstairs TV | 60 minutes |
| Car DVD | 75 minutes |
| Mommy's iPad | 30 minutes |
| Daddy's iPad | 15 minutes |
| Family Xbox | 0 |
| Early learning tablet | 30 minutes |
| Kid's learning tablet | 45 minutes |
| Daddy's cell phone | 20 minutes |
| Mommy's cell phone | 30 minutes |
| Desktop computer | 20 minutes |
| Laptop computer | 0 |
| Mommy's digital camera | 0 |

"Oh my gosh! That's . . . just not possible! I mean, it was a really busy day . . . the trip to the mall took forever, with the highway construction and all . . . waiting in the restaurant. . . . Six hours? No—that's terrible!" a shocked Colleen exclaimed.

The researcher just smiled. "Actually, it's pretty typical," she explained. In households across the country, parents who took part in one of our early Learning Habit surveys regularly reported that their child used between 90 and 120 minutes of media per day. Yet when asked specific questions about the devices, the total was commonly between six and eight hours per day.[2] Our findings were consistent with other media research. The "few minutes" of playing on Mommy's phone plus "one or two TV shows or DVDs" plus "some iPad games here and there" plus "the movie on the trip to and from the mall" don't seem like much—until all the minutes are added up.

# #GOODLUCKWITHTHAT

What the research team knew was that information on *media overuse* wasn't particularly meaningful to most parents. All the charts and data they could gather would be worthless unless parents could see how screen time could actually be detrimental to their own children. In October 2013, the American Academy of Pediatrics (AAP) had tried presenting a report on media use and youth. The AAP urged parents to limit media use to between one and two hours a day.

Referencing the new guidelines, an Associated Press writer immediately took to Twitter and joked "#goodluckwiththat."[3] The AAP's new policy statement and study had become a joke. The hashtag was so catchy that within hours, every major news organization in the country, including CNN and *The Today Show*, was reporting the findings using the hashtag #goodluckwiththat.

The AAP was screaming "fire"—but nobody was listening. As Dr. Pressman put it, "If we're going to scream 'fire' to a group of parents, there'd better be a *real* fire, and we'd better know how to put it out!"

*Nothing fools you better than the lie you tell yourself:*
*When you notice something on your own, only then does*
*the lie become penetrable.*

—Raymond Joseph Teller, comedic
magician of Penn & Teller

# CONNECTING THE THREE C'S

The Learning Habit Study findings presented throughout the rest of this chapter are intended to help parents link media consumption, creation, and communication to outcomes important in the lives of their own children: grades, social skills, and emotional learning.

In the rest of this chapter, we'll take a look at the three C's of media, one by one: consumption, creation, and communication. After reading these sections, no parent will be able to say they don't have a reason to limit their child's media consumption and communication to between one and two hours a day. Parents will also understand how media creation works and will be provided with some resources to help children who have an interest get started.

# MEDIA CONSUMPTION

## Case Study: Kelly's Sleep

Kelly (age 8) was in the second grade. As the oldest of three girls in her family, she was considered by her parents to be mature for her age. She was a very social little girl who was popular with her classmates and teacher. Because she had a late birthday, she had missed the cutoff for kindergarten in her school district and was older than most of the other children.

Kelly was given a certain measure of autonomy at home; her mother and father were proud of the way she helped out with her twin sisters (10 months old), often referring to Kelly as "the little mother." Successful at school, a pleasure at home, Kelly was the apple of her parents' eye.

Therefore, when she asked for her own TV ("if it doesn't cost too much") for her birthday, her parents were delighted to grant her request. At her birthday party after school on Friday, her friends saw the big box in Kelly's room, and thought it was the best present ever.

The TV had a built in DVD player, so Mommy allowed Kelly to take some of her favorite DVDs into her room; Kelly assured her mother that "the babies" could come in and watch with her, when they were a little older. Her parents thought that was totally adorable.

The first night, the whole family pretty much camped out in Kelly's room, eating birthday cake and watching movies. The little ones went to bed on time, but Kelly and her parents stayed up to watch the movies. It broke the bedtime rule, but it was a special occasion.

Saturday and Sunday nights, Kelly went to bed on time. Her mother did the usual routine, cuddling and reading; they had just started the first Harry Potter book. After Kelly's mom left the room, Kelly couldn't sleep. That big TV was just *right there*, waiting to be turned on. She crept out of bed and put the *Frozen* DVD in; she intended to watch it for only a few minutes. She ended up falling asleep, but was awakened when the movie started to replay. Finding the remote, she turned it off; it took her a while to fall back to sleep.

Over the next several weeks, Kelly changed. It was subtle at first—a bit of reluctance to get out of bed in the morning. The weather had turned cold and icy, so her mother couldn't blame her; she'd stay in her warm bed, too, if she could. Then she became more irritable with the babies and was less willing to play with them and help her mother feed and bathe them. She seemed to be less cheerful. Her father wondered if there was a problem at school, but Kelly assured them that everything was fine.

She was becoming tired during the day and her appetite was off. Her mother didn't like the way Kelly looked; she seemed drawn and pale.

Her parents became concerned. One of Kelly's cousins had recently been diagnosed with leukemia, and suddenly, it all made sense: The lethargy, irritability, complaining, lack of spontaneity, and wanting to be in her room, alone, instead of with her sisters, all came together in one awful revelation. Kelly might be really sick.

Her mother first called Kelly's teacher, who also reported concern about Kelly's lack of energy and attentiveness. She, too, had noticed the child's irritability and low tolerance for frustration, reporting an uncharacteristically heated disagreement between Kelly and her friend, just the day before.

Her mother next called Dr. Barrows, their pediatrician; when she explained her concerns, Dr. Barrows reassured her that "almost certainly, Kelly doesn't have a serious disease," but told her to bring her daughter in first thing the next morning. She would examine Kelly and draw the blood for analysis.

Kelly's parents had a rough few days; Dr. Barrows had found no swelling of lymph nodes, fever, or other symptoms that would suggest leukemia. She did note that Kelly looked pale and had circles under her eyes.

When Kelly's blood work came back, everything was within normal ranges. The pediatrician reported that Kelly was "as healthy as a horse." She was concerned, however, over the change in personality and the overall appearance of tiredness. With Kelly happily playing in the adjoining playroom, she asked Kelly's parents if anything had changed in their daughter's life: Any new baby-sitters? Any sleepovers at a new friend's house? Had she joined a team or group? Her parents were horrified by the implication of abuse and assured the doctor that none of those things had occurred.

Had they spoken to her teacher? Was she, perhaps, being bullied? "Yes" and "No," they answered. What about any changes in her daily routine? Dr. Barrows asked them to think back; could they remember when they started to see the changes?

Her parents thought back; they really couldn't remember anything unusual.

The pediatrician said she'd like to speak to Kelly alone. When the nurse brought Kelly in, Dr. Barrows was perched on the edge of her desk. She smiled at Kelly and said, "All right, young lady. What's going on with you? No matter what it is, I won't be angry, and I *promise* that you won't get in trouble. Why are you so tired and cranky? Where's my sunny girl? Come on, sweet pea, spill it."

Slowly, the story came out. Kelly said that she had been so excited to have a TV in her room—none of her friends did. She started by watching videos after she went to bed; they were ones she knew by heart though, so she usually fell asleep. She would then wake in the night, and because of either the sound or the light of the TV, she found it hard to get back to sleep, sometimes.

Then she decided to explore what was on TV—programs that she never got to see. So she started channel surfing. Her parents had installed parental controls, but there were still lots of programs to watch; she started watching some new programs and telling her friends at school.

As the story evolved, it was obvious that Kelly was:

✓ Falling asleep much later than normal.

✓ Having interrupted sleep.

Kelly's parents were greatly relieved. They were also confused about what to do. Kelly owned a TV; it was a birthday present from them. Were they just supposed to take it away?

They wrote her a note.

> *Dear Kelly,*
>
> *Mom and Dad have learned a lot over the past few weeks. Having a television in your bedroom is a big responsibility.*
> *So tomorrow, we'd like to talk with you about it.*
>
> Love,<br>Mommy and Daddy

The next day was Saturday. After a pancake breakfast, they sat with Kelly in her room. Kelly said she was sorry for using her TV after bedtime; mostly, she was afraid that her parents were mad at her. After she realized that they weren't mad and they weren't going to take her TV, she was happy to agree to some rules. These are the rules they posted on the refrigerator.

### Kelly's TV Rules

1. Kelly may watch her TV for two hours a day on the weekend.
2. While the TV is on, Kelly's door will stay open.
3. On Sunday night, the TV will be disconnected; on Friday, it will be reconnected.

*Follow-up: Within a week after the TV rules were in place, the old Kelly was back.*

## RESEARCHERS' CONCLUSIONS

Sleep and media consumption are even more closely related than researchers previously thought. In our research, we found that few deleterious effects appeared, regardless of the device, when children consumed fewer than 45 minutes of media time. With more than 45 minutes, sleep begins a downturn; after 180 minutes (three hours) of media consumption, the effect on children's sleep is substantial.

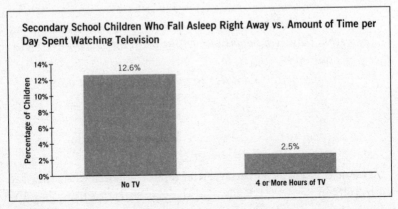

FIGURE 3.1

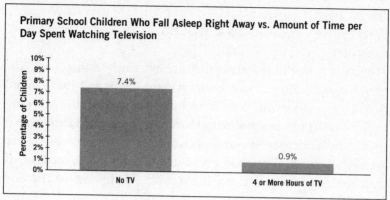

FIGURE 3.2

Parents rarely attribute sleep deprivation (symptoms include changes in mood, attention problems, decrease in grades, hyperactivity or lethargy) to electronics use. In fact, overuse of electronics is one of the top causes of sleep deprivation. An increase or decrease of just 30 minutes of sleep can have a dramatic impact on a child.

After polling families in 4,600 cities throughout the United States, our researchers found that *12.6%* of secondary school–age children who watched *no TV* fell asleep right away. In contrast, only *2.5%* of secondary school–age children who watched TV for *four or more hours* a day fell asleep right away (see Figure 3.1). To further compare, *less than 1%* of primary school–age children who watched TV four or more hours a day fell asleep right away (Figure 3.2).

The Learning Habit Study strongly suggests that, for many children, media use is a prime contributor to trouble falling asleep (known as sleep onset latency, or SOL).

# TV RULES

Television is one of the areas that are extremely difficult for parents to control. Parents who grew up in the 1970s and 1980s found that television viewing tended to limit itself naturally. Morning television was not an option until Saturday (unless children wanted to watch the news). Age-appropriate shows were on only a few evenings a week. That was about it. In high school, most of us watched 1.5 hours of television a week, including *90210* and *Friends*.

We didn't have rules about watching TV because we didn't need them. When it comes to television, old-school methods no longer apply. There are now so many programs that children can access—many of them grossly inappropriate—that both parental supervision and TV-viewing rules are definitely required.

## The *New* Rules for TV

✓ 30 to 60 minutes maximum in the evening—only *after* homework, reading, and household chores are completed.

✓ No electronics permitted in children's bedrooms.

✓ No morning TV on school days.

## Case Study: Andrea and Family Routines

"When I had McKenzie, I vowed not to let her watch television. I never thought I would be *that* parent," Andrea declared.

In fact, Andrea and her husband weren't huge media users. Andrea didn't introduce television to McKenzie until she was already pregnant with Jacob. She would get nauseated and need to run to the bathroom. She started turning on the television to keep Mc-

Kenzie busy. After she had Jacob, she would regularly let McKenzie watch TV while she fed the baby. The "cereal in front of the TV" routine became a morning staple.

Doing errands with one child was tough; with two it felt impossible. Andrea started letting the children play on her phone in the supermarket to keep them busy in the cart. If she didn't, they would get out of the cart, fight, or have a meltdown. Her new SUV had built-in screens for the kids, which, she thought, would be perfect for those long road trips. "But, though it hardly qualifies as a long road trip, on the way to the supermarket the kids always fight, so I let them watch a DVD," she said.

They'd play a game on her phone while waiting for a table in a restaurant. Sometimes, she'd pack a MobiGo for them to play on. Andrea's husband often worked late, so family dinners were a rare occurrence.

When you start tracking media use, as Andrea discovered, it adds up quickly. Andrea didn't leave her children in front of the TV for seven straight hours a day. Nonetheless, all those little increments of time added up to seven hours.

## Tracking

Media consumption extends far beyond television watching. Cell phones and tablets make it possible for children to play games and watch videos virtually everywhere. *Media tracking* is a powerful technique.

Start by making a list of your media devices and your children's. Track your children's media use by device. You'll be surprised how quickly it adds up.

When McKenzie started first grade, Andrea noticed she had a lot of trouble making friends. Her daughter had always seemed shy in kindergarten, but many children appear shy. Andrea tried enrolling McKenzie in gymnastics and soccer that year, but she cried and said she hated them. She kept running out of class or practices with excuses; "I have to pee" or "My ankle hurts." Andrea was exhausted. She was tired of dragging her daughter to activities she hated and then having to explain her daughter's embarrassing behavior to the other parents. "She's just overtired" was Andrea's go-to excuse.

McKenzie seemed chronically unhappy. She was always begging Andrea for toys she'd seen on a TV commercial. The more Andrea gave in to McKenzie's demands, the unhappier she seemed.

McKenzie's insecurity, mood swings, and shyness worried her parents, so they brought it to the attention of their pediatrician. Andrea's mother was being successfully treated for bipolar disorder, so Andrea was deeply concerned about her daughter. Their doctor told them the answer was most likely far less complicated. They had to cut back on her media consumption. His advice was to track it and then start cutting back on the most frequent activity. Andrea identified the game apps being played on their cell phones and learning tablets as the worst offenders, eating up about four hours a day. Television was the second.

Andrea didn't want McKenzie to feel like she was being punished by taking away activities she loved. She invented something she called the "swap-out" method. She swapped one media consumption activity a week with a non-media activity. She started with meals. All meals were eaten together at the dining room table. Since her husband couldn't always do family dinners, he swapped out 30 minutes of evening TV for playing board games with the family.

The positive changes in McKenzie's behavior were almost immediate. The focus on family dinners and family board games had a ripple effect, and Andrea began to make other changes to the routine over the next few months. She added chores to McKenzie's afternoon routine and saw a further decrease in her daughter's temper tantrums and demands.

*Follow-up: Andrea is no longer concerned about McKenzie's having bipolar disorder. Her daughter's social skills and behavior are markedly improved.*

"She complained for about a week, and then stopped asking," Andrea reported, who has also noticed an improvement in her daughter's ability to maintain eye contact and socialize with her peers.

Here is what worked for Andrea, who recommends using the swap-out method:

- ✓ Permit media in the car only for longs trips (longer than one hour of uninterrupted driving). "This immediately cut out at least a fifth of my child's media consumption," Andrea said.

- ✓ Phones are off-limits—period. "It stays in my purse," said Andrea.

- ✓ Media-free weekday family dinners at the table (with whoever is home).

- ✓ Evening game time: 30 minutes of family time, media free. Board games, word games, puzzles, or another type of non-media game; the specific activity is far less important than the quality of uninterrupted family interaction.

- ✓ Regular household chores. "McKenzie is a calmer, happier, and more confident child since she started doing chores; making her bed, putting her dirty clothes in the hamper, and setting the table are now her daily jobs."

## RESEARCHERS' CONCLUSIONS

"We found a negative relationship between children's media use and their social-skill development," reported Dr. Pressman. Andrea's focus on media-free family dinners and phone-in-purse tactics were more powerful than she realized. Children who eat dinner with their parents play 50% fewer media games.

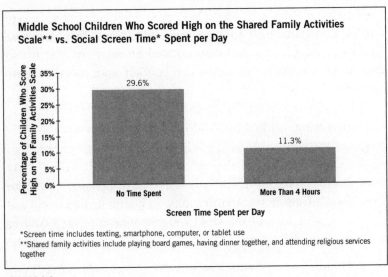

Middle School Children Who Scored High on the Shared Family Activities Scale** vs. Social Screen Time* Spent per Day

*Screen time includes texting, smartphone, computer, or tablet use
**Shared family activities include playing board games, having dinner together, and attending religious services together

FIGURE 3.3

# Case Study:
# Patrick and Social Skills—The Creator's Kids

Patrick, a graduate of Rhode Island School of Design (RISD), has developed some of the most popular video games of our time. His business, which is located just outside of Cambridge, Massachusetts, houses nearly every video game ever made. His staff looks like a cult of über-cool 30- and 40-somethings, dressed in Vans sneakers, Dickies pants, and graphic tees, and sporting three-day beards. Don't let the scruff fool you; each of these guys is worth several million dollars.

Rows of Xboxes and Nintendos fill the testing room, where

children are regularly invited in to play games and provide feedback. I asked the group of entrepreneurs if they have children, and they nodded their heads yes.

Patrick, the father of five children, openly admitted that he does not allow his children to play video games.

"I let them mess around on the computer, but that's about it," he said.

Patrick said he didn't grow up a gamer. "I fell in love with design work as a kid," he volunteers. "I spent all the time I could taking art classes."

I asked Patrick if he's familiar with the statistics on video game play and poor social skills in children.

He laughed, saying, "Why do you think I don't let my kids play video games?"

When asked if he was aware of how addictive video gaming can be, he just looked at me. "Are you kidding?" he asked, smiling. "My entire career is based on that. The goal of developers is to make the most complex, most captivating, most *addictive* games they can! I don't let my children play video games for precisely that reason. I don't want my kids spending time gaming, when they could be playing a sport or reading a book.

"If that makes me a hypocrite, then so be it," he said, with a twinkle in his eye. "I design games because I love the challenge; if parents just hand over my games to their children with *no rules* about their use, that's wrong."

## RESEARCHERS' CONCLUSIONS

According to the Learning Habit Study, children who game more than 90 minutes a day are twice as likely to have social problems, for example: difficulty making friends, inability to join other kids in play, fear of trying new things, and being unable to effectively communicate their feelings and needs.

Patrick may also be concerned about his children's grades. A dedicated gamer is *nine times* more likely to get a failing grade in both English and math.

As Dr. Pressman put it, "When the guy inventing the video games won't let his own children play them, that's a strong message. As a parent, I would think pretty seriously about that."

---

### Habits That Help

Try these best practices reported in the Learning Habit Study to reduce video game play by 50%:

> » *Eat dinner with your kids, unplugged:* Children who eat family dinners together play 50% fewer video games.
> » *Start a family activity night:* Children who regularly play board games with their parents are half as likely to play video games.

---

## Case Study: Simon's Grades

Simon (age 13) is the heavy-duty gamer we mentioned at the start of this chapter. His parents brought him in to therapy because gaming had taken over his life. The youngest of five children, Simon is different from his older siblings. All of them were goal centered; two were in graduate school and two had graduated with advanced degrees and were building their careers.

"Maybe we're just too tired to have a teenager," Simon's father, Antonio, commented sadly. "Lori and I work hard to provide a good home, but by the time we get out of work, we're both exhausted. Trying to get Simon to leave his 'cave' . . . we just give up."

Lori was sitting on the edge of her chair, a tissue clenched in her hands; she looked like a coiled spring about ready to pop. Simon, meanwhile, came for this first visit wearing a black hoodie, untied high-tops, and stained jeans that appeared to be two sizes too big.

He sat leaning forward, forearms resting heavily on his thighs, head down, with the hood hiding his face. I couldn't tell if he was listening intently or falling asleep.

According to his father, Simon goes to school, stays for home-room, and then, many days, returns home and spends the day gam-ing. His father reported that the school had called a few times, but that they had no idea how serious it was until they received a call from the guidance counselor the previous week. She said that Simon had exceeded the allowable number of unexplained absences from his classes, and that he was failing every subject.

They had called their pediatrician, who had them bring Simon in for a physical examination. He found that Simon had lost weight (10 pounds, from an already slight physique), which was troubling; a child Simon's age is normally gaining weight or at least maintaining his weight. He said that Simon appeared, otherwise, to be healthy. His blood tests had not shown any cause for immediate concern. The doctor referred Simon for therapy.

Simon played games on his laptop. His passion was first-person shooter games, especially the Call of Duty series, and violent, role-playing horror games (RPGs) like Pathologic.

"Simon begged, nagged, and made our lives miserable," his father described, "until we gave in and bought him the laptop he wanted. He said he'd be able to use it for school, to get into higher-level graphic design classes. Really, he wanted it because it was powerful enough to support his games."

Bottom line: Simon had an addiction—gaming. A loner, he had gradually given up on his family interactions, his schoolwork, and his friends.

"When his sister comes home on weekends from college, we try to do fun things—like bowling, the potluck suppers at our church, family game night (playing Scrabble or Monopoly), watching old movies—things that Simon used to love. Now he just ignores us. He's probably going to be held back in school. . . . I just feel helpless. I don't know who my son is anymore. I thought it was drugs, but his tests came back clean."

We came up with a plan for Simon; it was a media intervention. Simon was an addict. He didn't like the plan *at all*, but he needed a lifeline. Simon was drowning.

---

Gaming can be just as destructive to a child's academic performance, social skills, and emotional balance as other addictions.

---

We had a meeting in the office with the parents, to help them design a workable plan for Simon. We then explained the purpose of introducing him to the plan in a family meeting (see Chapter Two), with as many of his siblings present as possible. (Three out of four came home for the weekend; they were all frustrated and angry with their kid brother, but willing to do whatever they could to help.)

**Step 1: Normalize Simon's living conditions.** He and his father moved Simon's things out of the basement and into his room. Grudgingly, he cleaned his bedroom, changed his sheets, and collected his dirty laundry. His father installed a lock on the basement door. *As long as Simon was allowed to isolate, he wasn't going to feel a sense of belonging.*

**Step 2: Set up a team meeting with the school that both parents and Simon attend.** Simon had changed his focus from academic success to gaming. He had no confidence that he could raise his grades enough to pass for the year. With guidance, he came to realize that it was his *choices* rather than his *ability* that were holding him back. Finally, he admitted that being retained and not moving on with his classmates would be deeply upsetting. He set an academic goal: Finish the year with passing grades. The purpose of the school meeting was to get his teachers on board. His parents called the guidance counselor to set up the meeting. Most of the teachers had known Simon's sister and brothers; they wanted Simon to succeed. The counselor said that if there were any problems, she'd call one of his parents. *The teachers were willing to help; now Simon had to put forth the effort.*

**Step 3: Develop a contract.** Simon had to meet daily requirements to win one hour of computer time per day. Simon, of course, balked at this. His parents told him that the choice was one hour or zero hours. He chose one hour.

The contract included the following:

✓ *Daily maintenance of his room and himself:* Every day he was to shower, make his bed, gather his laundry, eat regular meals, and sit with his parents for dinner.

✓ *Time-limited homework routine:* Homework would be done at the dining room table. No media devices would be available. He would do his best for the allotted time and hand his work in on time.

✓ *No more electronics:* Simon lost the use of his cell phone, computer, and TV. If he had to make a call, he did it from the telephone in the kitchen. He no longer had access to other gamers, through social media.

✓ *Evening routine:* Simon got to choose an activity to do with his parents and whichever sibling was home, for 30 minutes after dinner. At first, he just sat, doing nothing. His parents read their books. After a few nights of silence, Simon brought a book from the school library and read, too. After a few more nights, he got into the game cupboard and pulled out some old games. They played Trouble and Sorry for a few nights, but Simon found them boring. He found an old back-gammon set of his dad's and asked his father to teach him. They now often have a game after dinner.

✓ *Church on Sunday:* Simon had to be up, dressed, fed, and ready to go by 9:30 on Sunday morning, to be on time for the 10:00 service. He was not required to actively participate. After the first Sunday of "active non-participation," Simon got bored. Thereafter, he participated in the service. When his mother commented on his nice singing voice and suggested that he might consider joining the choir, his response was, "Seriously? Are you on crack, Mom?" Even his father laughed.

✓ *Therapy:* Simon started group therapy on Saturday afternoons. His parents joined a parent group. At first, it was tough for Simon. He had low self-esteem and he had lost confidence in his social skills. It took several weeks before he felt comfortable talking. He eventually settled in and became a valued member of the group.

✓ *Computer use:* Every day that Simon met the conditions of the contract, he got his one hour of computer time. Any problems would be discussed at a Saturday morning family meeting.

Few parents want to acknowledge that their child has an addiction. Although Simon's parents had been a bit slow in recognizing the extent of their son's problem, once they did, they became active and appropriate participants in his recovery.

There were problems and setbacks for Simon. He became easily discouraged. His academic progress was slow, and he felt socially inept and lonely. The group therapy was helpful in developing his comfort with peer relations. Occasionally, he would break down and cry, begging to get his computer back just for one night or one weekend. It was really hard for Antonio and Lori to see him so desperate; they didn't give in, though. They were too afraid of destroying everything they had all worked so hard to repair.

Things got better for Simon. He discovered that he had more determination than he'd given himself credit for. One of his new friends was a karate student; he invited Simon to come watch a class. Simon, much to his surprise, found it fascinating. He joined the class, and the discipline and sense of mastery and pride in his body's capabilities gave a big boost to his self-esteem.

At the end of the school year, he passed all his classes with C's and B's. He was proud of his effort and his accomplishments. As he told his parents, "I'm really happy about this, but I know I can do better . . . and I will." Now *that* was music to his mother's ears!

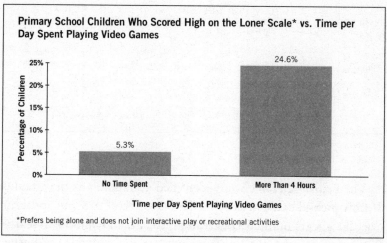

FIGURE 3.4

## RESEARCHERS' CONCLUSIONS

The trajectory for all grade levels was remarkably similar in areas of academic performance, social skills, and emotion. In Figure 3.5, which is similar to others we have published, progressive and statistically significant decrements in grade point average (GPA) began as children entered the 31- to 60-minute range of time spent, per day, on combined screen times. When comparing multiple measures, the team extrapolated that more than 45 minutes of screen time per day will likely result in decreased academic performance. Thus, when examining this chart, parents may weigh the *risks to benefits* of added screen time in a child's schedule. For some parents, a fractional drop in GPA may be acceptable, if they believe it is being offset by other gains stemming from added screen time. We doubt, however, that parents will choose total screen times that lower their child's grade point.

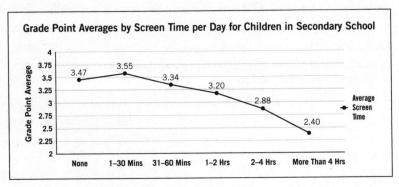

FIGURE 3.5

The Learning Habit Study identified 45 minutes as the amount of time a child can consume media before there are any apparent negative effects on their educational, social, and emotional learning outcomes. In reality, nothing devastating happens until after 180 minutes (three hours). However, at 90 minutes, on average, middle school children's grades drop nearly one grade level—not devastating, but certainly not good. At 300 minutes (five hours), a child's risk of getting F's is twice as great as that of a child who has only 15 minutes of screen time. That can be devastating.

## THE LONER PROFILE

There has been a tremendous amount of concern regarding certain types of video games and violent tendencies in children. The results of the Learning Habit Study unveiled a new profile when it comes to media consumption. As it turns out, *with whom* a child is gaming is as important as *for how long* they are gaming. Children who engage in video game play by themselves are more likely to have a decrease in grades, social skills, and emotional health than children who do not play video games in isolation. The Learning Habit Study asked a series of questions relating to media consumption and social skills. Violent and graphic video games such as first-person single-shooter games were correlated against children's social skills, ability to make friends, level of confidence, and anger. Children who played these games by themselves gamed for longer periods of time, were prone to self-isolation, and had a low rating on the social scale. In essence, they were *loners*.

The Learning Habit Study also measured *with whom* children were playing video games. The available choices were as follows:

✓ By themselves

✓ With friends

✓ With parents

Children who played the games with parents or friends had a higher threshold (greater resistance) to the deleterious effects of video games. Children who played the games by themselves were at the greatest risk for a series of problems, including diminished grades and increased incidence of emotional problems.

Although more research on the Loner Profile is recommended, it appears that when video games are employed as a shared experience—played with parents and friends—they are less destructive than when played alone. Even extremely violent video games, when played with a parent, seemed to have little to no measurable negative impact on a child—very different results than when the same games are played in isolation. One explanation is that, for children, the depth of fantasy and lack of reality checking is less problematic when games are played with others; children may not identify with the characters as much when they play games as an interactive activity. In a group, with a friend, or with a parent, children are also focusing on other skills, such as competitive social skills—which offset some of the negative intensity experienced when played without human interaction.

Although further research is needed, we strongly recommend that parents take the following findings seriously.

The results of the Learning Habit Study showed that children have a 45-minute threshold for television. With more viewing time than that, children at most grade levels show academic, social, and emotional decrements.

In fact, children who used computers and tablets moderately scored significantly higher than their non-user counterparts. After 45 minutes of use, however, grades slowly but steadily declined. After *three hours of use*, grades rapidly declined. After *five hours of use*, relatively few students could maintain a grade of A in math or English. After only 1.5 hours of television viewing, children's grades rapidly began to decline. After *four hours of television consumption*, children had virtually zero likelihood of academic success (see Figure 3.6).

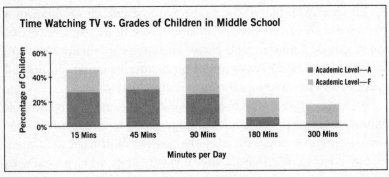

FIGURE 3.6

## Case Study: Jodie

Jodie (age 9) was in the fourth grade; she was the new kid and shy. Her family had moved from a small town, where she knew everybody, to "the big city," as her mother called it. The "big city" Jodie lived in was actually a suburb—a maze of interconnected streets ending in mysterious cul-de-sacs that never failed to confuse her when she rode her bike.

She missed her older brother, who had started at a boarding school for theater arts the week before they moved. Her brother, Richard, was her hero. He could always make her laugh with his crazy impersonations, especially the one of their father. Daddy could be kind of goofy, and Richard had him nailed. Even Daddy laughed when Richard spoke in the "let's talk about it, son" serious voice.

Before Richard left, he had given Jodie his iPad, and had loaded a bunch of apps onto it for her to play. She had a lot of time to play while they were packing, moving, and unpacking. Then Daddy started his "important job" in the city, and Mommy was busy decorating and looking for a job. More time to play her iPad. After school started, she still had lots of time to play. Her school didn't give homework until the fifth grade, which was good, but they expected every kid to play a sport, which was bad.

Jodie was not athletic; her mother always said, "We're thinkers, not runners." Jodie agreed. It didn't matter for Richard. He was such a great actor that people always assumed he was athletic, even though he wasn't. He was kind of a klutz, but he used to tease Jodie, saying, "I look like a *primo ballerino* compared to you!

The thing about having a brother like Richard was, he was always the center of attention—in a good way. She was free to hide in her room and read her books; her friends, where they used to live, were kind of *"bookish,"* as Richard said, with a *"veddy"* British accent.

Here, everybody ran around and kicked balls, or threw balls, or hit balls, or caught balls. They yelled a lot and jumped up and down, giving each other high-fives—or so it seemed to Jodie. They all had serious athletic interests.

At recess, the first couple of weeks, some of the girls asked her to play kickball. Jodie wanted to be friends, but she was too shy to join the games. Just thinking about it made her anxious. Her teacher didn't seem to mind if Jodie went to the library with her tablet; they used them in school, so lots of kids had them. What made hers different were the apps, especially the new one. She had an avatar who was also a superhero and math expert. Her avatar, Zora, had become her best friend. Zora was very cool and could do everything Jodie couldn't. The more she played with Zora, the closer they became.

Then came "the dreadful day." Miss Hanson, the gym teacher, said they all had to compete in the school's First Annual Olympics. Jodie tried to become invisible; a girl in her class, Perry, who was a little chubby but a fast runner, asked Jodie to be her partner. Jodie couldn't even speak. Perry asked her again; Jodie couldn't even look her in the eye. She didn't know what to say! Perry went away. Jodie hid in the locker room.

In the cafeteria, she could tell that Perry was talking about her. Perry didn't look mad; she looked . . . sort of hurt. Jodie thought, "What would Richard do?" He would make Perry laugh! So, working herself up to take her tray to Perry's table, she walked over, head down. *Do something funny! Do something funny!* she told herself. So, she opened her milk, and shouted, "Bombs away!" and poured the milk over her head.

Perry didn't laugh—no one laughed. Perry said, "Oooh! Gross!" as she tried to get away from the table. The girl beside Jodie jumped up, slipped on the milk, and fell down, getting ketchup all over her clothes. "You're disgusting," the girl said, trying to wipe the ketchup off her top. She looked like she wanted to cry. "Weirdo!" "What did you do that for?" and other shocked and disapproving declarations were heard around the cafeteria.

Mr. Wilson, the other gym teacher, came over. He had seen the whole thing. "Come with me, young lady," he said, leading Jodie out of the cafeteria. "You're not making yourself very popular with that kind of behavior," he said.

Jodie thought her heart was going to jump right out of her chest. She felt clammy and dizzy; it was hard to breathe. She just wanted to run—her iPad! Zora! It was still at the table! She broke away from Mr. Wilson and ran back to the cafeteria. She never made eye contact with anyone; just ran in, grabbed her pack, and started to run out. Mr. Wilson was racing in; he grabbed her arm and took her to the office.

Her mother came; Jodie was put in a small room beside the office, alone. Well, not exactly alone; she was with Zora—who was slaying a monster and doing math, all at the same time. Zora didn't feel like she was going to die; Zora could breathe just fine; Zora's heart wasn't pumping so hard she could hear it in her ear. Jodie was the only one who felt those things.

Jodie could hear voices—Mr. Wilson, the principal, her teacher, and her mother. Her teacher was going on and on: "No eye contact," "Can't talk to the other children," "Very dear child," "Was going to call you," and the worst one, "Too attached to her tablet; will always choose to play with it rather than with another child. She doesn't even look at me or make conversation; she just mumbles." Her mother said something she couldn't hear. Her teacher said, "She's anxious all the time. I'm very concerned about her."

## RESEARCHERS' CONCLUSIONS

Anxiety is a hallmark of children who spend too much time in front of screens. According to our interviews with teachers, anxiety is now a widespread problem for elementary school students. One group of elementary school teachers said that students' anxiety was their #1 concern.

Too much screen time is also a deterrent to learning social skills; Jodie was unable to relate easily with other children. This, too, is a trend teachers are noticing in elementary schoolers (see Chapter Seven).

## Family Responsibility

*If you want children to keep their feet on the ground, put some responsibility on their shoulders.*
    —Abigail Van Buren, "Dear Abby" columnist

When we look at the charts presented in this chapter, we can't help but agree with the wisdom of "Dear Abby." Children are more successful when they are occupied in activities that provide opportunities for growth. These include:

✓ Family activities

✓ Regular chores

✓ Community events, such as church or volunteerism

✓ Sports and games

✓ Playing with friends

✓ Taking classes of high interest (art, dance, karate)

Responsible children are too busy—and too tired at the end of the day—to become over-involved in passive media consumption. They have developed more productive, interesting learning habits.

## MEDIA CREATION

Not all media use is detrimental to children. Play through technology is the way children learn how to use technology. This play is often how they acquire valuable skills and gain access to beneficial content.[4] The goal for parents is to use media *creation* to both inspire and prepare our children with 21st-century skills. Children will have a distinct advantage if they possess the skills necessary to produce and distribute media and technology as well as to use and evaluate it.

Blogging, developing PowerPoint presentations, making videos, creating animation, learning code, and engaging in digital scrapbooking, are just a few of the many examples of media creation. Parents hear that children need to learn how to create and use media and then falsely believe children will gather these skills through communication media (texting, surfing the web, and social media). These are completely different forms of media.

In all of the combined research, we have found absolutely no evidence of children who were unable to *naturally regulate themselves* when it came to media creation. Media creation is hard, and after a while, it gets tedious. We have yet to find a child who is staying up all night teaching themselves HTML, Java, or touch typing! That's why school programs, designed to teach each of these skills and provide opportunities for students to *collaborate* and to *showcase* their creations, are so increasingly important. When children are actively involved in media creation, they are learning valuable skills that will help them move closer to their goals.

When children are given interactive forms of media that combine game play and learning, they flourish. One of the most successful ways to incorporate media creation into a child's life is through *online math games* and *fun, interactive flash cards*. They are visually appealing and promote autonomous learning. Best of all, educational apps or games can usually be explored in about 15 minutes. As long as the game is challenging enough, children will naturally stop playing, on their own, after a reasonable period of time. Another wonderful combination of education and media involves teaching through song and movement. For children in lower elementary grades, there are apps and websites that teach spelling through entertaining, interactive videos. When children are fully engaged, even in complex tasks, they learn.

## Case Study: Jayden

**Jayden (age 10):** For the past 2 years, I had the privilege of working with the Association of American Publishers (AAP) on their Adopt-a-School program.[5] This terrific national program is a collaboration between AAP, the New York City Department of Education, the Children's Book Council, and the schools' librarians. It is aimed at improving literacy and encouraging reading, through direct interaction with authors. During a visit to CS150X middle school in the Bronx, I spoke to children like Jayden, a fifth grader who loves to play video games.

Both Jayden's teacher and the librarian took great pains to explain to me the unfortunate financial situation these families are in. (Teachers at the school regularly have money and cell phones stolen out of their purses by students.) Naturally, I was caught off guard when Jayden said that at his home, where money is extremely tight, his family has an Xbox 360, three televisions, and a laptop computer. He also has his own smartphone, which he uses to text, play games, watch YouTube videos, and post on Facebook.

He explained that he plays video games from the time he gets home from school, about 4 p.m., until whenever he falls asleep, usually around 11 p.m.

His grades are poor, C's, D's, and F's. I asked Jayden what he wanted to be when he grew up. He responded, "I want to be a doctor." There is absolutely no connection, in Jayden's mind, between academic success and his future goal.

The new digital divide isn't about who has the tools, it's about how the tools are being used.

## Case Study: Sampson

**Sampson (age 11):** I met Sampson while interviewing students at a New York City middle school. The school has a serious robotics club, and Sampson—along with 12 other students—as preparing for a robotics competition. Although I was all set to interview Sampson, I found that *he* spent the majority of our time together interviewing *me*!

After learning about my book project, Sampson quickly asked if I had a website. I sheepishly admitted that it wasn't constructed yet. Sampson quickly offered to design one for me, and wrote down the names of two other websites he had created.

Impressed, I asked him if he actually knew code. He did. He had first learned basic logic loops and low-level HTML from playing games on Scratch, an MIT website. By eight years old, he began to learn early-level coding after playing a popular game called Minecraft. He went online and researched mods—how to alter codes to make changes to games. His parents, eager to feed his learning habit, enrolled him and a friend in a class that teaches Java to teens in a user-friendly way.

They gobbled up the experience like candy.

His parents then challenged him to start a business venture. He chose web design.

When I asked him how many hours a day he spent on the computer, he replied, "I'm only allowed to spend an hour on the computer."

Sampson's grades are strong. He maintains an A– average. When I asked Sampson what he wanted to be when he grew up, he replied, "An entrepreneur. I really want to design apps."

There is absolutely no disconnect between *how* Sampson is using technology and his future goals.

### RESEARCHERS' CONCLUSIONS

Sampson's parents did many empowering things that other parents can learn from. They set time-oriented rules about media consumption and used that play to introduce their son to media use in an exciting way. Then they replaced *consumption* with *creation*.

Some of the available choices for media creation are blogs, digital storyboards, video presentations, podcasts, mods, Facebook (an organization or business, not a personal account), video games, apps, websites, Wikimedia, and digital videos or music remixing. Many schools are now including classes in media creation as part of their curriculum.

## Case Study: Mrs. O'Kane and the School Newspaper

When Mrs. O'Kane took over the school newspaper, she realized that she had a wonderful opportunity to integrate media creation. The students were thrilled when she announced that the newspaper would *go green* and *go digital*.

The newspaper is formatted like a blog, and elementary school students learn the basics of the WordPress platform by participating in the school paper. Amelia, a third grader, suggested that they add a "how-to" section, for kids eager to learn something new or show off a skill through video.

One student gave a tutorial on how to play the violin. Another student recorded it, and uploaded it via YouTube. All of the writing for the newspaper is typed, and many of the students can already touch-type.

**RESEARCHERS' CONCLUSIONS**

When children are challenged to learn new material, they will probably persevere—as long as there is any reward or reinforcement. As the habit or skill builds, it becomes self-reinforcing and a learning habit has been established. That learning habit schedule is exactly what Mrs. O'Kane facilitated. The children were challenged to learn WordPress, typing, and new styles of composition. Because this was happening in a collegial atmosphere, children were not afraid to express original ideas to their peers (social interaction, communication skills, and reinforcement were all occurring simultaneously). They got to see their work as it evolved, and it was put forward to the entire school community. The newspaper experience is the epitome of productive habit building.

### Resources for Media Creation

✓ *Production-editorial (office-type) skills:* It is important that students learn word-processing and presentation skills for school projects and to prepare them for college. Have your children start by designing and typing thank-you cards on the computer.

✓ *Digital drawing:* Starting as young as kindergarten, children can learn to draw incredible images on a computer and gain familiarity with the keyboard and mouse.

✓ *USB-powered microscopes:* These amazing microscopes allow children to see what is under the microscope on the computer monitor and then research it.

✓ *Legos:* Those little toys you trip over on the floor have some incredible digital learning programs for children. Bricks in Space and WeDo Robotics are just two.

✓ *Podcasting:* Record narrations for animations, stories, and videos.

✓ *Apps:* iMovie, The Wheels on the Bus, BrainPOP Jr., SketchBook Pro, Brushes, iDraw, Explain Everything, Creative Book Builder, Book Creator, My Story, Toontastic, Puppet Pals, Inspiration, and Keynote.

✓ *iPad Boot Camps:* Apple is positioning the iPad as a credible source of educational technology, reaching out to students, parents, and teachers with these programs for media creation:
  - iPad Animation Boot Camp
  - iPad Filmmaking Boot Camp
  - iPad Artist/Photographer Boot Camp
  - iPad Rockstar Boot Camp

## MEDIA COMMUNICATION

*We're living in an era where capturing moments using our phones is more important than actually living these moments with whoever is beside us.*
—Posted by Blossom, on Unknown Quotes

## The Omnipresent Power of the Cell Phone

I can't think of another single device that changed the family dynamics of our home, and the relationship I've enjoyed with my son, as much as the smartphone. Our cell phone rules and experiences have been fluid. They started with the basics: passwords (we have always required them), parental controls (installed on his phone), and time limits. They have changed over the years, as we—as a family—have changed.

I'm much more careful about my own cell phone use since my son got his. I try harder to be fully present when I'm with him, because that's the behavior I want to encourage. I leave my phone at home, just to show that I can, and I feel better when I do. (Sometimes, I just take the pictures in my mind.)

Here are a few things I've learned along the way:

- ✓ I made my child wait until he was 14 to get a smartphone. I wish I had waited longer.

- ✓ That phone will become the most important thing in your child's life. Be prepared for it.

- ✓ Your child will walk around staring at their phone. They will seem distracted and irritated when they can't look at it.

- ✓ Your child now has another way of communicating with their friends, people they like, people they don't like, and you. Be prepared for a breakdown in verbal communication with you.

- ✓ When given a choice, they will send you a text rather than call. Have rules about calling—it's important that they don't forget how!

- ✓ "Quality time" with your child will never be the same. If they own a phone, they are multitasking. It's a new and strange feeling to constantly share your child, even when they are with you.

✓ The way they experience the world will forever be changed. The first time you catch them staring into their phone at a concert while videotaping it, you'll understand. Stress the importance of being *fully present* at their lives.

✓ As hard as you try, you can't place digital limits on communication—Snapchat and Twitter messages are just a few sites that allow children to get around parental texting limits. You'll have to monitor this, and it will make you feel uncomfortable to do that. You'll get over it and so will your kids, but your relationship with them will never be quite the same.

✓ You can control how your child uses their phone—in your presence—with clear rules. Don't give up that power.

✓ You can control where and when your child can use their cell phone in your house, by establishing clear rules. Don't give up that power.

✓ Your child will wake up exhausted if you let them take a cell phone into their room at night . . . so don't.

✓ Your child's grades will start to decrease if they don't turn the cell phone off during homework time.

✓ Explain to your child that digital footprints last forever.* Talk to them about respecting their body and those of other people. Have a clear plan about what will happen if your child uses the phone for sexting, bullying, taking or receiving naked pictures, and posting destructive content online. Make sure they know the plan, make sure you follow through the second it happens . . . *for sure*: Something, at some point, will happen.

---

* Except when they don't—Wickr and other apps claim that they delete messages after a specified length of time.

✓ Don't buy a child a phone as a gift. It's not a gift; it's a responsibility. If they want one, they can buy it with their own money. (My son also used his own money to replace the phone the two times he dropped it and it cracked.)

✓ Do get them a cell phone contract. (I pay my child's cell phone bill, but I know parents who go in 50/50.) I like being my son's communication provider—because he can't use his phone without me. He signed a contract with me, just like he would for a cell phone carrier. You can find many contracts drawn up by a bevy of wonderful bloggers, who have shared these—free of charge—online. If you don't know what to write in your own, borrow someone else's.*

## MORE DOES NOT EQUAL BETTER

More of something good isn't necessarily better. The results of the Learning Habit Study showed that a significant number of children have a 45-minute threshold for texting, computer, phone, or tablet use. In fact, children who used computers and tablets moderately scored significantly higher than their non-user counterparts. After 45 minutes of use, however, grades slowly but steadily declined. After 180 minutes (three hours) of use, grades rapidly declined. After four hours of use, fewer than 10% of students could maintain a grade of 90 or above.

Another trend discovered during the Learning Habit Study was that children were given complex media devices without exhibiting responsibility for even the simplest of household tasks or chores. *The study revealed that more elementary school children have cell phones than make their beds.* Take a moment to let that statistic sink in.

---

* Check mycrazygoodlife.com/cell-phone-contract-for-kids and cyberbullying.us/cyberbullying_cell_phone_contract.pdf for good examples.

## Case Study: Cody and Media Multitasking[6]

Cody (age 11) sat hunched over a bowl of cereal, wearing a blue hoodie. He was hopelessly grouchy in the morning. Both his parents had stopped engaging him in conversation before he left for school.

"His grouchiness would affect the whole family," explained his mother, Beth. "By the time Cody left for school, I'd feel incredibly crabby. Then I'd show up for work in a foul mood."

Morning grouchiness is not an uncommon complaint from parents, especially parents of teenagers. But what happens when your child's mood doesn't improve throughout the day, when your child seems to be terminally bad-tempered?

What about a bad mood that lasts not just for a day or two, but for several weeks or months?

"I woke up one morning and said to my husband, Kevin, 'I'm really worried about Cody,'" Beth said. "He rolled over and said, 'I know, I am, too.'"

Beth and Kevin made an appointment with a family therapist. Part of Cody's treatment at the Center included keeping a journal (tracking). His therapist asked him to record the highs and lows of the day; his mood, exercise, and sleep—and his media use.

Cody's journal revealed a disturbing pattern of relentless late-night texting with friends, coupled with additional hours on the computer while listening to music via headphones. Even on nights he would log off earlier, he was constantly being awakened by the *ding* of his cell phone or iPad with some sort of alert.

For a developing child, it's nearly impossible to resist the urgent impulse to reply to text messages, or restrain themselves from checking social media sites like Facebook, Twitter, Tumblr, Instagram, Reddit, Vine, and YouTube.

"After a few sessions with his therapist, Cody came home and announced, 'I'm done with Facebook,'" Beth recounted. "Kevin and I played it cool and said nothing. The next morning, at break-

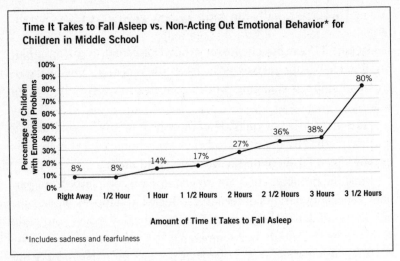

FIGURE 3.7

fast, he was like a different kid. He was awake, and pleasant, and actually speaking to us," said Beth.

"A few days later, he came home and asked us to move his computers out of his room," Beth reported. "Kevin and I looked at each

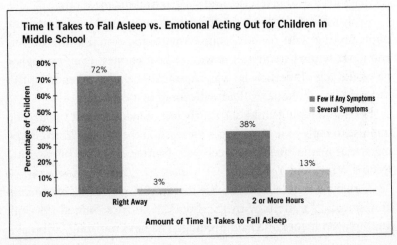

FIGURE 3.8

other like, 'Is this really our kid?' Before, we couldn't pry him off of the computer, even if we wanted to."

According to Cody's parents, the day Cody unplugged at night, his mood improved and his grouchiness disappeared. Cody still uses his laptop and has a cell phone, but leaves them outside his bedroom. He's remained Facebook free for eight months, and many of his friends have followed suit.

## RESEARCHERS' CONCLUSIONS

The deluge of digital stimulation combined with frequent multitasking via his tablet and cell phone was affecting Cody's sleep, concentration, and mood. Developing children and teenagers are particularly susceptible to media addiction and concurrent sleep deprivation.

Dr. Larry Rosen, a research psychologist and professor at California State University at Dominguez Hills, published a study in the May issue of *Computers in Human Behavior* on media multitasking while learning. The study cautions parents against a dangerous and growing phenomenon: attending to multiple streams of information and entertainment while studying and learning.

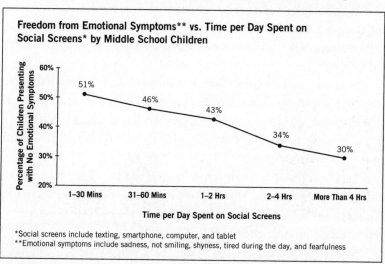

Freedom from Emotional Symptoms** vs. Time per Day Spent on Social Screens* by Middle School Children

*Social screens include texting, smartphone, computer, and tablet
**Emotional symptoms include sadness, not smiling, shyness, tired during the day, and fearfulness

FIGURE 3.9

When we parents put a cell phone, computer, tablet, or TV remote in a child's hand, we are giving them a powerful instrument. Why, then, are we debating our right to monitor its usage?

The next question is: How are we using technology to teach our children responsibility?

In 1964, Marshall McLuhan wrote about the effect that electronic media was having in terms of blurring regional boundaries and turning the world into a "global village."[7] PhilosophicalSociety .com reports in "An Overview of McLuhan's Thinking":

> A "friend" on television will be just as important to us
> as a "real-life" friend. The person we instant message on
> the Internet will "matter" as much as someone we just
> met at a dinner party. And so on.[8]

## Case Study: Ciara and Social Media

**Ciara (12):** Ciara's mother, Elise, was awakened by the sound of crying at 3:30 on a Wednesday morning. She got up, and discovered her daughter sitting on her bed, iPad on her lap, weeping.

Elise couldn't imagine why her daughter was awake—on a school night—on her tablet, and crying. "I felt like I was having an out-of-body experience," Elise related. "The whole scene was too bizarre for words."

She went on to recount, "My first thought was that my daughter was the victim of cyberbullying. I mean, Ciara's a dancer; with all that exercise, she's always in bed, dead to the world, by 9:30."

As it turned out, Ciara wasn't being cyberbullied—at least, not in the traditional sense.

Ciara had made a "really close friend" online. They had met in a dance chat room and started following each other on Facebook, Twitter, and Tumblr. Ciara told her mother that "Tiffany is like my sister; I'd do anything for her!"

As Elise uncovered the story, the "really close friend" had been sending Ciara increasingly disturbing messages about being sexually abused and about regularly visiting an Ana website. These websites, as Elise discovered, encourage anorexia nervosa as a "lifestyle choice," and provide strategies to help girls starve themselves in a disturbing—and dangerous—quest for "beauty." Tiffany had decided that not eating would give her control over her life and change her entire "look," so she had resolved to stop eating entirely.

That night, however, she confided in Ciara that she planned to kill herself.

"Tiffany had my daughter convinced that if she didn't stay on Tumblr with her, Tiffany was going to take a bottle of her mother's pills, go into the bathtub, and slit her wrists. Ciara felt totally responsible for keeping this girl—whom she'd never even met—alive."

Other than the obvious problem (nighttime computer use) and solution (no more media devices in Ciara's bedroom), the more disturbing factor, to Elise, was that her daughter would:

- ✓ Form a relationship with a stranger online.

- ✓ Believe that what that person was telling her was the truth.

- ✓ Believe that it was her responsibility to keep this girl alive.

- ✓ Think that it would be her fault if the girl killed herself.

- ✓ Feel unable to talk to her mother about it.

When the police and school authorities were contacted, Elise was told that there was nothing they could do. No one had been physically hurt and it wasn't technically bullying, because Tiffany was only saying things about herself. Furthermore, although there were stories about a girl in that school having done that kind of thing before, there were no grounds for speaking to the girl or calling her parents into the school.

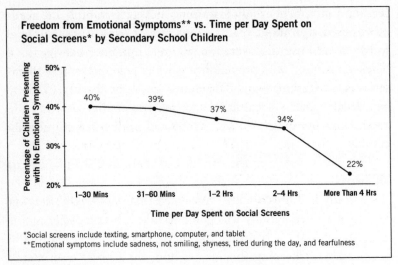

**Freedom from Emotional Symptoms\*\* vs. Time per Day Spent on Social Screens\* by Secondary School Children**

Percentage of Children Presenting with No Emotional Symptoms

50%
40%
30%
20%

40%    39%    37%    34%    22%

1–30 Mins    31–60 Mins    1–2 Hrs    2–4 Hrs    More Than 4 Hrs

Time per Day Spent on Social Screens

\*Social screens include texting, smartphone, computer, and tablet
\*\*Emotional symptoms include sadness, not smiling, shyness, tired during the day, and fearfulness

FIGURE 3.10

## RESEARCHERS' CONCLUSIONS

Ciara's story is not unusual. Kids who have "relationships" through social media are under the illusion that they are having real relationships. The danger is that they are setting themselves up for myriad problems. Although Ciara had outside interests and "real" friends, she was not a "media creator," in the new tech parlance; she was, as most kids are, a media consumer. She wasn't using her computer for any creative or learning experience; she was naively using it, only for entertainment.

This is the rule—not the exception, teachers and our own research tell us. As media consumerism rises (often to more than eight hours a day, our study found), communication skills fall.

When children are unable to be successful in interpersonal relationships, they are more drawn to digital ones. It's a chicken and egg situation. Which comes first, the alienation/isolation leading to media overuse or vice versa? We vote for the latter. As children become more screen involved, they have less need for communication skills and less time for/interest in socialization activities. This lack of ability to communicate their feelings, wants, and needs makes them feel like losers; that, in turn, breeds discontent and anger. Swallowing feelings—not believing that anyone wants to listen to you, or spend time with you, or genuinely cares about you—is like locking a pack of dogs in the basement and refusing to feed them; sooner or later, they'll break free and devour you.

If children can't talk to their parents about their feelings and get validation, they become closed off, frustrated, insecure, and angry.

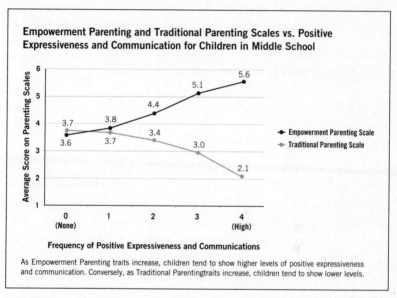

**Empowerment Parenting and Traditional Parenting Scales vs. Positive Expressiveness and Communication for Children in Middle School**

As Empowerment Parenting traits increase, children tend to show higher levels of positive expressiveness and communication. Conversely, as Traditional Parentingtraits increase, children tend to show lower levels.

FIGURE 3.11

You may have noticed that some of the charts in this chapter use the term *traditional parenting scale*. Traditional parenting includes characteristics such as:

✓ Lack of warmth: a judgmental, critical style

✓ Not inclined to "listen to the music" when children need to talk about how they are feeling

✓ Impulsive reactions: quick to correct; frequent use of *should*; impatient interrupting when children talk

✓ Reactive rather than thoughtful: more inclined to punish, hit, or spank

We use the terms *traditional* and *enabling* synonymously, because the effects are to shut children down—to correct and judge; not to allow children to vent their feelings or to make their own choices. This style of parenting is controlling and outcome oriented. It is antithetical to the open mind-set that creates learning habits.

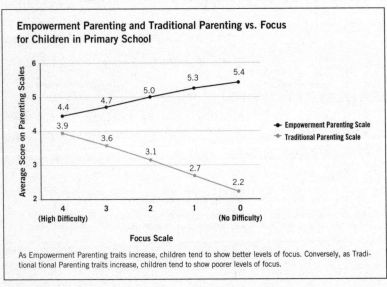

**Empowerment Parenting and Traditional Parenting vs. Focus for Children in Primary School**

As Empowerment Parenting traits increase, children tend to show better levels of focus. Conversely, as Traditional Parenting traits increase, children tend to show poorer levels of focus.

FIGURE 3.12

## Case Study: The Ding and Short-Term Memory[9]

I'm mid-conversation with my 15-year-old, and he's filling me in on the happenings of his day. They chose pseudonyms in French class. His "French" name? Bruno. I remind him that Bruno is Italian, not French, but he couldn't care less. "It's hilarious," he assures me.

Then I hear it; the faint but ubiquitous *ding* of an iPhone coming from his pocket, and he's transported someplace else. As we continue our chat, there is visible tension in his jawline and his stare is more vacant. He's suppressing the urge to glance at his phone, but he can't stop himself from thinking about it. He's looking at me, he's responding to what I'm saying, but he's not really there. I've already lost him.

I tell him that I'll be picking him up from swim practice tonight; I tell him about his cousin's birthday party next weekend. He walks away and makes it about five paces before he pulls the phone out of his pocket.

I find out later that he has no memory of my telling him either of these things.

So, what actually happened to my child's memory during the last two minutes of our conversation—the part after the *ding*?

## RESEARCHERS' CONCLUSIONS

In a 2013 article published in Sweden's Royal Institute of Technology (KTH) newsletter, Erik Fransén, a researcher and professor of computer science at KTH, explained that the problem with technology use has to do with our working memory, or what we often refer to as our "short-term" memory: "Working memory enables us to filter out information and find what we need in the communication. . . . It's also a limited resource."[10]

According to Fransén's research, working memory can carry only three or four items. When we add a new message to that (*Ding*, check your cell phone! *Ding*, check your cell phone!), we lose our ability to process information.

The effect of media multitasking on memory is still relatively unknown. Many parents think it's simply use of more than one media device at a time; like watching *The Voice* while texting. It's not that simple. When you ask a child to power down, it gives them permission to let go of whatever and whoever is virtually intruding on your conversation.

You wouldn't go to a party and converse with 10 people who

are scattered about a crowded room at the same time. You talk to one person at a time or the conversation loses relevance and passion. Yet that's exactly what our children are doing when they're on the couch texting 10 different people. It's social chaos, it's loud, and it's really not surprising that someone can't focus, sleep, or remember things after navigating that.

### Recommendations

- ✓ Have a *cell phone spot* in your home: Turn the phones off and place them there upon entering the house. It will become a habit, just like hanging up your keys.

- ✓ Whenever possible, power down before conversations.

- ✓ Cell phones should not be permitted in bedrooms.

- ✓ Cell phones should be powered down a minimum of one hour before bedtime.

- ✓ Have a cell phone contract that is clear and specific. Have your child sign it and post it in a common area of the house.

- ✓ No cell phones during meal time. Not for anyone.

Parents have *a lot more control* than they are choosing to exercise.

### Reminder

When you put a cell phone in your child's hand, it suddenly becomes as important as any other lesson you're going to teach them. Use it to help them develop media management learning habits by having clear, time-specific rules in place.

# CONCLUSION: WHAT THEY SAID . . . OOPS!

## About the Television

*Television won't be able to hold on to any market it captures after the first six months. People will soon get tired of staring at a plywood box every night.*

—Darryl F. Zanuck, head of
Twentieth Century-Fox, 1946

## About the Telephone

*This "telephone" has too many shortcomings to be seriously considered as a practical form of communication. The device is inherently of no value to us.*

—Western Union, internal memo, 1878

## About the Computer

*There is no reason for any individual to have a computer in their home.*

—Ken Olsen, president of Digital Corporation, 1977

*I think there is a world market for maybe five computers.*

—Thomas J. Watson Sr., chairman of IBM, 1943

Oh, dear. Unfortunately, these notable gentlemen were either born too early or not fully cognizant of Marshall McLuhan's writings on media. . . . Even in the infancy of electronic communication, McLuhan could see its potential.

The thesis of his work concerning media and its overarching importance becomes more true every nanosecond. We, as parents, are missing an absolutely essential opportunity to shape the way our children understand and use media, if we don't employ our influence and skill to point them in the direction of media management as a powerful *learning habit*.

# CHAPTER FOUR

# The Homework Habit: Supporting Academic Homework and Reading

"My life is a black hole of boredom and despair."
"So basically you've been doing homework."
"Like I said, black hole."
—*Kiersten White,* Supernaturally

**Lucy Hopkins (teacher)** stands in front of her kindergarten students with a puppet on one hand. The puppet is a teaching tool, and Mrs. Hopkins is using it to teach both vowel and consonant sounds to the class. The students use "sky writing" and copy Mrs. Hopkins's motions in the air with their tiny hands forming letters. Mrs. Hopkins then clicks a button on her laptop and a video projects onto the classroom screen. The two-minute video teaches the students songs to help them remember the words they just learned. The word is printed on the screen, and music plays. Today the students are learning *is* and *see*:

> I spell is "IS" i-s-i-s, it doesn't have a "Z"
> I spell "IS" i-s-i-s, there's just no foolin' me![1]

Today, 20 smiling five- and six-year-old children just learned how to pronounce, read, and write two new sight words! Mrs. Hopkins hands each student a worksheet with the new sight words printed on it, a "big-kid" homework assignment for her students.

Jessica (age 7) is in the first grade. She is being treated for ADHD and feels like her teacher is always reminding her to do things like *slow down* and *focus*. She says that her handwriting is "terrible" and thinks it's too hard to make the letters look neat if she is trying to think. She feels frustrated whenever she has a homework assignment and angry at her mom for making her sit for "so-o-o-o long" and do it.

Liz and Mauve (age 14) are cousins and BFFs. The girls are each starting a new college preparatory high school in the fall. Homework has never created an issue for either Liz or Mauve. The girls are both average students but are a little worried about the challenging classes at the college prep schools.

Ben Wallace (teacher) began integrating the Common Core State Standards (CCSS) into his classroom last year. The school district in which Mr. Wallace works purchased a digital mathematics program, which means all homework is to be done online. The year before, Mr. Wallace was involved in testing a beta version of the program in his classroom. The students' mathematics scores improved dramatically, and he was excited to integrate the online homework assignments. However, the program the school district purchased was very different from the model Mr. Wallace had tested; it wasn't as much fun for the students. It fact, the students and their parents found the homework module stressful. Regardless, he was required to assign digital math homework using the program the school district purchased.

# THE HOMEWORK HABIT

Homework habits teach children self-mastery, autonomy, intrinsic motivation, and self-efficacy.

The Learning Habit Studies revealed an unexpected skill set: the *homework habit*. For the researchers, this information was pivotal in its potential to enhance the quality of life for parents and their children. Why? Because the homework habit was the *only* habit that correlated with every skill identified as central for development of children able to be self-reliant and goal focused through every level of their education.

In Chapter Two, parents learned the best way to set up a rule so that it becomes self-reinforcing. The formation of habit will occur naturally, after the routine is done consistently without any parental cuing.

An academic homework routine is just like that: a system that the family decides on, so children can do their homework as efficiently as possible, within reasonable time limits. A school's curriculum may change, but the homework routine should stay the same. This is the only sane way to maintain balance. A homework routine includes leaving children time to play, participate in sports and clubs, and take lessons. Learning is not a race to the top; it is a gradual process that occurs every single day. As children are learning to develop multiple strategies and models for problem solving (especially in math), their minds are being challenged in new and unique ways.

Parents have commented that their children are tired, frustrated, and disengaged. Children's self-esteem is closely linked to their academic performance. That's why it's increasingly important for parents to implement a clear homework routine that includes activities that are interesting and fun for kids.

## HOW MUCH TIME IS NEEDED
## FOR ACADEMIC HOMEWORK?

Harris Cooper, professor of psychology at Duke, reviewed more than 60 studies regarding the amount of time a child might do homework to achieve the optimal results. In a paper, published in 2006, he recommended that this time was 10 to 20 minutes per grade in school. Therefore, a second grader would be expected to sit, distraction free, for 20 minutes, while a sixth grader would have approximately 60 minutes (an hour) allocated for homework.

✓ First grade: 10 to 20 minutes of homework

✓ Second grade: 20 minutes of homework

✓ Fourth grade: 40 minutes of homework

✓ Sixth grade: 60 minutes of homework

✓ Ninth through twelfth grades: 90 to 120 minutes of homework

The National Parent Teacher Association (PTA) and National Education Association (NEA) recommendations also agree with these general guidelines, recommending 10 minutes per grade, with the exception being 10 to 20 minutes in the first grade. Obviously, high school students may occasionally need more time; with good time management and scheduling skills, however, they can usually parcel out assignments to complete their homework within the suggested 10 minutes per grade.

## THE BETTER HOMEWORK HABIT

The homework habit is based not only on research but also on interviews with nearly 100 elementary- and middle-school teachers across the United States who have been actively involved in the development and implementation of their school's new curriculum. Teachers universally agreed that children should spend only 10 minutes per grade on homework and then stop. Not a single teacher interviewed felt that a child should spend more time than that.

This doesn't mean that these teachers assign only 10 minutes' worth of homework a night. As one third-grade teacher commented, "All children work at a different pace. I typically assign a worksheet. As long as a student is trying, that's what matters. Completion should not be the goal, especially with the new material."

The first step in creating a homework habit involves deciding where and when to do homework, then adopting a 10-minute rule. This means that children will sit and work on an academic activity for 10 minutes per grade. If they don't finish, that's okay. If they finish early, they'll read for the remainder of homework time. Have plenty of books on hand and available for your child. Elementary school homework assignments can be really inconsistent. There will be many days when your child doesn't have homework. On those days they will still read. Some days they may have a deluge of assignments, and parents will feel tempted to have children work longer. Don't. This is about forming a habit; working gradually toward a goal. When children know there is a start and a finish to a task, they relax and focus.

Perhaps the most rewarding part of the homework habit is that there is no need for a child to lie about having homework or not having homework. They are going to sit and work for the exact same amount of time, regardless of the volume of work assigned. Rushing through an assignment without focusing is not going to get them one step closer to playing a video game. They also don't get to drag homework out by complaining. Instead, they will have to go into school the next day and deal with the consequences of their choice.

The homework routine does not replace the 20 to 30 minutes of reading elementary-school children are required to complete every day. This should still occur, now more than ever. With *theoretical learning* and rapid, experimental curriculum changes occurring in most schools, the best way parents can help children is by encouraging *reading*.

Homework is a close collaboration between home, school, and community. It requires a delicate balance and an absolute commitment on the part of parents and children. It is important that parents support their children's teachers; conveying the impression that their school assignments are not of high value is doing your child—and the teacher—a disservice. Most teachers are doing everything within their power to help children succeed. They are under a tremendous amount of pressure to work with new material, and have been given very little guidance. With the implementation of different state standards, the classroom pace may feel rushed. This frequently results in an increase in homework assignments. That's why parents need a *consistent* homework habit. Having your child spend hours on a developmentally inappropriate assignment will teach them to dislike learning and school, and make them feel inadequate and angry. *Having them focus for a grade-appropriate amount of time and rewarding them for hard work and effort is a far better system.*

We discovered that each portion of the homework routine (not just the academic segment) affects good grades. This is probably not groundbreaking news to students in Shanghai, China—who have used a similar routine for years and claim the world's top-scoring and emotionally and physically healthy students.[2] However, this idea differs greatly from what American parents have been taught.

Removing sports, family time, social events, and dance classes with the hope of improving the quality of academic homework is a bad idea. When the routine becomes unbalanced, school performance declines, social skills decline, and students suffer from emotional problems.

## FIRST, YOU MUST BELIEVE . . .

When we interviewed a fifth grader about homework, he just stared for a minute and then said disgustedly, "Homework? That's what you want to talk to me about, *homework*? Are you *trying* to ruin my day? I can't think of anything to say about homework that isn't . . . rude!"

Most parents surveyed didn't indicate having a problem with children being *assigned* homework; what they didn't like was the stress, arguments, and anxiety that the *process of doing* homework caused throughout their families.

In countries where children maintain top scores in academics, there is a strong cultural difference in the way schoolwork is administered at home compared to how it is most often administered here in the United States. In these cultures, children are taught at a young age about the value of schoolwork and take complete ownership of it. They have clear goals and determination. Above all, they do not believe that they are born with a special talent, have a high IQ, or are entitled to anything. They understand that they are fully capable of learning and developing their brains. They believe in their ability to learn the material. The focus is always on developing a learning habit. Changing our schools' curriculum and simply raising our standards won't help a child to develop this vital part of the success equation. This is one of the most important parts of "homework": *children must believe they are capable of doing the work*. Introducing children to more challenging work, without using Empowerment Parenting, is a recipe for disaster.

> *In Shanghai, students are raised to be hard workers.*
> *We care about what we do and we believe in ourselves.*
> —Chen Jie, Shanghai student

## Case Study: Jessica

Jessica (age 7) has been in family therapy for several months. She was referred to us for an ADHD evaluation shortly after the start of first grade. Jess is the type of child who appears very *busy* all the time. Her body and mind seem to be in a constant state of motion.

What's interesting about Jess is that she is able to sit for relatively long periods of time for a seven-year-old. What continues to remain a challenge for Jess, her teacher, and her parents, however, is that she is not able to concentrate on *one specific thing* for any prolonged period of time. Children who struggle with either concentration or time-management skills have difficulty with academic homework skills. Jessica's mother, Kathy, reports that she and her daughter frequently have arguments during homework time. They're not full-blown screaming matches, but they add a measurable degree of tension to the house.

The following is an excerpt from Kathy's therapy session:

**Therapist:** So, what's actually happening when Jess does her homework?

**Kathy:** She rushes through it, as fast as she can. Last night she had a handwriting paper and she wasn't even trying. Mrs. Gamen, her teacher, gave them a page with five state names on it. Each of the states had a printed line below it, and they had to copy the state name onto the line, and then find it on the map and color it in.

**Therapist:** I hope Mississippi wasn't on the list!

**Kathy:** That's exactly what I thought! No, Mrs. Gamen was nice and started with short ones, like Utah and Ohio. Anyway, Jess is scribbling her answers down as fast as she can. She's not even capitalizing all the first letters like she's supposed to, and she's writing some of the letters backward.

**Therapist:** That's not unusual for a seven-year-old, Kathy.

**Kathy:** I know it's probably normal, but she's doing it because she's rushing. So I had her redo the letters, and capitalize them, but she's still writing them all messy. Finally I said to her, "You know what? If you're not going to sit and try your hardest, then don't do your homework!" I feel like she's just not putting in the effort. I tell her to slow down and relax, but she doesn't listen. She just doesn't *care* about it like I did when I was in school.

## RESEARCHERS' CONCLUSIONS

At the tender age of seven, Jess was already establishing an ineffective homework routine and developing some strong negative feelings about her schoolwork. The homework routine described here is a common one in the United States. It requires a couple of things to hold it together. The first is a parent's assistance, in this case, Kathy's. The second is negative feedback from the parent in the form of comments and commands, such as Kathy's instruction to "redo" the homework.

When these routines continue, they guarantee a pattern of habit building—but *unproductive* learning habits are being formed.

Children:

✓ Don't develop intrinsic motivation.

✓ Don't develop autonomy.

✓ Don't develop mastery.

✓ Don't develop self-efficacy.

## Missing the Target

Kathy's goal was to set up a positive homework routine that would happen automatically, without her needing to nag or fight with Jess. She felt sorry for Jess, who seemed to dislike schoolwork so much, but she was also frustrated by her daughter's behavior. Thanks to some well-meaning but enabling parenting techniques, Kathy was helping Jess build an ineffective learning habit.

## A BETTER HOMEWORK HABIT

Kathy and her therapist decided on a reasonable amount of time for Jess to spend on homework. Using the 10-minute rule, they agreed that 10 minutes was a good place to start for a first grader. Kathy was asked to help Jess set a measurable long-term goal for herself—something they could both feel good about and focus on. They agreed that sitting for 20 minutes and focusing on the same task was a reasonable long-term goal.

The next step was to move Kathy into the Empowerment Parenting mind frame. Kathy agreed to praise her daughter only for effort (hard work) and not outcome. "Nice job staying focused" or "I can see you're working really hard, Jess" were her go-to phrases. When Jess made a mistake, Kathy would not say a word. Even if she did not finish the assignment in the allotted time, Jessica would stop and pack up her things after 10 minutes.

This was challenging for Kathy to conceptualize and buy into. She found it hard enough to picture herself letting Jess turn in a sloppy assignment . . . not turning in a completed assignment? Inconceivable!

"Aren't I just promoting mediocrity?" Kathy asked.

## DEVELOPING AUTONOMY, SELF-MASTERY, AND MOTIVATION

Kathy isn't the only parent who has wrestled with this particular part of the homework habit. Many parents in the Unites States can't imagine encouraging this practice. Yet, in a recent study of 33 countries, the United States scored significantly lower than 17 of them on "motivation to learn."[3] Intrinsic motivation comes from students:

✓ Believing that they are capable of doing the work, and

✓ Making a connection to the work.

When parents do the work for the child, or take responsibility for their child's assignment, children lose that connection; they lose their motivation and autonomy.

It might feel counterintuitive, but when a parent allows a child to turn in an assignment with errors on it, they are allowing that child to learn from their mistakes.

When parents correct assignments for children or point out errors, children *will* make the changes, but they will learn *nothing*. It's robotic. That's why you end up telling your child the same thing, night after night.

Setting up a doable, time-limited, and reasonable homework routine, however, allows children to develop self-management, scheduling, time management, and goal-setting skills. Combined with your encouragement for their hard work, they will develop a successful homework habit and feel a sense of mastery and pride.

Many people, parents included, believe that they are fully capable of teaching. Teaching is a skill; it's hard to be an effective teacher, especially for children. Even if you have a degree in teaching and are actively teaching in a school, please don't attempt to teach your own child. You have a different job. You are Mommy or Daddy; only you can help with the most important *homework* of all—the essential skill sets. By allowing your children to do their own schoolwork, you are encouraging positive learning habits. In addition, if your child is having a genuine problem with either comprehending or completing the work, the difficulty will reveal itself sooner if you're *not helping*. This makes it possible to enlist the aid of teachers and other school personnel who are trained to deal with learning issues.

In a seven-week study, parents were taught how to use a technique that mirrored the combination of Empowerment Parenting and homework habits for a better homework routine.[4]

### Skills Learned

✓ *Intrinsic motivation:* Explaining to the children why learning the material is important; suggesting how their homework is preparation for making their world a better place and for helping them realize their dreams.

✓ *Autonomy:* Letting the child know that *you believe* they can do the work. It may be hard, but they have the control to make it happen. Standing aside and not doing the work for them or losing patience with them.

✓ *Self-mastery:* Highlighting the interesting aspects of homework topics and emphasizing that the process of studying enhances one's cognitive development (or "brain power," in kidspeak). Emphasizing learning and working hard over the grade they receive.

After the seven weeks, parents in the treatment group reported that their children were more intrinsically motivated to do their schoolwork, and children reported feeling more positive emotions about doing homework. They also reported less stress and fewer arguments during homework time.[5]

## THE HOMEWORK ROUTINE

The next part of developing a homework habit involved having Jess do the same thing every day after school so that it would become a routine. This meant that Jess would sit for 10 minutes each day, regardless of whether she had a worksheet or another assignment to complete for school. On the days Jess did not have a worksheet, she would read. (Jessica and her mother had always read for 20 minutes before bed. The reading portion of homework did not replace this activity.)

Kathy had a mix of books available at the table for Jess. Most were *easy readers* or *level one* books. She also had a timer set out on the table.

Kathy decided it would be best for Jessica to have some play time and exercise immediately after school, before sitting for homework time.

Jessica's homework rule was simple: "Between 4:00 and 4:10, I will sit at the kitchen table and do my homework. Afterward, my homework is packed in my backpack; then I can pick an activity I want."

The first day, Jess rushed through her assignment and finished it in a record *1.6 minutes*! It was barely legible. She looked at Kathy, who said nothing, but gestured at the stack of books. Jessica muttered a few choice words about "dumb books" and then asked her mother if she could watch TV.

"What's our rule?" asked her mother.

"I don't know," Jess replied.

Her mother repeated the rule: "Homework is from 4:00 to 4:10."

Jess picked up a book and flipped through a couple of pages. The timer went off and Jess looked at her mother, confused.

"Now you can do something you want," Kathy said.

After a few days of the homework routine, Jess began to slow down on her work. There was no reason for her to rush through it—she would sit for the same period of time, regardless of how long it took her. She began to take pride in her assignments and started trying harder. The combination of specific time, parental non-interference, consistency, and praise for effort yielded gratifying results.

Another surprising finding of the research team was the discovery that there really was no "normal" when it came to homework duration. What we found looked more like a swinging pendulum, marked by two extremes. The good news is that children actually have far less homework than has been previously reported.

## The Homework Habit

> » Eliminates children lying and saying they don't have homework; they're going to be at the table or desk, regardless.
> » Helps children avoid rushing through assignments; it's not going to get them even one extra minute closer to their PlayStation3.
> » Helps them work more efficiently. They don't drag it out with whining or complaining. When the time is up, they are done.
> » Eliminates children's staying up past their bedtime to complete an assignment.
> » Promotes a balanced life.

However, a significant number of children still have homework that exceeds five or six hours per day. What we gleaned from this snapshot was that there appeared to be very little middle ground.

What we also noticed was that there was a strong connection between children who spent a reasonable length of time on homework (10 minutes per grade) and an increase in good grades (A's and B's) in English and math.

The Learning Habit Studies and other research found only a marginal correlation between extended homework time and higher grades. In fact, as other researchers have also found, beyond a certain point, as homework time increased, grades leveled off or decreased. Moreover, extended homework time often means cutting out the very activities (like sports and sleep) that are equally necessary for academic success.

Children seem to have a maximum time threshold for homework; once they meet that threshold, their grades, organization, and self-management skills start to decrease.

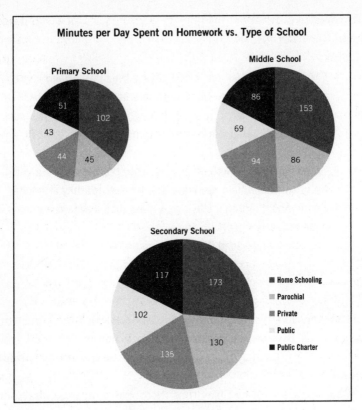

**Minutes per Day Spent on Homework vs. Type of School**

Primary School

51
102
43
44    45

Middle School

86
153
69
94    86

Secondary School

117
173
102
130
135

■ Home Schooling
▨ Parochial
■ Private
░ Public
■ Public Charter

FIGURE 4.1

Homework habits stay the same, even with digital assignments.

## HOMEWORK HABITS AND CORE CURRICULUM: BLENDING ENGLISH/LANGUAGE ARTS AND MEDIA USE

Our interviews with teachers, parents, and children have revealed enthusiasm for the raising of educational standards, to bring our schools more in line with the demands of a college. However, there is also deep concern about the implementation of the new standards, which are made all the more confusing by the pervasive use of "eduspeak." This educational industry terminology is frequently used in the new curriculum, and makes it nearly impossible for parents to understand. If it doesn't make sense to you, you're not alone.

According to the CCSS National Governor's Association:

> To be ready for college, workforce training, and life in a technological society, students need the ability to gather, comprehend, evaluate, synthesize, and report on information and ideas, to conduct original research in order to answer questions or solve problems, and to analyze and create a high volume and extensive range of print and non-print texts in media forms old and new. The need to conduct research and to produce and consume media is embedded into every aspect of today's curriculum.[6]

How, you may ask, does this affect the way your family manages the homework routine? In a word—it doesn't. The delivery systems will be altered (textbooks to online resources, paper tests to computer tests) but the principle remains the same. There will be a period of adjustment, of course; but children will still need to have balanced, healthy lives facilitated by sensible and empowering parents.

Teachers are trying to reach various learners: auditory, visual, and kinesthetic. The new approach to math and the online components may be helpful for some students and frustrating for others, depending on how they learn. As teachers and students become more familiar with the tools, they can use them to create individualized learning plans. The most important thing for parents to understand about these tools is that homework habits should remain the same, even though the device is changing.

## Case Study: Ben Wallace's Classroom

*The entire purpose of computer-based homework and learning is to develop autonomy in children.*
                    —Ben Wallace, second-grade teacher

**Ben Wallace (teacher)**, mentioned earlier in this chapter, is a second-grade teacher who loves bringing technology into the classroom.

"For one of my students, I'm mixing in elements of some first-grade computation problems with online homework games because this will help him to better understand our current lesson plan," he reported during an interview at his elementary school.

One of the most important things Ben underscores is that teachers and administrators are still working out the kinks with these programs. Homework time should remain the same for kids—now more than ever.

### BEN'S ADVICE FOR PARENTS

"Be patient with teachers and students when they start using online homework tools. In my classroom, we use an online math program and every child in the class can receive a different playlist (that's what the tutorials are called) based on their individual level. However, we [teachers] have received little to no instruction on how to use these programs. As we become more familiar with the programs, we will be able to use them with greater proficiency. For the next few years, we are all learning these tools *together*. Don't allow them to turn your life upside down. Many of the programs will change over the next few years and improve as we continue to get feedback from parents and students. It's a team effort."

### HOW IT SHOULD NOT BE USED

Ben continues, "Students *should* make mistakes on homework. This is a time for them to practice. I know what they are doing in the classroom. When they come in with assignments that are perfectly written or typed—without a single misspelling—I think, 'Nice job, Mom or Dad, for doing your kid's homework.'

"When I see that a child is spending 70 minutes on a computer program because they are *correcting* all their work—it really upsets me.

"The entire purpose of computer-based homework and learning is to *develop autonomy* in children. If a parent is forcing a child to make corrections or hand in a perfect paper, they are missing the point of the assignment. With the new computer-based homework assignments, we know how long the kids are spending on them. I would rather they spend a reasonable amount of time and make errors. That's how they learn."

## MORE EDUCATORS' COMMENTS

The CCSS are intended to assist students in using the online tools that are necessary for them to train and compete in the workforce. Familiarity with these tools can be achieved through online assignments and new media forms. One of the ways parents can assist children is by teaching them about Internet safety.

Today's students live in a world in which they have access to unlimited information and must discriminate between what is accurate and what is not. Children whose parents have taught them about Internet safety, online commercialism, and the importance of analyzing sources can successfully conduct research and find solutions to problems.

And students who understand how to successfully produce and create media are surpassing their non-media-educated peers. Perhaps the biggest *homework* challenge for parents is to steer children away from consumption media and toward creation media. There are a plethora of interactive math and English language arts (ELA) games available online, and apps that align with the CCSS. If your child is struggling with the new material, talk to the teacher about supplementing with an interactive tool—an engaging learning game that your child can have fun playing.

## NOT ENOUGH HOURS IN THE DAY

In October 2013, the *Atlantic* published a special report called "The Homework Wars: How Much Is Too Much?"[7] The author, Karl Taro Greenfeld, was concerned about the amount of time his eighth-grade daughter was spending on homework, so he did her homework for one week. The article was entertainingly written; regrettably, it shared special-report status with another article, "Two-Thirds of Americans Flush Toilets with Their Feet." (No, I did not make that up.) However, what drew my attention were the more than 800 comments at the end of the online version of this article.

While the posted comments varied in topic and focus, they all seemed to see the need for children to *complete* whatever homework was assigned—no matter how unreasonable the amount or how long the child had to work to finish it, often staying up until the middle of the night. Only one or two writers voiced the thought that *parents* could decide how much time was reasonable for their child to spend doing homework and then cap it at that amount of time—just have them stop and do something else.

## RESEARCHERS' CONCLUSION

At what point do parents decide what's best for their children? At what point do we rethink our goals for our kids? Parents, as we noted previously, have much more power than they are choosing to exercise.

As parents, our responsibility is to empower our children to explore all the opportunities for learning that are available—and most of those have *nothing* to do with academic homework. We are the ones who must determine the quality of our children's lives, until they have the experience to make those reasonable decisions for themselves.

**We need to decide:** What quality of life do we really want our children to have? What kind of parents do we want to be?

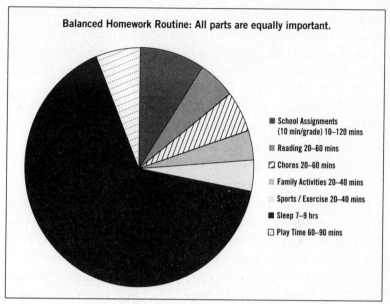

Balanced Homework Routine: All parts are equally important.

- School Assignments (10 min/grade) 10–120 mins
- Reading 20–60 mins
- Chores 20–60 mins
- Family Activities 20–40 mins
- Sports / Exercise 20–40 mins
- Sleep 7–9 hrs
- Play Time 60–90 mins

FIGURE 4.2

Balanced Homework Routine: All parts are equally important.

## FEEDING THE BRAIN THROUGH EXERCISE

The WebMD article "Train Your Brain with Exercise" supports our contention that our brains work better after we exercise our bodies. Children are calmer, happier, and more able to focus when they have some physical activity. "When one exercises," Christin Anderson of the University of San Francisco says, "you can think more clearly, perform better, and your morale is better. This is pure science—stimulate your nervous system and function at a higher level."[8]

What may come as a surprise to many parents is the link between athletics and professional success, not just for men but also for women. In a 2011 *Forbes* article, Jenna Goudreau interviewed a group of power women (CEOs and other top executives of global companies) and found that all of them equated their success in the highly competitive corporate world with the skills acquired through team sports.[9] Goudreau cited an Oppenheimer study that found:

> A shocking 82% of women in executive-level jobs had played organized sports in middle, high or post-secondary school. Moreover, nearly *half* of women earning over $75,000 identified themselves as "athletic."[10]

Participation in athletics and other high-interest extracurricular activities are not only physically and psychologically beneficial for children, they also give them occasions for social contact not found in the classroom or online. They provide kids with a different kind of opportunity to excel, to work as part of a team, and to set reasonable goals for themselves and achieve them.[11] When a child is engaged in athletics, they learn to manage frustration, to remain focused in high-pressure situations, and *to stay in the game*. They learn to deal with their emotions; they don't quit (discussed in Chapter Ten).

As the Oppenheimer study suggested, these children's grades do not suffer and their chances of financial success in adult life may actually increase. Make no mistake: to ensure our children's financial security, we must connect a college degree with employability. Unemployment rates are twice as high for those with just a high school diploma compared to those with a bachelor's degree or higher.[12]

## Case Study: Liz and Mauve

**Liz and Mauve (age 14)** were best friends and cousins; they attended a private Catholic middle school. During the spring and summer of 2012, the girls were faced with an extremely important decision: Where would they attend high school?

There were three outstanding private college preparatory schools in the area. Liz and Mauve were given a choice. Liz chose the Tailer

School and Mauve chose Chase Academy. Chase, previously an all-boys school, had recently become coed. Due to the apparent shortage of female students, all of the girls were required to play three high school sports: field hockey, basketball, and soccer. They weren't even given a choice of sports. At Tailer, a high school well known for their students' athletic prowess, it was difficult to make the high school teams.

Both girls had participated in sports during elementary school, but stopped in middle school, when things began to get competitive. Mauve described herself as "having zero athletic ability."

Mauve regularly complained about how horrible it was that her school "forces me to play sports. This is America for goodness sakes!" she told her mother.

Despite her complaining, Mauve seemed to be having fun. "We were all being forced to do it, so it's not like we judged each other for being bad. *All* the girls were pretty bad," admitted Mauve.

Her cousin Liz was not forced to take any sports at Tailer. Instead, the school simply required that a parent sign a quarterly slip saying that the student got physical activity at home. This fulfilled the PE requirement for the school.

"My parents just signed mine," said Liz.

During the 2012–2013 school year, Mauve began to blossom. Participating in sports gave her a new group of friends, she felt proud of her body and the muscles she was building, and she seemed about as happy as a 14-year-old girl can seem. The school curriculum was hard, and between sports and studying, she had no free time during the week. However, her grades that year were the highest they had ever been.

Liz, on the other hand, was struggling. She had trouble breaking into the tightly formed cliques at her new school. She began to gain weight and felt depressed. She spent hours at night trying to keep up with the difficult curriculum, but her grades that year were the lowest they had ever been. It didn't make any sense to her; she was spending all her time studying.

What's interesting to note is that both girls scored within five points of each other on the entrance exams to the schools. They both had B averages on admission. In many ways, they were more like twins than cousins. Tailer and Chase had almost identical academic curricula—but dramatically different physical requirements.

## RESEARCHERS' CONCLUSIONS

In the many family interviews we conducted, both children and parents were happier and more focused when exercise of some kind was part of the homework routine. The children were having fun, while learning new skills and building habits that increased their organizational skills and social awareness; sports participation encourages time management, prioritizing, and willingness to act in the best interest of the team—all traits that build character and self-esteem. The learning habits encouraged by athletics are almost always positive.

As one mother said, "I keep them really busy: between sports and chores and schoolwork, they don't have time to get into trouble. The kids they've met through their school and community teams have all been great kids. And, believe me when I say a baseball glove or lacrosse stick is a whole lot cheaper than a video game system."

The December 2013 issue of *Frontiers in Human Neuroscience* postulated that:

> If you're an athlete, you warm up before practice or a game because it helps you perform at your peak. But what about when you're preparing for strenuous mental activity—y'know, like homework? You probably go straight from Facebook to your physics worksheet without batting an eyelash. It might be time to rethink that approach.[13]

## Case Study: Alex's Advice

**Alexis Wooten (teacher):** Alex is a middle school teacher who started incorporating math CCSS into her classroom in 2013. "I've never seen kids so mentally drained as they have been this year with the mathematics curriculum. They are fully capable of understanding this material, but it is enormously taxing," she told us.

She had some unusual advice for parents. "When your children get home, have them exercise. Run around and play sports. *They need physical activity*; I can't stress this enough.

"They are working so hard during the day—in a way they simply weren't before. When they get home, they need to move. This new material is truly mentally exhausting and they get very little exercise at school. If we are raising the academic standards for our children, then exercise needs to increase as well. They are closely connected."

## WHAT THE COMMON CORE STATE STANDARDS ARE MISSING

While East Coast researchers worked to measure learning outcomes through an online study, researchers in England were running around measuring sweaty children. They were able to provide statisticians with valuable results on physical activity and the developing brain. Nearly 5,000 students participated in a study that measured the biological effects of exercise on children's achievement in school.[14]

The British team measured both duration and intensity of 11-year-old students' daily physical activity for a period of three to seven days, using a device worn on the kids' belts. Both boys and girls got fewer than the recommended 60 minutes for daily exercise. The boys clocked 29 minutes, on average, and the girls, 18 minutes.

Those who exercised the most did better in national academic exams. At age 11, the kids who exercised most had better performance in three subjects: math, science, and English. The activity especially helped the girls raise their science grades. At ages 13, 15, and 16, the link between more exercise and better grades held.[15]

## THE MESSAGE TO PARENTS: WORK HARD, PLAY HARD

Higher-intensity activity has biological effects on the brain that improve academic performance. (Walking or light play may have additional benefits, particularly social benefits if done with a friend, but didn't affect academic performance.) What did have an impact was the *intensity and duration* of physical activity, the type of exercise that is typically found through sports, exercise classes, or running.

According to the British researchers, the findings have important implications for education policy, suggesting that schools should value physical activity as a way to improve classroom performance.[16]

At the Center, we place a high value on exercise, especially for kids with ADHD or academic challenges. Encourage your children to ride bikes to school, where possible, and add 30 minutes of vigorous exercise a day, as part of their homework. Children would benefit enormously from making this a non-negotiable part of their homework habit. Because sports combine exercise and social skill building, they help busy children multitask and stay well rounded. Many children who dislike group contact sports find that they feel comfortable with swimming, karate, skiing, dance classes, fencing, or other team sports/activities with elements of individual performance. Any kind of exercise, even a vigorous game of tag, makes a big difference for kids.

## FEEDING THE BRAIN THROUGH SLEEP

Compared with their counterparts in Japan and South Korea, on average, Chinese high school students sleep the longest, suffer the lowest psychological pressure, and have the greatest self-confidence, according to a comparative survey report on the mental health status of teens in these countries issued by Shanghai Academy of Social Science.[17]

According to the Learning Habit Study, too many children are getting too little sleep. The prime cause is media in the bedroom; the secondary cause is *lack of an established homework habit*. Especially in the higher grades, kids with no homework habit put their schoolwork off until late in the evening, and then get to bed too late. This causes problems with cognition and mood, which are reflected by poor grades and diminished social contact. Nobody likes to hang with a grumpy, irritable kid!

## RESEARCHERS' CONCLUSIONS

We know that the homework habit is positively correlated with a number of things, such as:

- ✓ Empowerment Parenting
- ✓ Low sleep onset latency (SOL)—falling asleep quickly
- ✓ No media in the bedroom; limited media at other times
- ✓ No media or any distractions during homework time
- ✓ The 10-minute rule (10 minutes of academic homework per grade)
- ✓ Regular exercise
- ✓ Social skills and opportunities
- ✓ Daily family time, including 30 minutes of media-free family activity (meals, games, talking, or reading together)
- ✓ Regular household chores
- ✓ Rules for homework, chores, and bedtime
- ✓ Screen time as a reward (after tasks are done, never before)
- ✓ Effective communication skills

## THE READING HABIT: SAVING THE BEST FOR LAST

*Whatever our bedtime was as kids, we could stay up an extra half hour if we were reading. My parents didn't care as long as I was under the spell of a Stephen King or a*

*Douglas Adams. Now I read in bed. I read at work. I read standing in line. It's like, "Hello, my name is Nathan and I am a reader."*

—Nathan Fillion, award-winning actor

The average three-credit college course requires two to three hours of reading a week. If your child is taking the five courses per semester necessary to graduate in four years, this translates to 10 to 15 hours of reading a week.

Lack of self-management, poor study skills, and a deficit of reading habits are three primary reasons for the high rate of college dropouts.[18] After completing the necessary reading, students then have to budget time to complete written assignments, study, and attend labs and classes. *That amounts to between 50 and 60 hours a week.* The goal of obtaining a college degree is not so easy to achieve, especially when students are distracted, frustrated, and unable to persevere and accomplish long-term goals.

## READING AND THE COMMON CORE

*Never trust anyone who has not brought a book with them.*

—Lemony Snicket, pseudonym of
Daniel Handler, author

All the teachers we interviewed agreed that the biggest challenge with the CCSS is the need to be able to read math problems rapidly and with comprehension; then be able to translate the words to mathematical constructs and actually do the problem—in a time-limited setting. Common core mathematics is more theoretical and less computational. It requires two additional skills not usually associated with math:

1. Speed reading.
2. Careful reading.

The content is more challenging, so by its nature it takes the students longer. Students' reading abilities are, by and large, not up to the challenge.

## Case Study: Anna's Classroom

*It's the reading that's slowing them down!*
—Anna Slovak, third-grade teacher

**Anna Slovak (teacher):** Anna is a third-grade teacher who worked on a task force to assist in implementation of the new math curriculum at a Rhode Island elementary school.

"I've always assigned one worksheet for math homework," she told us. "That remains the same, even with the new standards. But let's face it: theoretical problems are harder for students. They're complaining more this year and seem much more frustrated. It's not the math that's slowing them down. It's the reading. Last year I had some students who could breeze through math, but struggled with ELA. This year, they can't do that because of the word problems."

### ANNA'S ADVICE FOR PARENTS

"Have your children read more," Anna recommends. "I would always prefer that a child came into school and told me they couldn't finish an assignment rather than know that a parent 'helped' them. I hate to see them spending too long on digital math assignments;

we know, because we can track them. I'd prefer they stopped after a reasonable period of time and read a book. *Reading is the key to success with the core curriculum.* These children have to read, read carefully, and learn to read quickly. I would never feel disappointed if a child didn't do their homework because they spent an hour reading."

## The Evidence on Reading

A longitudinal study* of 54 children examined reading and writing. It concluded that the good readers read considerably more than the poor readers both in and out of school, which appeared to contribute to the good readers' growth in some reading and writing skills. Poor readers tended to become poor writers. Early writing skill did not predict later writing skill as well as early reading ability predicted later reading ability.[19]

**RESEARCHERS' CONCLUSIONS**
The frequency with which children read is an important factor that is directly tied with intrinsic motivation. The longitudinal study showed that the children who see reading as a desirable activity read more frequently and thus develop better reading skills.[20]

If parents read, children will read. It's that simple. It doesn't matter how the book is delivered—hardback, paperback, ebook, comic book—reading begets reading. Empowering Parents read to their children and allow their children to read *to them* and *with them*. Unplug the media and bring out the books; you'll be helping

---

* A longitudinal study is a research technique that involves studying the same group of individuals over an extended period of time.

your child master a skill that will get them both into and out of college—with a degree.

## READING AND TEST ANXIETY

Every teacher interviewed for *The Learning Habit* offered an opinion on standardized testing. Many teachers voiced concern over the students' emotional well-being. One student teacher described her first experience with the tests:

> "The tension inside the school was palpable. I didn't remember, walking into the school that day, that testing was scheduled. What I felt, after setting foot inside, was both indescribable and instantaneous. I thought perhaps something horrific had occurred to one of the students, so I immediately started walking, as quickly as I could, toward the office. Then I saw the 'Shh! Testing in Progress' sign on the classroom door and remembered that state testing was that day."

We can spend time debating them, we can sound the alarm on how emotionally detrimental they are, but it's not going to change the immediate testing landscape for our children. The fact is that stakes are high when it comes to standardized testing. They are required for college admission, they often determine school curriculum and funding, they might determine your child's ability to graduate from high school, and their effects are far reaching.

Students aren't the only ones who suffer. These tests are draining for teachers, who are often forced to "cram in" information before and after the testing process, in an effort to keep the productivity level of their students steady; mandated testing is often predicated on the premise that all children in a grade are progressing at the same rate and have been able to master the same material. Low scores by students are depressing for the students and a source of anxiety for the teachers, as they can be seen as a reflection on a teacher's effectiveness.

One of the biggest challenges for students is that the individual tests are timed, and the testing day is long. Children who are not used to sitting and concentrating, for a specific period of time, have extreme difficulty with standardized tests. It is often less of a *comprehension* issue and more of a *concentration* issue. Children who are accustomed to spending hours on homework or to having unlimited time for writing assignments, find that they run out of time or "freeze up" on standardized tests.

The homework habit necessitates a combination of time management skills *and* reading skills. These skills are mentioned time and time again throughout this book, because they cultivate long-term learning habits. Not only do these habits assist children with homework, but they greatly decrease the amount of test anxiety children feel during the ever-increasing incidence of standardized testing.

It's unrealistic to ask a third grader to sit still for several hours and take a test.

However, it's a lot less stressful for a child if they are accustomed to:

✓ Sitting for specified periods of time, as part of a regular academic homework routine

✓ Working within a limited time frame

### RESEARCHERS' CONCLUSIONS

The statistics on reading motivation are particularly alarming. According to the National Assessment of Educational Progress, 73% of children do not read frequently for enjoyment.[21] The general lack of intrinsic motivation to read is in accordance with the finding that the United States is ranked number 33 out of 35 countries on a survey of reading motivation.[22]

However, I'll bet we score near the top on texting skills—if that's any comfort!

# THE BIG PICTURE:
# ACRONYMS MAY CHANGE,
# HOMEWORK ROUTINE MUST NOT

The goal of education is to develop lifelong learners. As acronyms for tests and various state-mandated curricula continue to change, our home environments should remain the same. These are rapidly changing times in education, for the United States and the rest of the world. Educators and parents want our children to learn the skills that prepare them for college and assist them in participating in a global community. There are exciting changes to school curricula that have many parents jumping for joy. There are also several reasons, noted earlier, why parents may have genuine concerns.

In our opinion, the homework methodology outlined in this chapter is the only guaranteed way to stop the pendulum from swinging. I have a kindergartener who attends public school. By the time she's in high school, I imagine there will be a different curriculum, with a new acronym, and new state standardized testing. (*Big sigh.*) My goal is to keep things consistent, calm, and happy for my child. And I can do that— because I have complete control over the two most important academic areas of my child's life: *homework and reading.*

Parents of children in grades K–5 have probably begun to notice a shift in the volume and content of school assignments being sent home. When a new curriculum and teaching materials are introduced in the classroom, it can take several years for administrators to gauge the pace and speed at which the material should be taught. After this is done, tests can be developed to measure competency. This is typically done during a period of field testing, or beta testing. However, this doesn't always happen, and parents and children often notice a rigorous change in classroom pace in the form of homework. Specifically, worksheets ... so many worksheets!

## A BETTER WAY

Veteran teachers and parents understand that learning is not about cramming for a test. A child isn't doomed for life because they didn't do well on a third-grade spelling test or a fourth-grade state exam. Parents and teachers are both equally guilty of feeding into the hysteria and hype concerning new achievement testing and curricula. The goal is to integrate best practices, gradually, into our children's everyday lives, so that they can develop familiarity with the concepts necessary to succeed. In establishing self-reinforcing homework habits for our kids, we want to:

✓ *Ensure they get a reward*, usually an activity they enjoy, for working on their homework and reading. We all need things to look forward to; like it or not, media consumption is a powerful reward for children. If you are going to allow your child to use media during the week, make sure they earn it: *first* we do our schoolwork and reading, *then* we get some TV or game time.

✓ *Praise them for effort.* The other powerful reward is your acknowledgment of their hard work; praising for effort is invaluable.

✓ *Help them to learn self-soothing relaxation techniques.* Children need to be able to self-soothe and relax themselves in the presence of homework, classroom, and testing stresses. Anxiety and panic attacks are now the #1 reason for pediatric referrals to the Center (for years it had been ADHD); our kids are under increasing educational stress. We can't change the school pressures, but we can change how our kids are able to deal with them. Relaxation techniques are presented, in depth, in Chapter Nine. These relaxation exercises are enormously helpful for anxiety-ridden kids. Children as young as five years old are receptive to the concept of "calming my body" through a combination of deep breathing and positive self-statements. This is a skill that will benefit them for their entire lives.

✓ *Build a media-free requirement into the academic homework routine.* Media consumption makes it difficult for children to concentrate—that's why it's allowed only *after* academic homework time and reading are completed. Make sure children turn in their cell phones before starting homework and never allow a child to watch TV or listen to music or have any other distractions while working. It will only slow them down.

✓ Guard against the "just this once" impassioned pleas of our children to modify or break the homework rule. They'll thank you for this later—much later.

Academic homework and reading are, however, only part of the big picture. Homework is influenced by virtually all other parts of your children's daily routines and activities. For all-round healthy homework habits, take note of the following rules:

## Homework Hygiene Rules

✓ 10 minutes of schoolwork per grade, every school day. If schoolwork is not assigned, then children sit and read for the full time.

✓ 30 to 40 minutes of vigorous exercise or play (team sports or group exercise allows children to see friends and build social skills as well as develop brain power).

✓ Regular, media-free bedtime ritual that allows for at least 8 hours of sleep a night.

✓ Performance of daily household chores.

✓ 30 minutes of media-free family time every day.

✓ Parental praise for effort and tenacity, without "helping."

✓ Integrate deep breathing practices as part of the family homework routine.

# CHAPTER FIVE

# Time Flies:
# Mastering Time Management

---

The secret to your future
is hidden in your daily routine.
You have to be self-disciplined
to spend your time wisely.
—*Michelle Moore, leadership coach*

Bobby's coach benches him. Lily's friends go to the movies without her. Jared's teacher keeps him from going on a field trip. Sophie has a meltdown before school and begs her mom to let her stay home. Chloe has a panic attack over a book report. Geremy's last-minute rush costs him 25% off his midterm grade. Lindsay's best friend, Aime, gets her feelings hurt.

Different kids experiencing different stressors. However, the Learning Habit Study findings suggest that all of these children have the same problem: significant difficulty in scheduling and efficiently managing their time.

In our interviews with children in grades K–12, we heard story upon story of children who suffered because of poor time management habits. These children were anxious and unaware of how to set up a workable, regular method for keeping track of their academic, social, and other responsibilities. Few, at any age, wore a watch; most of the children in primary school (grades K–4) could not read an analog clock.

In this chapter, you will read a number of vignettes told to us by students and teachers. You may have experienced one or more similar painful and frustrating incidents with your own children but may not necessarily have realized that they had to do specifically with time management.

**Bobby (age 12)** has been consistently late for hockey practice. He can't seem to remember where he dumped his equipment, so has trouble locating and collecting it. He's always rushing to make it to practice on time. He is a valued and popular team member, but his coach has a rule: *Be on time or sit behind the line.* Bobby is angry, hurt, sad . . . and sitting.

**Lily (age 9)** is expected to have her room cleaned and her bed changed by noon on Sundays. One Sunday morning, Lily chose to watch TV, play Minecraft, talk on her cell phone to her cousin, and try out a few hairstyles. At noon, she was frantically shoveling her clothes into the hamper, as she started to clean her room. She was grounded for the rest of the day and missed going to the movies with her friends. She is mad at her parents and sad and embarrassed that she had to tell her friends she couldn't go. She could tell that her best friend, Marie, was mad by the way she wouldn't even let Lily explain.

**Jared (age 10)** hates English. He thinks his ELA teacher is boring and stupid. They are doing a unit on poetry and are required to write a haiku, a six- to eight-line poem in free verse, and a two-stanza, eight-line nursery rhyme. The project was in place of a midterm exam; Jared had three weeks to complete the project. He waited until the night before, when he also had to study for his social studies midterm. He didn't complete the English assignment. In spite of his compelling arguments, his teacher sent him to detention—while his class went on a scheduled field trip. He was furious and disappointed. He felt like a loser having to stay behind and finish his poetry project, while all his friends went to the city to see a play.

**Sophie (age 13)** has an ELA/American history teacher, Mr. Bennett, who's a really good teacher and she likes him. She thinks he's smart and funny—but she never wants to get on his bad side. He can sometimes be very sarcastic and kind of mean. A B+/A– student, Sophie relies on her good reputation (and her considerable charm) to get away with some occasional . . . slacking. The one thing about which Mr. Bennett is inflexible is "the notebook." Students are required to keep a notebook containing their class notes, quizzes and tests, homework assignments, and two relevant news articles per week. They don't hand the notebooks in, but are required to bring them to every class, and Mr. Bennett does unannounced spot checks. If the notebook is incomplete, the student gets an F, which is equal to two quiz grades.

When Sophie goes online to check for relevant news articles, she frequently gets distracted. Sometimes she has a nagging feeling that she really needs to make the time to catch up and get her notebook in shape, but, thus far, she has managed to successfully ignore it. This morning, just before she was ready to leave for school, she got a text from her best friend, Lisa, whose mother is in Mrs. Bennett's tennis group: "Today—B's notebook! ☹." Sophie can't believe it. She knows how mad he can get, and all her friends are in that class. She panics, starts to cry, and begs her mom not to make her go to school. She promises never to do it again. Her mother relents and lets her stay home, but she is to stay in her room and work on the notebook all day. After all, her mom rationalizes, it's "just this once."

> *So. Much. homework. Such poor time management.*
> —Anonymous Tweet

Time management is such an essential skill, you'd think we'd all be experts at it! That's not the case, however; both children and adults suffer from a seeming inability to manage their time judiciously. This deficit affects every area of our lives, from inconveniencing family, friends, and team members to damaging us academically, professionally, financially, physically, psychologically—and even legally.

**Chloe (age 10)** forgot about a book report due the next day; it had been assigned two weeks previously. She was freaking out, as she had read only 30 pages and had 200 more to go. She stayed up reading, until she fell asleep on the couch. She still hadn't finished the book, let alone written the report. Chloe had a hysterical meltdown before school. Her parents sent her to school anyway, but Chloe went immediately to the nurse's office, complaining of an upset stomach and headache. The nurse called Chloe's mother, who explained what had happened. When the nurse told Chloe that her mother said to send her back to class, Chloe had a full-blown panic attack. Her mother picked her up and took her to her pediatrician. He recommended counseling for Chloe to help her with her anxiety issues.

**Geremy (age 9)** worked for hours on an important science project. Before school, he was playing Wii tennis with his sister; the bus arrived, and he neglected to pack the project in his backpack, so couldn't hand it in. It counted as 25% of his midterm grade.

**Lindsay (age 11)** decided not to ask her friend, Aime, to join her group for an English project. Aime was in tears. Aime's mother and Lindsay's mother were friends; when Lindsay's mother heard the story, she asked her daughter about it. Lindsay told her, "Aime's my best friend, but she's just too unreliable; I always have to remind her about everything, so I can't count on her to do her part and get it to me on time. She's so disorganized; it makes me nervous. This project is a big part of our term grade and I'm the team leader; I picked kids I could count on to do the work according to our schedule."

## ORGANIZING TIME

When I was a little girl, my mother frequently said, "If you need something done, give it to a busy person." I thought that was odd; after all, if a person is already busy, why would you expect them to be able to do more?

As has happened many times, I've discovered that my mother was right. People who are busy are usually highly organized; they make the best use of their time by planning ahead, knowing approximately how long a task will take, using the calendars and reminders in their smartphones or planners, and wearing a watch. They leave early for appointments in order to be punctual, giving themselves an extra few minutes to account for the unexpected—like getting stuck behind a school bus or having to take a detour.

We all know really organized people who always plan ahead—maybe we are those people. If we're not, we are in awe of them (and perhaps, sometimes, just a tiny bit annoyed by their seemingly effortless efficiency!).

### Developing an Internal Clock

Most adults have developed what we like to call an *internal clock*. This allows us to estimate how long tasks should take. It also alerts us when things are taking too long. However, when we are truly immersed in a task, our internal clock can shut off. Most parents have had the "Oh no!" moment—the moment when we look at our watch and suddenly realize we are late to pick up our child. It's a pretty frightening feeling, as no parent wants to let down their child or leave them waiting for a ride. My "Oh no!" moment happened in the third week of school, when I was so immersed in a project that I forgot to walk out to the bus stop to pick up my five-year-old daughter. Lesson learned! Now I have two alarms set on my phone as reminders.

One of the most wonderful things about children is how open

they are to fully turning themselves over to an experience. Watch them play, take in a movie, dance, or daydream. They are virtually transported someplace else. This almost magical ability to get lost in projects and dreams makes time management challenging for them. They don't *want* to annoy their parents—leave them waiting, or make them late. They are simply having an "Oh no!" moment, every day. It's not fun. I've been there.

A challenging part of time management has to do with developing an internal clock. This is developed after children understand what a certain period of time feels like in their body. A six-year-old understands past, present, and future but has no concept of how *long* in the past something was; it could have been a week or a year ago. An eight-year-old understands there are seven days in a week, but probably can't tell you how many minutes an average movie is. The concepts of time and estimating time are complex.

Kids don't grasp time. It doesn't happen until they are much older. Use visual reminders of time for all children: calendars, pictures, and so on. Have them wear a watch, but realize that unless they internalize a certain period of time (know what an hour feels like or five minutes feels like), time means very little to them.

To teach children time management skills, the first step is to have them internalize the amount of time something should take. Make it time specific. Here's an example.

## Case Study: Seth and the Lost Time

Seth (age 5) gets "lost" in his room, playing with his Legos, every morning. Every morning, Tony, his father, has to remind Seth to get dressed and come downstairs for breakfast. Every morning, Seth is surprised to rediscover that he actually has to put on a shirt, pants, socks, and shoes *before* he can have his favorite Cheerios with strawberry milk—then he has to *run* back upstairs to brush his teeth. Every morning, he plays with his dog, Sparky, for a while, before he feeds him and gives him fresh water. Every morning, he feels as if he's *really* hurrying; he doesn't understand why his dad gets so cranky as he runs with Seth to the bus stop.

One afternoon, when Tony picks up Seth from his after-school program, he tells Seth that they're going to do a "very important experiment"; he retrieves an interesting-looking bag from the trunk. *Ohh! It's from the Dollar Place—Seth's favorite store.*

After an early supper, Tony sets up a work area on the kitchen table: a big piece of shiny white paper, a pack of colored markers, a bigger black marker, a roll of packing tape, two glass bowls—one large, one smaller—and three bags of multicolored foam balls; the balls range in size from "fat marble" to "golf ball" to "tennis ball." Seth thinks the balls are very cool. His dad outlines the shapes of three balls across the top of the paper. The smallest one, he colors yellow; the medium one, green; the largest one, blue; he writes the numbers 5, 10, and 20 on the corresponding ball with a fat black marker.

Seth opens the three bags of foam balls: the "fat marble" ones are yellow; the medium-sized "golf balls" are green, and the biggest "tennis balls" are blue. Seth is fascinated. Tony explains:

> Tony: I know that mornings have been tough for us; it's hard to figure out how long it takes to do stuff. So, I thought you might like to *see* and *feel* how much time morning jobs really take. First, we're going to do an experiment; then, we're going to make a poster for your bedroom door.
>
> Seth: Cool! Do I get to play with the balls?
>
> Tony: You certainly do. *You're the one* who's going to do the experiment with the balls.
>
> Seth: Cool! Do I throw them . . . into the bowls?
>
> Tony: Sort of. First, I need to put a label on this bowl. [He sticks a piece of packing tape on the smaller bowl; with the fat black marker, he writes, "**1 Hour = 60 Minutes.**"] This bowl represents the amount of time you have, from when your alarm

goes off to when you leave for school—that's 1 hour, or 60 minutes.

**Seth:** 60 minutes! Wow! That's a lot of time! 60 minutes . . . sounds like forever.

**Tony:** It does, doesn't it? Well, here's where those colored balls come in. Can you see how I labeled them on the paper?

**Seth:** Uh-huh. I can see numbers. The little yellow one says 5 and the next one—the green one—says 10 . . . but I don't know what the blue one is.

**Tony:** Good reading skills, champ. The blue one says 20. Those numbers mean minutes; like how many minutes it takes to do something. For example, let's say that you play with your Legos for 20 minutes.

**Seth:** Is that a long time?

**Tony:** Hmm . . . 20 minutes is about how long I read to you at night. So, let's see. Put a blue 20-minute ball into the little bowl. [Seth does it.] Now, how long does it take you to get dressed, do you think?

**Seth:** I don't know—maybe . . . the baby one, 5 minutes.

**Tony:** Okay. Put one into the bowl. [Seth adds a yellow ball.] How about brushing your teeth? [Seth adds another yellow ball, for 5 more minutes.] Eating breakfast?

**Seth:** [Thinking] Hmm . . . I think a big blue ball. [Adds it to the bowl, 20 minutes.]

**Tony:** How about going to the bathroom? [Seth adds a yellow ball, another 5.] Oh! Here's an important one—feeding Sparky and getting him his water!

**Seth:** I like to play with him, too. Let's give Sparky a big blue ball! [Tries to get the 20-minute ball into the bowl; it teeters on top, then rolls off.]

**Tony:** Oh, no! Sparky's ball won't go in!

**Seth:** What does it mean, Daddy?

**Tony:** Well, I think it means that we know why mornings are such a hassle! Maybe you're trying to do too many things, or maybe . . . you're taking too long to do them. If it's taking the full 60 minutes to do your other morning jobs—like Legos and dressing and eating and bathroom stuff—that leaves no time for Sparky! The big blue ball can't fit into the one-hour bowl. Can you think of a way to get everything done in the time you have every morning?

**Seth:** [Looks concerned and shrugs his shoulders.]

**Tony:** I have an idea. Tomorrow morning, let's use the timer on my phone and we'll time everything you do. That way, we can come up with a plan! Then, after school, we'll make the poster, so that every morning, you know what order to do things and how long it's going to take you. You can write the numbers on the balls, too. Then, every morning, you can start with an empty bowl and fill it up as you do your jobs. Okay?

**Seth:** Okay! It will be like an expur-ment! Do I get to use that black marker on the balls?

**Tony:** [Laughing.] Right! Sure.

As you can guess, the time it took Seth to do things was quite different from the time he imagined; Seth realized, for instance, that he didn't have time to play Legos before school. He played with them only after school—after he played with Sparky and did his "homework." He and his dad came up with a reasonable timetable so that Seth could "do his jobs" without rushing. They made the bedroom door poster, with illustrations by Seth, of the order of the chores. They also made a pie chart so that Seth could see the relative duration of activities. He did, indeed, write the numbers on the balls; fortunately, there were quite a few balls in each bag—that black marker was pretty messy!

For the first week, Seth used the digital timer on his clock; it helped him gauge if he was getting his jobs done in the allotted time. After that week, his internal clock took over.

When teaching a child about time and time management, it's imperative that they develop an internal clock. This is the only way they will learn how to self-regulate, as opposed to relying on a parent's reminders. For each task, make sure you:

✓ Make it time specific (for example, 5 minutes).

✓ Have a timer, chart, or other cue (that's not you) to help them learn the specific increments of time it takes to complete a given task; use it until they've developed a habit.

✓ Use statements about time, for example, "That show was 30 minutes," or "Let's see if we can get this done in 10 minutes—I'll set the oven timer, and then we can make popcorn!"

✓ Consider getting your child an analog watch (no digital display); that way, they can learn to spot 5-minute, 15-minute, and 30-minute increments of time. (Tony and Seth picked out an inexpensive analog watch: Seth liked the lizard pattern on the strap; Tony liked the plain white face and large, easy-to-read numbers—it included every number from 1 to 12.)

✓ Again, praise your child for trying! We all have days when we lose a shoe or temporarily space out; when that happens, use nonverbal cues (like pointing at their chart or a clock) to help them refocus.

Tony used an effective strategy with Seth. Very young children enjoy visual charts; to help a primary-school child understand the morning routine, draw a picture of their morning chores. It might include going to the bathroom, getting dressed, making the bed (not well, but trying), eating breakfast, and brushing teeth. Put the chart on the bedroom door. Your child will learn to consult it every morning. This kind of on-the-door chart can be adapted to a pie chart to show children the relative length of time that different activities take. (Next, Seth is going to tackle making his bed—5 minutes!)

# THE LEARNING HABIT STUDY RESULTS

According to the Learning Habit Study, the learning habit of time management develops in children most often when parents use Empowerment Parenting techniques. These children have scheduling expectations and practices such as:

- ✓ Having a regular bedtime.
- ✓ Checking a calendar, chart, or smartphone to keep their schedule.
- ✓ Consistent homework routines.
- ✓ Participation in athletics, clubs, and reading for pleasure.
- ✓ Doing household chores regularly.
- ✓ Making their beds regularly.
- ✓ Wearing a watch—analog for younger children.
- ✓ Keeping their possessions in order.
- ✓ Not using media in their rooms after bedtime.
- ✓ Falling asleep quickly.

These children score higher in English and mathematics than children whose parents use enabling parenting. Such parents:

- ✓ Do not establish rules about household chores.
- ✓ Do not institute a regular bedtime routine.
- ✓ Make their kids' beds for them.
- ✓ Allow more time to be spent on media use and less time on academic activities (reading) and physical activities (sports, exercise, playing).

The Learning Habit Study showed that children who do not have schedules, who are not expected to do chores, who do not have to keep their belongings in order, who do not engage in regular extracurricular activities, and in general, who have not established productive routines—do not learn the habit of time management.

## An Interesting Finding

According to the Learning Habit Survey, children who *wear a watch* and *check a calendar, chart, or smartphone to keep their schedule* are also children who *go on sleepovers with friends.*

Huh? How can those three factors correlate? Actually, it makes sense if you think about it. Especially in middle and high school, children have to *plan* social activities and keep track of them. Conversely, children who are chronically disorganized can be a source of stress for teammates and friends. Few children appreciate friends who are always late.

There is a way to structure your home to facilitate an organized child who internalizes the concept of time management. Look at how Rosie's mother did it for Rosie.

## Case Study: Rosie

**Rosie (age 12)** is a sixth grade honors student at a parochial school in New England. Rosie characterized herself as a "very busy kid." She sings in her church choir, plays soccer and basketball, and wants to start tennis in the spring. She volunteers at an after-school activity group for disabled children two days a week and has regular chores she does at home. She has a best friend and a select group of girls with whom she regularly socializes on the weekends.

**Interviewer:** How did you learn to manage your time to balance an active extracurricular life with studying and homework?

**Rosie:** [laughing] My mom is, like, the most organized person on the planet. She has a calendar on the refrigerator, and all our appointments or special things we have to do are on it. When I get home from school, we sit down, I have a snack, and we look over my school assignments from my planner. If I have long-range projects, like book reports, I put them in my phone's calendar with reminders. If there is a project that I need special supplies for, my mom writes it on the big calendar. I usually know how long my homework will take, so I try to get as much done in study period as I can. What's left, I do when I get home—after snack.

**Interviewer:** Tell me about the family schedule for evenings, like dinnertime and bedtime.

**Rosie:** We eat dinner at 5:30, right when my dad gets home. Thursdays can be the exception; my mom works until 7:00, so my dad has to heat up the dinner or we get takeout.

I go to bed at 8:30 and read until 9:00; then I have to shut off my light. Sometimes, I have late practices or rehearsals, so I come home, eat dinner, and then finish my homework. My mom doesn't want me doing homework after 7:30, so I can have time to be with my family. Sometimes we watch a show together—right now we're watching *Downton Abbey* on Netflix. Or, I can text my friends or use the computer, if I want, during that hour, until I take my shower. I usually don't, though; it's too much drama!

Fridays, we have homemade pizza and movie night.

**Interviewer:** When did your family start this scheduling routine? How old were you?

**Rosie:** It started when I was five. I was the only kid in my kindergarten class who had a watch and could tell time. I was so proud of it—it was pink and had Tinker Bell on it. I felt like a big shot when another kid would ask me what time it was.

Then every day after school, we did the same things as now. Snacks and talking, looking at my homework—usually coloring or learning a word—and my mom would read with me for a while, maybe half an hour. I felt important doing my "homework," and my mom gave me a sticker when I was done. If there was anything special, she put it on the big calendar. Then, I'd get my homework and stuff it into my Tinker Bell backpack, and put it by the door. Then I'd play until dinner. My mom would put my lunch or lunch money in my backpack in the morning.

**Interviewer:** I see that you have a Kindle. Do you like to read?

**Rosie:** I love to read; when I was really little, my mom would come in, and we'd cuddle in my bed, while she read to me. . . . *Where the Wild Things Are.* I must've made her read that a thousand times! My mom always read to me before bed. When I was in fifth grade, I got this Kindle for my birthday. I mostly like to read *real* books, so I can keep them; but in an emergency, I can just go on my mom's Amazon account to get a book.

**Interviewer:** Do you have regular chores around the house?

**Rosie:** My mom's favorite saying is, "Work first, everything else after!" When I was little—like maybe four—my mom started to teach me how to make my bed. I wasn't very good, but my mom always said, "You're trying, that's what's important; you'll get better, if you keep practicing." By kindergarten I could make it pretty well. I was supposed to do that and put my dirty clothes in the hamper before breakfast. I think I got stickers for doing that stuff. I had to put my wet towels in the hamper after my shower; my mother was really strict about that! She still is, and about leaving my room neat, with the bed made, in the morning. I just do it. It's no big deal.

**Interviewer:** Now that you're older, are there other chores that are part of your regular routine?

**Rosie:** I think I started setting the table around the same time.

I still do it, but now I also clear the dishes and load the dishwasher.

**Interviewer:** Anything else?

**Rosie:** You have to understand—my mom is a clean freak! My room has to be really cleaned every Saturday; *now* the rule is that I do it before I can go out or do anything else. So I do it. One time, last year—before we made the rule—I'd forgotten to put my dirty underwear and socks in the hamper, so I stuffed them into my underwear drawer. Mom found them—she was *not* happy! I couldn't watch TV for three days; I missed *Cake Boss* and *Honey Boo Boo.* I never did that again!

## Time Management Techniques

Rosie is an example of a well-organized child with excellent time management skills. Her mother's wisdom in starting Rosie on the path of learning the habit of time management at an early age has resulted in a happy, successful child who excels in academics and enjoys an active social life. She has responsibilities at home (chores) that are part of the rules that govern the house. She has a regular bedtime and reports that she falls asleep within minutes after turning out her light. The only media device allowed in her bedroom is her Kindle.

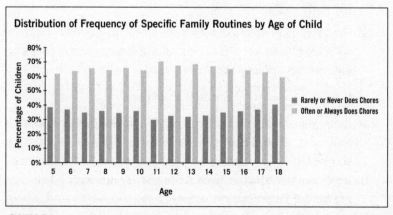

FIGURE 5.1

**RESEARCHERS' CONCLUSIONS**

We found that children who did household chores also scored high on measures of academic success and time management. The habit of doing chores (or not) is a stable one that starts very early and persists through adolescence.

## TEACHING—NO.
## CONSULTING AND MODELING—YES!

Parents play an integral part in showing their children how to effectively manage their time. They do this by modeling good time management for their children and by acting as consultants to their kids in helping them to:

✓ Judge how long tasks are likely to take and setting aside enough time to complete them.

✓ Set up reminders for long-term assignments/projects, so that the child learns to break down the assignment into manageable steps.

✓ Participate in family meetings to establish (or explain) rules for bedtime, media use, and chores and making them part of the child's schedule.

✓ Understand how to use their planner or the calendar on their smartphone to keep track of school assignments, projects, and extracurricular activities.

✓ Get used to wearing a watch and consulting it.

✓ Keep their belongings organized. When children's backpacks and folders are organized, they are unlikely to be missing completed assignments when they get to school or to be missing the materials they need to *do* the assignments when they get home. Organization is both a contributor to and a benefit of time management.

## SHORT-TERM GAIN: IT ISN'T WORTH IT

Parents who subscribe to the "just this once"[1] theory honestly believe that if they do something for their child *that is the child's responsibility*—for example, run out at the last minute to buy a backboard for the project they forgot to do or relax the homework rule because "just this once" they want to see the final contest on *The Voice*—that they are being understanding and helpful in a special circumstance. They believe that the child will learn from the experience and never get into that situation again. Wrong!

On a potentially humorous note regarding the "just this once" phenomenon, the researchers offer the following chart (Figure 5.2) showing the frequency, by age of children, with which a parent often or always types the child's assignment. On balance, fewer than 5% of the parents who participated in the study indicated that they typed their child's assignment "often or always." What is of particular interest is the consistency of the rate. It seems that once a parent starts typing their child's homework, they do so throughout the child's school tenure. Reviewing the findings, one of the Learning Habits Study researchers commented, "It appears that the adults have been well trained by their children."

As Albert Einstein (apparently never) said, "Insanity is doing the same things over and over again, and expecting different results."[2] That's exactly how nutty it is when parents subscribe to the enabling parenting behavior of "just this once."

The only things the child learns are that:

✓ If I forget something, Mom or Dad will get it for me.

✓ If I mess up, Mom or Dad will fix it for me.

✓ If I can't/won't/don't want to do something, Mom or Dad won't really make me do it; they'll do it for me.

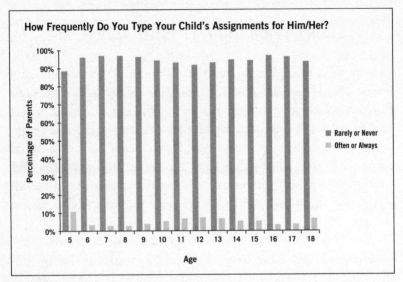

FIGURE 5.2

✓ If I don't want to follow a rule, I can get Mom or Dad to be flexible about it.

✓ I can't rely on myself; I can't do what needs to be done.

And then, Susie or John goes off to college. Whoops! All that reading, all those essays and papers, all those cool distractions at party central, and no:

✓ Time management habits.

✓ Parents to pick up the pieces.

One of the top five reasons college freshmen drop out is—you guessed it!—inability to effectively manage their time.[3]

In terms of role-modeling, parents can keep a calendar in a prominent place (for example, on the refrigerator) and keep it up to date. Social obligations, doctor's appointments, school projects,

TIME FLIES    149

sports practices, dance or music classes, and other practices and
events are all on the calendar. If one of the parents has a meeting
or business trip that will last late or take them away from home, it
goes on the calendar.

The purpose of a family calendar is so that each family member can see—at a glance—what appointments and obligations all
family members have coming up. There are no last-minute sur-
prises, like discovering on Thursday that your son or daughter has
an awards banquet on Friday night, the same night for which you
accepted an invitation to a dinner party at your boss's house.
Ouch.

Parents also model good time management by preparing children
in advance for time-sensitive events. For example:

> Susie, your dental appointment is at 8:30 tomorrow. There
> is a lot of traffic at that time, so I want to leave by 7:45.
> You may want to pack your Nook in your backpack to-
> night; if we get there early, we can read. You can just leave
> it when I drop you at school; I'll bring it home. We'll have
> breakfast at 7:15, so please be ready to eat and run.

Making the time—every day—to have "a little sit" with your
child to talk about their day, look over their planner, see if there's
anything unusual or special coming up that may require extra supplies or time, is extremely helpful for kids. If that special time comes
with a snack, that's even better. Once children master the time
management behaviors set forth in this chapter, the habit becomes
self-reinforcing. Children *like* to feel in control and independent;
they enjoy feeling proud of themselves. And they especially benefit
from the absence of anxiety about *how or when or if* their work
will get done. Learning how to effectively manage their time gives
them these feelings, and they have acquired a skill for life.

## RESEARCHERS' CONCLUSIONS

The most powerful influence on a child's ability to acquire the habit of time management happens at home. With the wise consultation of caring, focused parents who provide sensible rules and consistent routines, children, over time, internalize the principles of time management until, as Rosie said, "I just do it. It's no big deal."

# CHAPTER SIX

# Wanting Isn't Enough:
# Setting Educational Goals

---

*Set a goal to achieve something that is so big,
so exhilarating that it excites you and scares you
at the same time.*
—*Bob Proctor, author and life coach*

The space between wanting something and achieving it can seem daunting to an adult. For children and teenagers, it's even more intimidating.

One of the more powerful examples of goal setting and visualization comes from actor Jim Carrey. As a young actor and comedian, Carrey was broke. He described himself as literally having nothing. Even so, every night after a day of seemingly useless effort, he would sit on Mulholland Drive and visualize having specific directors approach him, because they were interested in his work. He would picture the audition and visualize what they would say to him.

Carrey believed that these things were out there, they just hadn't happened yet. He could see them, and they were extremely specific.

The vision of his bright future would lift his mood, and give

Carrey the excitement he needed to move forward with his action steps the next day. He would return to Mulholland Drive every night and repeat the process. It became a habit. One evening in 1990, Carrey took his visualization a step further, and wrote himself a check for $10 million for "acting services rendered." He dated it for Thanksgiving Day, five years in the future. It sat in his wallet deteriorating for five years. Every time he reached in his wallet he could feel it, a tangible reminder of his long-term goal. In November 1995, Jim Carrey's first big contract was signed—for exactly $10 million![1]

*Carrey's lesson for children:* Visualization and goal setting are powerful motivational tools that work hard if *you* work hard.

It's easy for children and teenagers to idolize the rich and famous and covet what they have. As kids, they see only the end result—not what effort it took to get there; the daily grind of hard work, practicing, improving, and overcoming setbacks along the way.

The rejections we receive, for those who don't take them personally, provide some of the best clues for success. It's that feedback that allows us to make necessary changes to our plans. Navigating the space between where we are and where we want to be means updating our routes based on new information.

> *I take rejection as someone blowing a bugle in my ear to wake me up and get going, rather than retreat.*
> —Sylvester Stallone, actor, screenwriter, and film director

## PREDICTIVE ABILITY

Scientists used to rely only on a child's IQ to predict academic success. With data from the Learning Habit Studies, we now know that educational goals account for *an additional 25%* of our ability to predict what a child's grades will be.[2]

Educational goals are one of the most significant factors in children's educational success.

In the course of researching this book, we interviewed hundreds of families. There were many stories about how these families worked toward having children acquire the habit of goal setting. The following story, however, was the most profound example we came across of how setting the goal of "getting into a good college" and implementing the steps to attain this goal changed a boy's life.

## Case Study: Cameron and His Mother

Cameron (age 17) was in the twelfth grade, an honors student, an athlete, and the treasurer of his class. The day we interviewed him, he had just gotten his acceptance letter from his #1 college choice, Stanford University. Cameron was, by most measures, an extremely successful young man. That had not always been the case. Cameron's academic and social life fell apart in the seventh grade.

> Interviewer: As I understand it, you were on the honor roll most of the time from first grade through sixth grade. What happened in seventh grade?
> Cameron: When I started middle school, I didn't know most of the kids. I was lonely. Mostly, I didn't care about grades or classes; I just wanted to make friends. I had always gotten good grades, but I never considered myself a geek; I wasn't a team sports guy, either. I just had my friends, who were kids I'd grown up with, and they didn't belong to any special group. They were just . . . my friends.
> So, when I got to the new school, I didn't have anything special to make me stand out; I wasn't a geek, or a jock, or

a stoner, so I didn't automatically fit in with a group. I had always liked playing my [video] games, but it wasn't that big a deal. That changed; the way I entertained myself was by gaming. That's how I finally made friends.

Interviewer: How did this way of building new friendships affect your life—your homework strategy, grades, scheduling—your daily routines?

Cameron: When I got home from school, I'd dump my stuff, grab some food, and go to my room. I'd see who was playing, and I'd game, and text, and connect with my friends that way. I did Facebook and Twitter too, for a while, but they're really lame—even then I thought they were stupid. . . . Now, I don't even have a Facebook account. I'll probably start up again when I get to college, so I can keep up with my friends and family without having to use the phone. . . . I really don't use my phone that much.

Interviewer: So, texting and gaming were pretty much what you did?

Cameron: Mm hmm. When Mom got home with my little sister, I'd sometimes hang out with them while she made dinner, eat, and then go back to my room. I'd try to do my homework, but I kept getting distracted by the texts and the games. I didn't have any homework strategy or study skills; I'd never had much homework in elementary school. I used to like to read; I read all the Percy Jackson books and the Alex Rider series—I really liked those. But I pretty much gave that up. The books that were our "required reading" were boring, so that made it hard for me. I was a pretty slow reader, so if a book didn't grab my interest right away, it was too much work.

Interviewer: How were your grades?

Cameron: I didn't know how to study for tests; even when I tried to study, I got bad grades, anyway, so it seemed pretty pointless. Obviously, my grades started to slide. By eighth grade, I was getting all C's and D's. My mom was upset; she didn't

know what to do. She'd see my report card, and take stuff
away [game systems, cell phone], but then I'd get them back.
I never got in trouble in school, I was just one of those kids
who sits in the back and tries to disappear.

**Interviewer:** Cate, as Cameron's mother, what did you think?

**Cate:** It was a gradual process. I'd gone back to get my MBA,
and Cam was just such a normal kid. I thought I was spending quality time with both kids, but the change in schools
for Cam was devastating. His friends were his support system; when he got separated from them, it was . . . bad. I had
known his grades were slipping, of course, but he was still
the same sweet boy with his sister and me. It was only, really,
in the eighth grade that he started to isolate. He was irritable;
he usually looked like an unmade bed. He got up late, barely
ate any breakfast, and ran to catch the bus. I started to wonder if he was taking drugs or was depressed. I kept thinking
that things would get better. I didn't want to be a nagging
mother, so I . . . just kept hoping.

   I was working like crazy, I had two kids to support, and
I just didn't want to believe that my happy boy was depressed and isolated. I kept hoping—believing—that things
would get better for Cam. He wasn't a troublemaker; I never
got calls from the school. . . . Looking back, I can't believe
how purposely blind I was.

**Interviewer:** So what happened?

**Cameron:** When my final report card came at the end of eighth
grade, I had just barely passed. That made me pretty ashamed.
The only good thing was, there was only one regional high
school, so I'd be in the same school with all my old friends.
I knew everything would be better then. I'd get back on
track.

   I was pumped for the first day of school. I knew I'd be
with my friends, and it would be like it used to be. I was
excited. And then, it all fell apart. The first week of school
was just hell. Yeah, I got to hook up with my old friends

around the halls, but not in my classes. My classes were horrible; they were filled with losers. I didn't belong in classes with those a-holes—I wanted to be with my friends.

So I went to the guidance counselor and told him I wanted him to get me out of those classes and put me in the ones with my friends. I told him which classes I wanted. He had this look on his face, like this was amusing him. His exact words—I'll never forget them—were, "Now, why on earth would I do that? Those classes are for students in the college track. If you're serious about getting into AP classes, young man, you've got a hell of a lot of work to do."

I knew he was right. I was a lousy student in middle school, barely passing even the easy classes. I made up my mind that I wanted to change. I was sick of being ashamed of myself, of feeling like a loser, of not being with my friends. When I looked at the previous two years, I felt like an idiot. Really, what had I done? Beat someone at Halo? Be the fastest under-the-desk texter? I was feeling . . . about as bad as a person can feel. I thought about my family; what a disappointment I must be.

I went to my mom's desk and got a Post-it note. I wrote: *"I am going to graduate from high school with at least a 3.5 GPA in all AP classes. I'm going to go to Stanford University School of Engineering, with a major in Aerospace Technology."* I stuck it on the mirror in my bedroom. Every day, I saw that note. I added a picture that I got online—it's an aerial shot of the campus with this building that almost looks like a rocket—and the caption on the picture says, "Freedom." It's still there, on my mirror.

This was the defining moment for Cameron. He set his educational goal, and wrote it down. He got an image to help him visualize his goal, and he put it where he saw it every day.

## BUILDING HIS LEARNING HABIT

**Cate:** That night, after dinner, Cam and I sat and talked for hours. We both cried. I told him I would do anything I could to help him. I am very organized; I believe in schedules and structure. We made a pact: he could ask me for suggestions about how to organize, set up a routine, build his study skills, and get help from teachers—anything at all. I would act as his consultant. There were just two conditions.

**Interviewer:** And those were?

**Cameron:** First, that Mom wouldn't give me advice unless I asked her. Second was that, no matter what she said, I didn't get to get mad at her. I just had to suck it up.

**Interviewer:** What was that like?

**Cameron:** Well, it was kinda hard at first. She suggested three things that would probably have the biggest impact on my teachers. She said that, not right away, but by the end of the first 6 weeks, I would probably see results:

- The first thing was to do my homework, every single day, even if I didn't understand it, and hand it in.
- The second thing was to move my seat, in all of my classes, to the front of the room.
- The third thing was to raise my hand and ask questions if I didn't understand something or if I knew the answer.

**Interviewer:** Did you do them?

**Cameron:** Not all at once. But over the next few of weeks, I did. My ELA/English teacher was actually happy that there was somebody who *wanted* to sit in the front.

Over the next few weeks, Cameron identified the habits he had formed that were not going to help him reach his goal. He had a cluster of behaviors that were self-defeating:

✓ Not entering his assignments regularly in his planner.

✓ Not leaving school with all the materials he would need.

✓ Grabbing a snack and taking it to his room.

✓ Getting involved with texting and gaming immediately, while he had his snack.

✓ Fitting the homework tasks into media breaks.

✓ Getting to bed late and sleeping poorly.

✓ Getting up late and feeling anxious, disorganized, defensive, and unprepared for the day.

Cameron worked diligently to change those habits; he worked out a series of small steps (short-term goals). The first goals he implemented were:

✓ Checking his planner before he left each class, to make sure he had written the homework assignment in it.

✓ Checking his planner before he left school, to make sure he had everything he needed in order to do his homework.

✓ Reviewing his planner with his mother, after dinner, to help him set up his schedule for maximum efficiency.

> *The first step is you have to say that you can.*
> —Will Smith, actor, producer, and rapper

These three behaviors quickly became habits. Because they made him feel more in control and lessened his anxiety, they were emotionally self-reinforcing.

In a meeting with his mother, however, Cameron confessed that he still had problems with homework completion. He was distracted, and it took him too long to do it. He asked his mother for help. Cate suggested that they work out a homework routine, so Cameron would have a limited amount of time to work (90 minutes), but during that time there would be no media. He would get himself set up in the kitchen and stay there for the 90 minutes. If he finished his work before the time was up, he would remain at the table to read. He had permission to buy any book that interested him, but he had to read.

Eventually, he developed a cue to help him develop his homework routine.

His cue: Hearing the *clink* as he dropped his cell phone and house key into the brass dish his mother kept on the hall table. As soon as he walked in the door, Cameron would take his phone out, turn it off, and drop it and his key ring into the dish. That action— phone out, off, and in the dish—was the trigger for him to get himself into his homework routine. He took his backpack into the kitchen, got a snack, and then sat down at the kitchen table.

He didn't go to his room until he had finished his homework, put it into the right folders, put everything into his backpack, and placed the backpack by the door.

**Interviewer:** That sounds like quite a challenge. Did you ever get discouraged?

**Cameron:** It was hard at the beginning. I made a lot of mistakes, and nothing much changed with my teachers or grades. Yes, I got discouraged. But I knew that I had to keep trying. My mom was really there for me; she'd set aside time after dinner for me to talk and go over my planner, so I could ask for her opinion about stuff I was doing. She kept her word and never gave me advice unless I asked for it; when I did, she was always honest. Sometimes, it made me mad. But she was usually right, and her suggestions were good.

After a few weeks, I realized that she had been right; sitting in the back of the class had not been a good idea; as soon as I moved to the front, I felt different. After I got up the nerve to raise my hand, I began to get called on more. And because I was actually doing the work and studying, I usually got the answers right. When the first midterm report came out, my grades showed the effort—C's and B's.

They weren't the A's I was aiming for, but they were a lot better than I'd been getting.

**Cate:** When Cam called me with his grades, I was so happy, I cried, which was a little embarrassing, as I had to go back into a meeting. I didn't care! I told him we were all going out to dinner to celebrate—his choice.

**Interviewer:** So, you began to see some results from your efforts. What happened after that?

**Cameron:** I started raising my hand whenever I didn't understand something and asking the teacher to explain it more. When we had a project, I thought it would be a good idea to decide what I was going to do—or how I was going to do it—and then check with the teacher to make sure it was what they wanted.

Also, my [class] notes were bad; messy, disorganized. . . . I started taking better notes. It got easier this year, because we can use our tablets to take notes in honors classes.

**Interviewer:** Did these new habits change anything else besides your grades?

**Cameron:** Well, yes. After that, everything just kind of snowballed. I was getting my homework done early, I wasn't depressed or anxious, and my friends all played sports, so I joined the track team. I worked out a lot and made varsity track my sophomore year. I also joined the basketball team.

Every day, I looked at my Post-it note and the picture of Stanford. *Every single day.*

**Interviewer:** So, Cate, what do you think about Cam, now?

**Cate:** Cam is a centered person. He knows what he wants, and he understands what he has to do to get it. I see these teenagers who look . . . aimless, like they're just . . . waiting for something to happen. Cam went out and made his future.

I read all the horror stories of kids who go off to college and have no study skills, whose emotional adjustment is so fragile that they can't take the pressure of the work or the distractions of the partying. I don't have those worries about Cam. He has the study habits and the life habits to meet any challenge that may be thrown at him. He won't be deterred or distracted from his goals. He wants to be an aeronautical engineer; he got his letter of acceptance from Stanford, with a scholarship. The rest of his expenses we can handle with other grants and some minimal loans. Cam's life is what he designed.

# HOW KIDS GET FROM POINT A TO POINT B

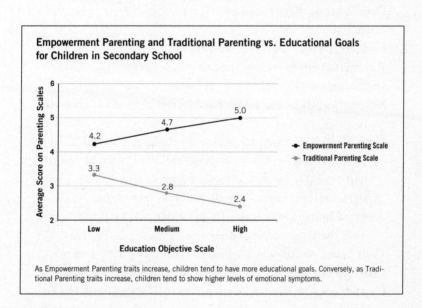

FIGURE 6.1

When helping your child discuss a goal (be it learning to make their bed, managing media usage, getting on the honor roll, graduating from college, or successfully riding a two-wheeler), there are steps to consider.

## Case Study: Aaron and Dad

**Aaron (age 10)** was frustrated. "I can't believe I have to write a book report. It's gonna take too long, and I'm gonna hate this book. I can't do it," complained Aaron, as he chewed his lasagna.

"Well," his father replied, "The first step is to read the first word in the book. Have you done that yet?"

**Aaron:** [rolling his eyes] Yes.

**Dad:** Then you're making progress. The next step is to read the first paragraph. Have you done that?

**Aaron:** Yeah, Dad, I'm on page 14, but it's taking forever.

**Dad:** When is the report due?

**Aaron:** Next Friday.

**Dad:** So. That's nine days away, right?

**Aaron:** It might as well be nine months!

**Dad:** How many pages are in the book?

**Aaron:** Um [checking the book], 243, but a couple of them are pictures.

**Dad:** Well, if you had to read it all tonight, that could be a problem! But your teacher says that 20 minutes of reading will probably get you through 20 pages, right? That's why she asked you to read for 20 minutes every night.

**Aaron:** I know, Dad, and if I'd done that, I'd be through and have the report done and—

**Dad:** Hang on, buddy; no blame, no foul. What I was going to say was that if you read—no distractions—for 30 or 35 minutes after supper, you'll get 33 to 35 pages read and finish the book in seven days. That leaves you two days to write the report.

**Aaron:** [laughing] Good math skills, Dad! But, *only* 35 minutes of reading?

**Dad:** It isn't that long, if you're really involved in doing something. That's about the time we've been here eating supper.

I have a proposition for you; let's set aside 40 minutes after supper, and you and I will go into the den and read. Just the two of us, no TV, no phones, door closed; sit on the couch and read.

**Aaron:** You'd do that?

**Dad:** Of course! I like to read, Aaron; sometimes I just get so caught up in stuff I have to do that I don't make the time. I have that new mystery that Mom put on my Kindle, and I'd enjoy having some dedicated time to read it. Do we have a deal?

**Aaron:** Yeah. OK, I guess. It doesn't sound that bad.

**Dad:** I can see it now—Aaron brings home his book report, with a **big A** and a written comment on the top, **"Great job, Aaron!"**

**Aaron:** [groaning—but smiling, too] Whatever!

Aaron's father facilitated the setting up of a realistic goal that:

✓ Was important to Aaron (read the book and do the report)

✓ Was time-limited (nine days)

✓ Was broken down into small steps (35 to 40 minutes a night)

✓ Had measurable short-term outcomes (33 to 35 pages a night)

✓ Had a visual image to capture the goal (the report with an **A** and the teacher's comment)

✓ Had an attainable outcome (finish the book with two days left to write the book report)

## RESEARCHERS' CONCLUSIONS

We've discovered how powerful an effect a child's educational objectives can have. Children who have the goals of making the honor roll, graduating from high school, and going to college were found to have:

✓ 60% better grades

✓ 40% fewer emotional problems

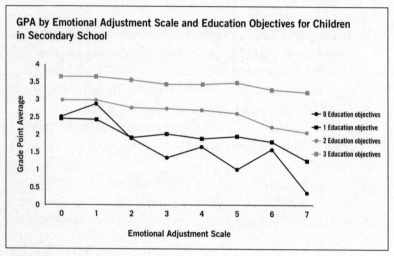

FIGURE 6.2

# CHAPTER SEVEN

# Message Sent = Message Received: Communicating Effectively

---

When we change the way we communicate,
we change society.
—*Clay Shirky, author, consultant on Internet technology*

I can't imagine how strange it must have seemed for people when they first used a telephone. The idea of being able to have a conversation with someone without seeing them must have been mind boggling. It did, indeed, change society. Probably, if you showed a group of children in 2014 a black rotary telephone from the 1950s, many of them wouldn't even know what it was.

In terms of momentous events, people born before 1960 may play, "Where were you when you heard that President Kennedy was shot?" In our generation, New Yorkers ask, "Where were you during the blackout of 2003?" For me, I vividly remember the first time I heard someone use the term *email*. It was a journalist who said it, and I was embarrassed that I didn't know what he was talking about!

Our ability to communicate rapidly is truly astounding. Even more astounding, however, is how our ability to relate to others— one on one, in person—is deteriorating. If you doubt that, just ask any teacher of grades K–12. We are raising children who can communicate through screens, but have diminished ability to initiate conversations, ask to join other kids on the playground, ask for help, make eye contact, apologize, listen and understand, convey sympathy, make friends, and perform a host of other interactive skills—that most adults take for granted.

## A CAUTIONARY TALE

A red-faced young man, sweating profusely under his black hoodie and gray T-shirt, squirmed in obvious discomfort as his eyes darted nervously around the room. His answers to questions were largely conceptual and rambling, failing to directly address the issue. Was this an FBI interview with a convicted felon?

No, it was Facebook founder Mark Zuckerberg, in the now famous interview conducted by Walt Mossberg and Kara Swisher about Facebook's privacy controls.[1] At the All Things Digital D8 conference, Zuckerberg's 60-second answer to a question was interpreted as blatantly arrogant by many; others simply wondered if he had any communication skills at all. For those not familiar with it, Zuckerberg essentially angered 350 million Facebook users by stating that he didn't care about their privacy. Whoops!

**Lesson 1:** *Failure to learn one of the essential skill sets will eventually catch up with you, regardless of how rich or famous you are.*

The now epic snafu created by Zuckerberg's lack of such skills reminds us that we can't avoid the inevitable face-to-face conversation. Of course, it was more than a little ironic that the creator of the world's largest communication and social network had failed to learn even basic communication skills. LOL!

What did Zuckerberg do to recover from the gaff? He hired a media trainer to teach him how to effectively communicate with the world. In subsequent interviews, the American public commented on how much more "likeable and social" Zuckerberg seemed. It appeared Zuckerberg had learned another important lesson.

**Lesson 2:** *It's not all about proving, it's about improving.*

"He's now able to convey, through storytelling, how his vision of the Facebook offering has evolved," said Clarity Media Group CEO, Bill McGowan. McGowan has media trained dozens of Facebook staff, including Zuckerberg. If the media is indeed the message, then strong communication skills are the vehicle.

**Lesson 3:** *Effective communication skills are as important to kindergartners as they are to CEOs.*

## RESPECTFUL ADULT COMMUNICATION

In her Chief Inspector Gamache mystery series, author Louise Penny shares with us Gamache's code for the four sentences that lead to wisdom:

I'm sorry. I was wrong. I need help. I don't know.[2]

These are simple phrases, aren't they? Why, then, do so many of us have difficulty in saying them?

Early in my career, I realized that both children and adults have difficulty in employing assertive communication. As a high school teacher, I seemed to spend a great deal of my time trying to get my students to tell me, clearly and succinctly, how they felt and what they wanted from me.

When I became a therapist, I initially worked with adults and was surprised to discover that they, too, were unable to clearly express their feelings. Often, they didn't even know *what* they were feeling, or if they even had the *right* to feel the way they did, so that made it triply hard!

In our culture, we are not brought up to say, "I feel . . ." Adults—especially males—think it's embarrassing, inappropriate, or weak to talk about feelings. In other cultures, the prohibitions against talking about one's feelings are even stricter. And yet, the ability to identify and express our feelings is an essential element of effective communication.

Look at these two common dinner table scenarios:

1. Cindy to her older sister, Leah: "You always interrupt me! You're so mean!"
2. Sandy to her older sister, Lois: "I feel so hurt and angry when you interrupt me. It makes me feel . . . stupid. I wish you'd let me talk sometimes."

In the first example, Cindy is accusing her sister. She is attacking her and calling her *mean*. In other words, Cindy is on the offensive. After she says, "You always interrupt . . . ," Leah has stopped listening to her; Leah is being attacked, and she is preparing her defensive counterattack.

1. Leah to Cindy: "Oh, yeah? Maybe if you had anything interesting to say, someone might want to listen!"

Nothing constructive is going to come from this conversation. When we call names, raise our voices, make accusations, say "you always" or "you never," people stop listening.

In the second example, Sandy is not accusing or attacking. She is talking about herself, how she feels. Then, she simply states what she wishes would happen. Lois has no need to be defensive and strike back because there is nothing to fight against.

When someone starts a sentence with the words *I feel*, people listen. They are curious, because it so rarely happens. *I-feel* statements are interesting, descriptive, and non-threatening; they describe the *speaker*, not the listener. They are respectful of both parties, and they stand an excellent chance of being heard. There is no defense to prepare, because there is no attack to defend against. Most of the time, a simple *I-feel* statement is enough to resolve the situation.[3]

2. Lois to Sandy: "I didn't know you felt that way. I really didn't mean to hurt your feelings. I'm sorry. And I don't think you're stupid—at least most of the time. [laughter] I don't want you to feel stupid. So talk; I won't interrupt. Really."

This is the way respectful adult communication (RAC) comments usually work out. We teach this technique to children with great success.

## HOW TO USE RAC: WHAT IT IS AND WHAT IT ISN'T

> *Anything that's human is mentionable, and anything that is mentionable can be more manageable. When we can talk about our feelings, they become less overwhelming, less upsetting, and less scary. The people we trust with that important talk can help us know that we are not alone.*
>
> —Fred Rogers, educator, Presbyterian minister, songwriter, author, and television host

Mister Rogers (of the *Mister Rogers' Neighborhood* TV show), wearing a shirt and tie, but made "comfy feeling" by adding a cardigan and a warm smile, always spoke to children softly, kindly, and welcomingly. He made them feel accepted and understood. He didn't talk down to kids, and didn't tell them what they *should* do. He asked them how they felt and what they thought. This calm, respectful, and supportive approach undoubtedly accounted for the show's popularity and almost 40-year run. His emphasis on talking about feelings was spot on.

RAC communication is simple but not necessarily easy. The words *I feel* are followed by a . . . *feeling*. Bad, happy, nervous, sad, angry, hungry, tired, scared, stupid, left out, ignored, proud, special—these are all feelings.

However, as soon as you say, "I feel that . . ." one of those annoying buzzers they use to signal out-of-time on game shows should sound. You are now about to express a *thought*, and probably an accusation or correction, not a feeling. The phrase *I feel that* is almost always followed by the word *you*. This is the end of a respectful, productive conversation and the beginning of an argument.

In our child therapy groups, we start small. Since the expression of feelings is such a novel idea, we want the kids to get used to the concept of feelings. We ask them to make a feelings list. Two groups of eight-year-olds came up with the list of feelings shown in Figure 7.1.

| angry | scared | confused | respected | lucky |
|---|---|---|---|---|
| sad | ashamed | bullied | helpless | **furious** |
| **hungry** | nervous | curious | disgraced | welcomed |
| **tired** | **good** | lame | foolish | **grateful** |
| depressed | **annoyed** | pissed | clean | overwhelmed |
| grumpy | embarrassed | **bored** | hyper | **stupid** |
| endangered | **excited** | **unwell** | ignored | brave |
| successful | wanted | **smart** | needed | **goofy** |
| invisible | unimportant | selfish | alone | hurt |
| proud | **thirsty** | mean | **happy** | beautiful/handsome |

FIGURE 7.1

We asked them which of those feelings they would feel comfortable talking about at home. Those words are in **bold** and shaded in the chart. As you can see, the children felt comfortable talking about physical states (hungry, tired, thirsty, unwell, good) and about some that are purely emotional (angry, happy, grateful, furious, stupid, excited, confused, annoyed, goofy, smart). They also said scared—but qualified it to mean "of scary movies, Bloody Mary, vampires, ghosts, the devil, etc." They wanted us to understand that they were absolutely *not* scared of failure, ridicule, or anything that might indicate vulnerability (Figure 7.2).

| angry | scared | confused | respected | lucky |
|-------|--------|----------|-----------|-------|
| sad | ashamed | bullied | helpless | furious |
| HUNGRY | NERVOUS | curious | disgraced | welcomed |
| TIRED | good | lame | foolish | grateful |
| depressed | ANNOYED | pissed | clean | overwhelmed |
| grumpy | embarrassed | bored | hyper | stupid |
| endangered | excited | UNWELL | ignored | brave |
| successful | wanted | SMART | needed | goofy |
| invisible | unimportant | selfish | alone | hurt |
| proud | THIRSTY | mean | HAPPY | beautiful/handsome |

FIGURE 7.2

We then asked them which feelings they would be comfortable talking about at school or with friends. Those are in UPPERCASE and shaded. Again, the kids indicated that speaking of physical states was okay; that feeling unwell (sick) was okay because you got to go to the nurse or go home, and that it was sometimes okay to indicate annoyance if someone was bothering you—but it had to be done carefully or you might get in trouble. You could talk about being happy about something specific—a good grade, a special event, or an acquisition (like a new video game). Some kids said it was okay to say "I feel smart," but most kids thought they could never talk about being or feeling smart in school or with friends—unless someone was making fun of them and they wanted to one-up them.

When asked about what they felt comfortable about discussing "in here" (in the group), they indicated pretty much all of them, with some exceptions. Those exceptions, I was to understand, were because, "They're not what *I* feel, but I know that *some kids* feel this way." Uh-huh. *These exceptions* are in **BOLD UPPERCASE** and are shaded (Figure 7.3).

| angry | **SCARED** | confused | respected | lucky |
|---|---|---|---|---|
| sad | **ASHAMED** | bullied | helpless | furious |
| hungry | nervous | curious | **DISGRACED** | welcomed |
| tired | good | lame | foolish | grateful |
| **DEPRESSED** | annoyed | pissed | clean | overwhelmed |
| grumpy | **EMBARRASSED** | bored | hyper | stupid |
| **ENDANGERED** | excited | unwell | **IGNORED** | **BRAVE** |
| successful | wanted | smart | needed | goofy |
| **INVISIBLE** | **UNIMPORTANT** | selfish | **ALONE** | **HURT** |
| **PROUD** | thirsty | mean | happy | **BEAUTIFUL/HANDSOME** |

FIGURE 7.3

Except for "feeling beautiful—or handsome," which none of them could acknowledge, the other feelings were the important ones; the ones that showed vulnerability. Even expressing pride or bravery makes a kid feel vulnerable, as it may invite ridicule.

After a lot of trust has developed and the steps we outline later in the chapter are followed, the "shaded feelings" are gradually brought out. In the best of all possible worlds, children will learn that it's safe to talk about all of their feelings, including the difficult ones, with parents, trusted teachers, and friends.

## FEELINGS ARE REAL, AND THEY'RE NOT ACTIONS

I was visiting a nursery school recently when I heard the following exchange between Billy and his mother:

> **Billy (age 4):** I hate Josh! He's mean!
> **Mother:** You don't hate Josh; don't say that. We don't use that word. And Josh's your best friend!
> **Billy:** [in tears] I do hate him! He's mean. And I hate you, too!

That went well, Mom. The thing is, at that moment Billy was in pain and didn't know how to describe how he felt. At that moment, he felt "hate," and he was trying to have a conversation in which:

✓ His feelings would be heard and understood.

✓ He could get support.

✓ He could be comforted.

Instead, he was shut down.

Some parents feel that words are magical, that the *expression* of negative ones will somehow be a gateway to the child *performing* bad actions. Actually, the converse is true. When children are allowed to talk about their negative feelings and process them with an understanding adult, they are far less likely to act them out. The very term *acting out* describes what people do when they either:

✓ Don't have the words to express how they are feeling, or they

✓ Have the words, but aren't allowed to say them

When our children are feeling angry and hurt, the best thing we can do is to *listen to them*.

What if you came home from work absolutely incensed at a

coworker who had taken your idea and passed it off as her own? How would you feel if the following conversation occurred?

> **You:** I could just kill Kimberly! That lying witch stole my pro-
> posal for the Kendry project and gave it to that idiot Lathrop,
> who actually believed that *she* had come up with it!
> **Your spouse:** We don't talk about killing people, and we don't
> use name calling in this house. You don't really feel that way.
> You like Kimberly, and Ms. Lathrop has been very good
> to you.

Now, you would probably have distinctly unfriendly feelings about your spouse, too!

Neither you nor Billy got the reaction you wanted. Unfortunately, the *bad-word police* showed up instead of the loving and supportive spouse or mommy. Both of you feel even more angry and hurt after your feelings are ignored and—even worse—denied and corrected; this kind of conversation never ends either quickly or well.

## LISTENING TO THE MUSIC, NOT THE WORDS

> *The most important thing in communication is to hear
> what isn't being said.*
> —Peter Drucker, management consultant, educator,
> and author

When children are using words or acting out, they often have underlying feelings that are not being expressed. The concept of "listening to the music" is an important one; the purpose is to help children talk about those hard-to-express feelings. This *inability to express* can be true for angry words and for shy words and for all the words in between. What kids *aren't* saying is often far more important than what they *are* saying. Take the statement made by four-year-old Billy:

**Billy:** I hate Josh! He's mean!

If Billy's mommy is listening to the music, she may respond quite differently from before:

**Mommy:** Oh, Billy, I'm sorry. You sound so upset.
**Billy:** I am upset! I'm so mad at him! He's a jerk.
**Mommy:** Do you want to talk about it? It sounds like Josh hurt your feelings.
**Billy:** [crying] He did hurt my feelings. He got to be leader and pick his team, and he didn't pick me!
**Mommy:** [giving him a hug] I'm so sorry, honey. That must have made you feel mad *and* sad.
**Billy:** [stops crying] Yeah. I felt sad. He was being a poophead. Do I have Tee ball today?

## "I Feel . . ."

By listening to the music, Billy's mother opened the door to what Billy was really feeling—hurt and sadness. He felt betrayed by his best friend, and he just needed to vent a little without having to censor his words. Once he knew he had been heard, it was done. He wanted to move on.

Billy's mother neither underreacted—a lecture about *blah blah blah*—nor overreacted—"I guess Josh isn't a nice boy; maybe we shouldn't invite him over anymore." Both of those techniques serve to make a child feel worse—and pretty much guarantee that they won't rush to confide their feelings to their parent anytime soon.

When parents can act as a beneficent mirror for their child's expression of feelings, then the child can communicate without fear, knowing they will get comfort. They won't feel angry or guilty; they won't get "helpful hints" about how they *should* feel or what they *should* have done or *should* do in the future, and they won't have to deal with their parent's feelings on top of their own.

## MOLLY AND DAD HAVE A TALK

**Molly (age 12)** is a sixth grader. She has just found out that she has been put in all AP classes for next year.

> **Molly:** I hate my school! They are so stupid!
>
> **Dad:** Wow! Something terrible must have happened.
>
> **Molly:** It did! I got put in all AP classes for next year.
>
> **Dad:** Oh. Well . . . that sounds like good news, honey. Congratulations? But . . . maybe it's not such good news to you?
>
> **Molly:** It's all nerds in those classes!
>
> **Dad:** Hmmm . . . nerds. Really?
>
> **Molly:** All my *real* friends are in regular classes. I want to be in regular classes, too.
>
> **Dad:** Oh, so . . . you won't be with your friends?. Everyone will be new?
>
> **Molly:** Yes! What if I can't do it? What if the nerds don't like me—I mean, if I don't like them.
>
> **Dad:** So, you're worried that you won't make new friends?
>
> **Molly:** Exactly! And what if my friends are all, like, "She thinks she's so smart! Now she's too good for us." What if Katie forgets about me? So, what if it's like, I'm *too good* for them, and the new kids think I'm *not good enough*?
>
> **Dad:** I can see how that could be a big problem . . . if it happened. Honestly? I really don't think that there's *anything* that could make Katie forget about you, but that's just my opinion. Molly, I have to ask you something.
>
> **Molly:** What, Daddy?
>
> **Dad:** Is there any part of you—just the tiniest bit—that feels kind of proud that your teachers think you deserve to be in AP classes?

**Molly:** I don't know . . . maybe . . . I guess . . . kind of. But . . .

**Dad:** Sweetheart, it's okay to be proud of yourself. You can even say, "I feel proud! Yay, me!"

**Molly:** [rolls her eyes, giggling] Dad!

**Dad:** I'm serious! Yes, you can! You worked really hard this year, Molly. I don't think a little, "Yay, me!" is too far out there. It's *important* to feel proud of yourself, honey. Your teachers obviously see how hard you've worked; they think you earned it or they wouldn't have recommended you.

**Molly:** Do *you* think I deserve it?

**Dad:** Yes, I do, and I'm very proud of you; all your hard work is paying off. Honey, I know it's a change, but you'll figure it out. Really.

**Molly:** Thanks, Dad. Can we go out for ice cream? To . . . celebrate? Can we take Katie?

Molly's dad is a great listener, very intuitive, and a good communicator. By being an empowering parent, he was able to tap into his daughter's conflicting feelings, without telling her how she should feel or giving her tips about how to shore up her friendships or how to have an open mind about "the nerds" or anything else. He allowed Molly to decide how *she* feels, in a situation that is confusing for her.

Many parents would see this as only a "win" and pooh-pooh their child's fears of losing her friends or of not being good enough. Molly will doubtless have more conversations with her father about this topic, and if she actually asks for advice, she'll probably get a thoughtful answer. But—*only if she asks!* As Hunter S. Thompson said:

A word to the wise is infuriating.

Loving parents empathize with their children; they can almost, literally, feel their pain.

However, the greatest gift they can give their hurting child is the gift of listening, without becoming overly emotionally involved. For kids, emotion-filled "*you*" statements often mask a deeper message: *I feel hurt. I don't understand. I need your help.* When we really listen, when we hear the music, when we make it possible for our children to say that they feel sad or hurt or scared or stupid, we are teaching them the first step in effective communication. We are teaching them how to *say it* in a way that others will be able to *hear it.*

## "I WANT . . ."

*Assumptions are the termites of relationships.*
—Henry Winkler, actor

The next step is to clearly say what it is that we would like to see happen. The words will vary—*I wish, I want, I don't want, I need, I wish you wouldn't*—it doesn't matter, as long as the listener doesn't have to guess what you are trying to say.

Even very young children can learn to communicate effectively.

### Case Study: Baxter and Manuel

Baxter (age 7) is a ball of energy. He has galloping ADHD, which has been effectively moderated by therapy and medication. When Baxter misses taking his stimulant medication, he can still be helped to focus with non-verbal cues. We use them in his group, and we showed his mother how to use them at home. Because Baxter has a number of learning disabilities, his self-confidence is still quite low. As with many kids who suffer from difficulties with their schoolwork, Baxter tends to exaggerate his non-academic achievements and often resorts to bragging. This can be extremely off-putting behavior for other children as well as for adults.

Baxter is in a group with two other boys; we often play foosball in this group, as it's a good outlet for their seven-year-old energy. It's a great tool for developing hand–eye coordination as well as for teaching good sportsmanship, the following of rules, and being a supportive team member—all important social skills for making friends. One of Baxter's issues is the need to tell other kids "how to do it" because "I am the best at this—I am a pro foosball player."

One Saturday morning, the kids and I were having a great time playing foosball, when Baxter said to his partner, "How could you miss that? You need to block those shots. You change with me; I'll play defense." The other child, Manuel, looked as if he were trying not to cry. His little face, all lit up with joy the minute before, just fell.

I stopped the game, and we all sat down. I asked Manuel how he was feeling right now. He said, quietly, "Angry." I asked him how he felt when Baxter said those things to him. He said, very quietly, "Angry . . . and . . . hurt."

I asked Manuel if he could turn his chair and look at Baxter; then, if he could tell him how he felt and what he wanted. I knew I was asking a lot of him, but I also knew that he needed to say it—and that Baxter needed to hear it. Manuel looked at me, and I smiled and nodded at him; he turned his chair, so that he was making eye contact with Baxter. He said, "I felt hurt and angry when you said those things to me. It made me feel bad . . . stupid and embarrassed. I don't want you to do it anymore."

Baxter looked genuinely horrified. He said, "I'm sorry. I feel bad. I didn't want to make you feel bad. You're my friend, and . . . I'm sorry that I hurt you. I promise I won't do it again." He obviously meant every word.

I asked Manuel how he felt. He smiled and said, "Better." Baxter volunteered, "Me, too." Manuel stuck out his hand and they shook hands. Baxter looked a little misty, but he hung in there, asking (in typical Baxter fashion) "*Now* can we get back to the game?" The boys both laughed.

At the end of the group, I told the boys that I thought they were brave. They looked surprised. I explained that it takes courage to talk about feelings—especially to say, "I feel hurt" and "I'm sorry." I also addressed the third boy (Pete) and congratulated him for his courage, in being able to listen to Baxter and Manuel, without get-ting embarrassed or trying to create a distraction.

After they left the group with their parents, I heard the waiting room door open and someone knocked on my door. When I said, "Come in," Manuel came running in, gave me a hug, and whispered, "Thank you."

Baxter's behavior changed dramatically after that day. He became kinder, he gave compliments, and he started saying "thank you." He still occasionally brags, but much, much less. The rewarding part of RAC is that *both* parties feel respected. In this case, Manuel was able to clearly say how he felt and get positive recognition and val-idation. Baxter was accorded the respect of being spoken to in a direct and kindly manner, instead of being ignored, ostracized, judged, or punished for his behavior.

The third child in this group, Pete, was relatively new, and had been reticent to talk about anything very personal up to that point. The RAC exchange affected him, too. He learned that it was safe to say how he felt and that we would listen to him with respect. He became an active member of the group from that day on.

### THE DEFINITION OF COMMUNICATION SKILLS: WHEN THE MESSAGE BEING SENT IS THE MESSAGE THAT IS RECEIVED[4]

I doubt that Mark Zuckerberg, in the interview discussed earlier in this chapter, intended to convey that he didn't care one bit about Facebook users' privacy concerns; nonetheless, whatever his inten-tion, that was the message received by the viewing audience.

> *The single biggest problem with communication is the illusion that it has taken place.*
> —George Bernard Shaw, Noble Prize–winning
> Irish playwright and co-founder of the
> London School of Economics

Zuckerberg's unfortunate interview is as illustrative of the Shaw quote, as is what is happening, online, with our children.

From teenagers to kids as young as eight and nine years old, communication—as in, genuine exchange of ideas and feelings—is assumed to be occurring in online "relationships." It is usually not.

*The ability to fully communicate involves more than words. It is a whole-body experience.*

- ✓ *Body language:* The position of the body, presence or absence of eye contact, stillness or movement of the whole body or of the extremities, facial expression, changes in facial muscles and/or coloring.

- ✓ *Voice:* The volume, intonation, word emphasis, intensity, congruity of voice and body with the words used.

- ✓ *Pace:* The pauses between the words and what they may indicate, the pressured or measured way the words are delivered.

- ✓ *Word choice:* Are the words themselves delivered in a way that is congruent with the meaning (for example, the delivery of the phrase *I don't mind* can mean genuine indifference or anger, hurt, or caring)?

This is one of the problems with online relationships, which can form within minutes. Children can believe that they know the other person *really well*, when they *really know* absolutely nothing; virtual reality is not reality, yet virtual is what online relationships are. Thinking that the person sending the messages is a close friend, children can reveal all sorts of information they would never give to a complete stranger—details including their address, personal information about themselves and other family members, where they go to school, family routines and patterns, even photos are routinely shared.

# HOMEWORK:
## PARENTS AS COMMUNICATION PARTNERS

*Every word, facial expression, gesture, or action on the
part of a parent gives the child some message about self-
worth. It is sad that so many parents don't realize what
messages they are sending.*
>                   —Virginia Satir, psychotherapist and author

Parents are the #1 role models for their children. No matter what
they may *say* to us, our kids look to us for the right way to do things.

It is up to us to remember that *our biggest homework* is to be the
kind of learners that we want our children to be; to show them the
habits and behaviors that we value, *by living them.* For example,
when they see us constantly on our phones or texting, how can we
preach media management skills without looking like frauds? I can't
tell you how many times I've seen children trying to talk to their
moms, while their moms are nodding and making *uh-huh* noises—
but still texting. The kids invariably walk away or become angry,
sometimes crying. "Do as I say, not as I do" will not fly with Generation M²; it's *so* last century!

As empowering parents, we *actively listen*; that's how our children learn to listen and to communicate effectively. They can't get
that from a screen. There is a comfort level necessary for kids to be
able to be assertive, to make friends, to share opinions, to solve
problems. They develop that only from learning how to talk to and
listen to others, in vivo. There need to be media-free zones and times
in all our homes if we want children to develop good communication skills.

As all parents know, children usually pick the most inconve-
nient times to want to have a conversation. Small children hate it
when their moms are on the phone or are talking to someone else.
Teens invariably want that heart-to-heart when it's bedtime and
you're totally exhausted.

Modeling good communication skills will help *you,* because it will make your *kids* more observant and polite. If you don't want them to interrupt you when you're talking to someone, then don't interrupt them! Give them a cue, like holding up your hand in a "stop" gesture or making the finger-to-lips "shh" signal—and then holding up your fingers to signal how many minutes before you'll be available.

If you have to excuse yourself from your conversation, then do so, but model "I feel . . . I want" when you ask your child to let you finish your conversation. They'll know that they're important, and that you're not blowing them off. Then, when you do start to listen to them, unplug or walk away from your friend; or squat down to be at eye level with them, if they're little.

After all, isn't listening to your child more important than almost anything? Not only will you advance their learning habit in the area of communication, but you will gain their trust in being able to communicate with you.

# CHAPTER EIGHT

# Options Versus Consequences: Making Responsible Decisions

_____

Everyone has to make their own decisions.
I still believe in that. You just have to be able
to accept the consequences without complaining.
—*Grace Jones, actor, singer, and model*

**Jonas (age 16)** has a decision to make. His father's family has an annual Christmas party the weekend before Christmas. He looks forward to it every year: all his cousins, great food, funny games, Santa Swap—everyone has a blast. This year, however, a YMCA swim meet is happening that weekend. It is not required that he participate; it's not for his school swim team. However, it is a qualification meet and he already qualified; Jonas wants to do everything he can to increase his chances of getting an athletic scholarship for college.

    *Choice: Annual party or swim meet*

**Madelyn (age 5)** had an arithmetic assignment. Madelyn's mother was at a meeting. Usually, Madelyn and Mommy unpack her backpack and Mommy stays with her while she does her important homework. Madelyn didn't unpack her backpack and get out her worksheet, because she wanted to spend time playing with Daddy. When he suggested they watch her favorite video before bath time, she had to make a decision.

**Choice:** *Worksheet or video*

**Noah (age 12)** was quite small for his age. An honors student, he was self-conscious about his height. His dad and older brother, both tall, kept reassuring him that he would have a growth spurt in a couple of years, but Noah was worried that he wouldn't; his mother and sister are both very small. Noah was sick of being called "Shorty" or "Short Stuff" by the guys in his school, even though he knew they were just fooling around. Every time he had to get something from the top shelf of his gym locker, someone said, "Hey, Shorty, you need a ladder to reach that?" He could usually think of a funny response, and everybody laughed. Those guys were his friends, and they knew he could always come back with a fierce remark.

One of the guys, Howard, wasn't a friend and wasn't innocently fooling around. He was a bully, and loved to single Noah out for ridicule. If he passed Noah in the hall, he'd always bump into him, elbow him, knock his books, or trip him. He really seemed to have it out for Noah, for reasons known only to himself. Therefore, Noah was careful not to get caught alone with Howard.

One day, Noah forgot his ELA textbook and had to run back to his locker to get it at the end of school. Howard was there. He started pushing Noah and taunting him, calling him names, and daring Noah to punch him. Noah was frightened. Normally he just tossed out a wise remark to level the playing field and everyone laughed. Clearly, that wasn't going to work this time. Howard was a huge kid, looking for a fight; there was no one in the corridor.

Noah felt like crying; he was scared out of his mind. Howard pushed him into the locker and said, "Go ahead smart-mouth, you're not so funny now. Hit me, you little piss-ant!" At that precise moment, he heard girls' voices—and the command, "No running in the halls!" from the scary vice principal.

*Choices: Yell for help; do nothing and take the beating; punch Howard*

## THE CHOICES AND THE MISTAKES

*We need to accept that we won't always make the right decisions, that we'll screw up royally sometimes—understanding that failure is not the opposite of success, it's part of success.*
    —Arianna Huffington, editor in chief, *Huffington Post*

One of the hardest things for parents to do is to give their children the opportunity to make choices that may not turn out well. Helping children learn through making both right and wrong decisions is tough, but it's the only way that a sustainable habit of decision-making can be learned. Once children have acquired this skill, they can make realistic decisions that are likely to feel satisfying. Realistic decisions are based on an assessment of the worst-case scenario and a willingness to live with that consequence. As Michael Jordan can attest, making mistakes—failing—is how we learn and ultimately triumph:

> I've missed more than 9,000 shots in my career. I've lost almost 300 games. Twenty-six times, I've been trusted to take the game-winning shot and missed. I've failed over and over and over again in my life. And that is why I succeed.[1]

## RESPONSIBILITY AND CONTROL

One of the hardest things for children to do is to take responsibility for the things they control—namely, themselves and their actions. It's a great feeling to be given choices, but it's hard to accept responsibility when things don't work out. Learning to say, "I made a mistake," "I blew it," "It's my fault," "I'm to blame; what can I do to make it up to you?" is tough. Our natural instinct is to make excuses, complain about injustice, or blame someone else. "My alarm didn't go off!" or "The dog ate my homework" are classics; the new classic is, "My computer died."

Doug Baldwin Jr. was a wide receiver for the Stanford University football team. His lifelong dream was to be a professional football player. An outstanding wide receiver, he nonetheless got very little playing time during his first three years at Stanford. That changed his senior year—when his attitude changed:

> [Due to an ankle sprain] my starting role was downgraded to backup. When I did step back on the field, it was with a chip on my shoulder. I was angry. How could I lose the starting role that I worked so hard for to an injury that was out of my control? . . .
>
> My focus was in the wrong place. While being angry and upset, balls slipped through my hands during practice, routes were sloppy and easily covered by defensive backs. . . .
>
> I was searching for answers to why things were happening to me, but I never stopped to think how I could get myself out of those situations. . . .
>
> [I realized that] I had to stop worrying about things that were not in my control. I had to start controlling the things that I could and have faith that everything else would work itself out. I focused on responding to obstacles in the right way. I focused on overcoming them and not letting them hold me back.[2]

Baldwin's statement is a perfect example of the perspective necessary for developing a habit of responsibility. Once he stopped worrying about things that he did not control (coaches' decisions regarding his playing time) and instead started taking responsibility for what he actually did control (the way he was playing), everything changed for this outstanding scholar-athlete. When he graduated in 2011, with a degree in science, technology, and society, he had been inducted into the National Honor Society, the Math Honor Society, and the Spanish National Honor Society. A few months later, he achieved his goal; he was signed as an undrafted free agent by the Seattle Seahawks and became a professional football player.

> The most successful children are the ones who are able to take responsibility for things only within their area of control and let other things go.

And the converse is true for parents.

> The most helpful parents are the ones who are able to *not* take responsibility for things that their children can control.

We previously mentioned the definition of insanity as "repeating the same behavior over and over, each time hoping for a different result." I would like to propose an additional thesis: Taking responsibility for things you don't control will drive you nuts! The corollary to that one is: *Not* taking responsibility for things you *do control* will drive everyone else nuts!

## THE BACKBONE IS EMPOWERMENT PARENTING

In our work, we've learned that helping children understand what specific parts of a task are their responsibility allows them to feel in control. It's also a great way to help refocus parents on Empowerment Parenting; the entire focus is on *learning* rather than *out-*

*come.* The first step is to understand the limits of our control and then—within those limits—put forth our best effort. Even if we don't achieve the outcome we want right now, we are building learning habits that will ultimately result in success.

This is how empowering parents help their children: They encourage effort and reflect reality in discussions about what their kids control. Knowing that "I am in control of what I think and say and how I act—that's my responsibility, no one else's" is a terrific start.

## Case Study: Graham

**Graham (age 6)** was playing with his friend, Danisha. Graham's mother had bought some new coloring books and suggested that the children might like to color a picture to hang on the refrigerator. Both children thought that was a great idea. Danisha chose the *Dora and Diego* coloring book; Graham picked *Spider-Man*, his hero.

Danisha started coloring immediately, humming a little song while she concentrated on her picture. Graham, however, kept looking at Danisha's picture.

"People aren't purple," Graham said. "You can't make Dora purple. That's not right. My mom won't like it."

Danisha kept on coloring. She turned the page, and started on a picture of Boots. She thought that the monkey would look beautiful with a red head and a blue body and started in on the new picture.

Graham, meanwhile, was becoming agitated. "No, Danisha," he said. "You can't go on to another picture until you finish this one!" he exclaimed, pointing to the purple people picture. "You need to do it the *right* way. Your way is *wrong.*"

Danisha put her crayon down. "You're not the boss of me!" she stammered and started to cry. Graham's mom came in and squatted down by the sobbing child. "Danisha, honey, what's wrong?" she asked.

Danisha just shook her head and kept crying. "I want to go home now," she sobbed.

Instead of focusing on what he controlled—how he colored *his* picture—Graham was trying to control how Danisha colored. His agitation over her lack of "doing it the right way" kept him from taking responsibility for his own picture, and in fact, he barely even started it. Trying to assume responsibility for how Danisha's picture looked and whether it would be acceptable for hanging on his mother's refrigerator ended with unhappiness and frustration for both children.

Danisha was hurt and angered by Graham's bossiness and criticism; Graham was frustrated and hurt that Danisha wouldn't take his instructions and do it "the right way."

By trying to be the boss of Danisha, Graham ended up not even being the boss of himself.

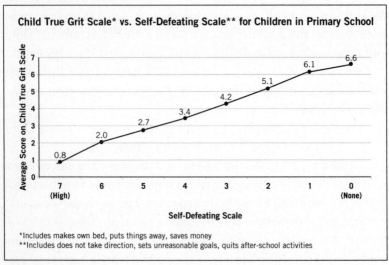

FIGURE 8.1

## CONTROL AND ACADEMIC HOMEWORK

Children do not control:

✓ What homework their teachers assign.

✓ Whether or not their teacher adequately prepares them to do the work, such as giving them clear instructions about exactly what is expected.

✓ What grade the teacher will give them.

They do, however, control:

✓ Asking the teacher for clarification if they don't understand an assignment.

✓ Making sure they go home with the materials they need.

✓ Putting in the effort to do the work as best they can.

✓ Making sure the homework gets handed in.

And those things, within their control, are their responsibility.

## CONTROL AND SPORTS

Children do not control:

✓ If the coach is fair, kind, or competent.

✓ If practices and games are held at convenient times and under optimal conditions, such as good or bad weather.

✓ If they are chosen to play or to sit on the bench.

They do, however, control:

✓ Showing up for every practice.

✓ Using criticism, mistakes, and embarrassments as learning opportunities.

✓ Following the rules.

✓ Being on time and with the right clothing and equipment.

✓ Trying their hardest, all the time.

✓ Being a good sport, in winning and in losing.

✓ Being a supportive team member.

They need to assume responsibility for those.

## Case Study: The Group Project

Hank (age 15) was a tenth grader in an AP science class; the class members were assigned group projects. Hank was partnered with another boy, Jeff; each was responsible for 50% of the project that counted as a single test grade for both of them.

Hank handed his part of the project in. He'd put a lot of effort into his paper and knew he'd get an A. The next day, at the end of the period, the students received their project grades: Hank and his partner got C's. The teacher's note read, "Incomplete." Hank asked Jeff what that meant; the other boy confessed that he hadn't handed his paper in—he hadn't finished it. Hank was furious.

When Hank got home from school, he slammed his backpack down, yelled at his little sister, and was rude to his mother. He complained about her not having any A.1. steak sauce for his burger and refused to touch his salad, saying, "You *know* I hate salad!" He went directly to his room after dinner.

After his little sister was in bed, Hank came into the living room, where his mother was looking through the mail.

**Mom:** Do you want to talk about it?

**Hank:** I got a C on my science project; my a-hole partner didn't hand anything in. I can't believe it! Mrs. Thorsen gave me a C! I did my part. I deserved an A!

**Mom:** I guess that explains why you've been so horrid since you got home.

**Hank:** Yeah, I'm sorry. But, Mom, it's so unfair. Can you talk

to Mrs. Thorsen about changing my grade? You saw my
paper; you know it deserved an A!

**Mom:** I thought you did a great job! But Hank, if Mrs. Thorsen
gave you a C, she had a reason. This was a *group* project
and, evidently, only half of it was done. You need to talk to
your teacher, honey.

The next day, Hank asked Mrs. Thorsen if he could talk to her
after school.

**Mrs. Thorsen:** I imagine that you're not pleased with your project grade, Hank.

**Hank:** No, I'm not. It's not fair to give me a C! I worked really
hard on my paper. That was a good paper.

**Mrs. Thorsen:** I agree; it was an excellent paper—I gave it an A.

**Hank:** You did? Oh—now I feel kind of stupid. I didn't realize
you'd already changed my grade. Thank you!

**Mrs. Thorsen:** You misunderstand, Hank; I didn't change your
grade. The grade you received was for the project. Your part
received an A; your partner's part received an F. The C was
really a gift.

**Hank:** A gift? How is getting a C on an A paper a gift?

**Mrs. Thorsen:** Let's say that your A is equal to a number grade
of 100%; your partner's grade is a zero; he didn't hand anything in. The average of those two grades is 50%—or an F.
I'm assuming that you'd prefer a C to an F. This was a *group*
project, Hank. The grade reflects the work of the *group*, not
of one person. When I assigned the project, I was clear about
my expectations. On the hand-out I gave you, I underlined
the words "group project will be given *one grade* that reflects
the complete project." Did you not read that?

**Hank:** But that's not fair! I'm not responsible for what my partner does. He is; it's not like I can control if he does his work.

**Mrs. Thorsen:** That's the point of a group project, Hank; learning how to work with another person to produce a unified result. Each member *is* responsible for the success of the *project*. Let me ask you something: Did you ever talk to Jeff? Ask him how he was doing?

**Hank:** Well, no, but . . .

**Mrs. Thorsen:** In reality, there were a number of things you *did* have control over. For instance, you could have called Jeff or talked to him in class or met him after school. If it was apparent that he wasn't doing his part, you could have talked to me about your concerns. When *your* grade is 50% dependent on *someone else's* work, then it's sensible to do whatever you can to monitor that other 50%.

Hank wasn't happy about the C, but he learned a valuable lesson about the extent of both his responsibility and his control.

## MODELING OPTIONS AND CONSEQUENCES

### Case Study: Landon's Decision

**Landon** (age 9) was in the fifth grade. On Monday afternoon, he was putting a clean bag in the trash can when he got a call from Caleb, inviting him to come to his house, play his new game system, and stay for supper. They could go to chorus practice together, and then Caleb's mom would bring Landon home. Landon was excited. Caleb was the cool new kid, he had the newest PlayStation Vita, and Landon was dying to play it. He begged his mother to let him go.

Landon's mother told him that they needed to discuss it, so to tell Caleb that he'd call him back in a few minutes. Landon protested; Mom told him that if they couldn't discuss it, the answer would be *no*. Landon told Caleb he'd call him back in a couple of minutes. Caleb said to hurry; they were on their way back from the mall and would be near Landon's house in 10 minutes.

Mom asked him about homework; he told her that he just had some math problems that wouldn't take long. He explained that he could do them later or during homeroom, but that getting invited to Caleb's was a big deal. Mom reminded him that he barely had time to shower after chorus and get to bed on time, so later was probably not an option.

Landon was starting to get upset. Mom told him, "I didn't say you couldn't go; I just want to make sure that you make a decision you can live with."

Landon didn't understand. Mom explained, "When we make decisions, choices, we don't make them in a big rush, unless it's a fire or something, which this is not. We look at the *best* that can happen and the *worst* that can happen. For instance, if you stay home and do your math, what's the worst that can happen?"

**Landon:** I miss going to Caleb's and he'll never ask me again!

**Mom:** What's the best that can happen?

**Landon:** Nothing!

**Mom:** Come on. If you show up with your homework done tomorrow, what's the best thing that is likely to happen?

**Landon:** Mr. Price will give me a check-plus in the book, and then I will probably have 10 checks in a row and can skip the next quiz or take it, and if I get a bad mark, it gets thrown out.

**Mom:** Okay, that's good. That's choice *number one*. Now, choice *number two*: You go to Caleb's. What the best thing that's likely to happen?

**Landon:** I get to play the newest, awesomest game and go to the coolest kid's coolest house.

**Mom:** What's the worst thing that can happen?

**Landon:** I told you, nothing. I'll get my homework done.

**Mom:** That's not how you make a decision, based on what you *hope* will happen. That's like deciding to rob a bank because you're pretty sure you'll get away with it. Nobody believes they'll get caught, Landon. To make good choices, you always have to believe that the *very worst thing* will happen. If that very worst thing happens, can you live with it? That's how you make realistic decisions, not based on hopes and prayers but on what can actually happen in the real world. So, what's the very worst thing that can happen if you choose to go to Caleb's?

**Landon:** Okay. So, maybe, something happens and I can't finish my homework. Mr. Price will be mad, he'll give me that "I expected more from you, Landon" speech, and I'll have to start all over again on the check-plus list.

**Mom:** Anything else?

**Landon:** Well, he could give me detention.

**Mom:** Okay. So, now you have two clear choices:

1. *Go to Caleb's*: The best is you get to play Vita, hang out in a cool house, and have lots of fun. The worst is you get into trouble with Mr. Price, who may be disappointed or mad, will make you start the check-plus list all over again, and could send you to detention.

2. *Stay home and do your homework*: The best is that you get praise and a reward of no quiz or drop the bad quiz grade from Mr. Price. The worst is you miss out on going to Caleb's, you don't get to play an awesome game in an awesome house, and you may never get invited back.

   Does that pretty much sum it up?

**Landon:** Yup. So, are you telling me that I get to choose?

**Mom:** Yes. But—

**Landon:** I *knew* there'd be a "but"!

**Mom:** Just listen a minute, please. You get to make this choice for yourself. But whatever choice you make, be sure that you can live with the "worst that can happen" scenario, because the worst happens more than you think.

**Landon:** So, you're saying I can go to Caleb's?

**Mom:** Whatever you think will turn out best for you, honey; it's your choice.

**Landon:** Great! Thanks, Mom. You won't regret this, you'll see.
I've gotta call him right now!

Due to inexperience, children have a natural tendency to over-inflate positive outcomes and underestimate negative repercussions. They tend to believe that "It won't happen to me; everything will work out the way I want."

## LIVING WITH THE CONSEQUENCES

When he got home after chorus, Landon reported that he did get to play the new game system, which was "totally awesome!" Caleb's mom was "nice"; dinner, however, was sandwiches, as opposed to Mom's "world-famous meatloaf and mashed potatoes." He said that the house was, indeed, awesome, but the boys pretty much stayed in Caleb's room. Landon got home just in time to shower and go to bed, as was his family's rule. When she went in to kiss him goodnight, he thanked his mother for letting him go.

The next day, Landon was unusually quiet after he got home from school. To his mother's, "How was your day?" he said, "Fine." He got his snack, then sat at the kitchen table to do his homework. His mother finished up the report she was writing and came into the kitchen to start dinner. She noticed that Landon had his math book out.

**Mom:** So, were you able to get your homework done in time?
**Landon:** I don't want to talk about it. [big sigh] No, I didn't. And Mr. Price was really steamed. He was so mean to me! He gave me two extra pages of homework. *And* I have detention tomorrow. I have the paper here; you or Dad have to sign it. Detention is two hours! Can you pick me up? I really don't want to wait for the late bus.
**Mom:** Honey, tomorrow is Wednesday, remember? I go into the office on Wednesdays and don't get home until 5:30 or 6:00.

**Landon:** What about Dad? Can he pick me up?

**Mom:** You'll have to ask him, but I sincerely doubt it. His regional manager is in for the week; ducking out early would *not* be the smart choice.

**Landon** [burying his head in his hands] Smart choice, right! I guess I didn't. Now I'm on Mr. Price's *slacker list*, where I'm sure Caleb is. I have all this homework . . . and the detention tomorrow? I asked if he could make it for Thursday, because Mrs. Jenkins is having that party after school and I'm going to miss it! Of course he said, "You should have thought of that before you decided to ditch your homework."

**Mom:** Oh, that's right. Tomorrow's the Science Stars party, isn't it?

**Landon:** Yes. And those parties are sick! But, stupid me; I have detention. You'd think Mr. Price could give me a pass, just this once.

**Mom:** I am truly sorry about the party, honey. I know how hard it is to believe that the *worst thing* can really happen; it stinks when it does—but it does, often. You're not stupid, Landon; I think you just got your first lesson in realistic decision making.

**Landon:** But Mr. Price . . .

**Mom:** Uh-uh. Landon, you made your choice; Mr. Price made his.

**Landon:** I know. I'm just so . . . I kind of knew I was making a mistake—the whole time I was at Caleb's, it felt . . . weird . . . wrong. I felt . . . like I was breaking a rule.

**Mom:** Well, you didn't break a rule. You just have a habit: You come home, take out the trash, get a snack, and do your homework. You made a decision to try something different, and it felt weird because you didn't do what you usually do—that makes us feel uncomfortable.

**Landon:** I felt bad when Mr. Price was talking to me. I don't think he likes me anymore.

**Mom:** I'm sure he still likes you, honey; he was probably annoyed and felt like you let him down. [smiling] I guess you'll just have to work extra hard to get back into Mr. Price's good graces. Look, your choice didn't turn out the way you hoped. Everybody makes mistakes, decisions we regret; fortunately, we can learn from them.

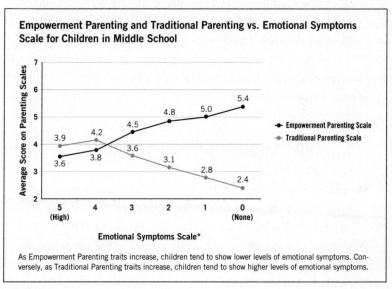

**Empowerment Parenting and Traditional Parenting vs. Emotional Symptoms Scale for Children in Middle School**

As Empowerment Parenting traits increase, children tend to show lower levels of emotional symptoms. Conversely, as Traditional Parenting traits increase, children tend to show higher levels of emotional symptoms.

FIGURE 8.2

## THE PARENTS' ROLE

The learning habit of good decision-making doesn't just happen. Several pieces have to be in play for a child to internalize the real-world concepts of:

✓ Looking at the options at their disposal.

✓ Defining the possible consequences of each option.

✓ Deciding which consequences are the ones that are more in line with their goal(s).

Often, the choice of consequences is between bad and worse; that's why having goals is so important in the whole decision-making process.

When parents are able to embrace this concept—looking at decisions in a non-moralistic, non-emotional, impersonal way—it makes it easier for the child to go through the process without fear of judgment, of disappointing a parent, or of making a bad decision. *Bad* decisions are mistakes: we only know for certain that they are mistakes *after* the fact. That's why recriminations and overreactions by parents are so unhelpful. When parents are tempted to use the word *should*, that's a cue; the next words out of their mouths are guaranteed to be *not* helpful.

## NO "SHOULDING" ON YOUR KID!

When someone says "You should . . . ," that means that they are expressing what they want you to do; what they think is best. It has nothing to do with what you want, need, think, or feel.

When you say to yourself "I really should" that translates to "I don't want to . . . but someone or something out there thinks it's the *right* thing for me to do."[3]

By working with your children on a non-urgent, non-emergency basis, you will help them understand the process. One of the traps that parents fall into is the "breathless demand." This is when your child of five or fifteen comes running in with a request—which is really a demand—for you to make an instant decision without all the facts. In their world, they are in a life-altering circumstance and they need an answer *right now*!

Unless someone is holding an acetylene torch in proximity to an open gas can, there is probably no real emergency. Your child has a strong desire for immediate gratification—that's all. The best response is usually, "If you need an answer before we have a chance to discuss it, then the answer will be *no*."

*Sometimes it's the smallest decisions that can change your life forever.*                    —Keri Russell, on *Felicity*

The small decisions don't have to be life threatening to have impact. Decisions that are made on the fly, that allow a modification or nullification of a household rule, can make establishing productive learning habits far more difficult. This is because every time a rule is modified or ignored "just this once," then children feel it incumbent on themselves to, once again, go through a testing period to see if the rule is an *always* rule or just a *sometimes* rule. It gives them license to ignore the rules—even the ones that were established to protect them.

## Case Study: Jonas's Decision

This chapter opened with a brief description of the decision 16-year-old Jonas had to make: to either go to his family's annual Christmas party or participate in a YMCA swim meet.

His father really wanted Jonas to attend the party. All his cousins were flying into town and this was probably one of the last times they would all get together before Jonas was off to college. Jonas's mother agreed; there was really no need for him to swim in the YMCA event.

Neither parent tried to influence Jonas; they trusted him to make the best choice for himself. They encouraged him to talk it over with his coach.

Jonas checked with his coach, who couldn't really give him any advice; it wasn't a team meet. The coach volunteered, however, that it was a well-known event, sometimes attended by college scouts. He told Jonas that some of his other teammates had wanted to swim in the meet but hadn't qualified for it. Jonas had.

Jonas decided to swim; he was focused on winning an athletic scholarship to college. His parents and siblings were shocked. As far as they were concerned, it wasn't a big deal for him to miss the event.

"I really can't explain it, but I'll just feel terrible if I miss the meet. Are you upset?" Jonas asked his father.

"Nope, just disappointed that I won't get to see you that weekend," answered his dad.

His father didn't totally understand it, but he knew that Jonas was deeply committed to his goal of winning a scholarship; if he felt it was important to go, then he probably needed to trust his gut.

As it happened, there were three scouts at the meet; they were all impressed by Jonas's performance. He ultimately got an excellent scholarship to the university of his choice, where he became a member of the swim team.

## Case Study: Madelyn's Dilemma

Let's revisit Madelyn, the five-year-old we introduced you to who was spending a special night with Daddy. She had to choose between telling her dad about her math homework or watching a video. Madelyn reasoned that her teacher wouldn't care when the paper was handed in, so decided to enjoy a wonderful night with Daddy . . . until she got in bed. Madelyn tossed and turned; the homework paper was "calling" to her. Finally, she couldn't help herself; she got out of bed to knock on Daddy's door.

As soon as he came to the door, Madelyn burst into tears. She told him about the homework and that she felt like she had "made a bad choice; that's what Mrs. Crosby says, 'Good choice or bad choice?'" She was very worried about what Mrs. Crosby was going to think about her. She loved Mrs. Crosby and didn't want her to be angry or sad or to think that she [Madelyn] wasn't a good girl. Madelyn asked Daddy if, just this once, she could stay up and do her paper.

Daddy said, "No. Now it's time for sleeping; that's our rule. But I bet that you'll find a way to get that paper done before school." He walked her back to her room, and tucked her in.

The next morning, Daddy asked Madelyn if she didn't usually work on her *Hello Kitty* scrapbook before school.

Madelyn said, "Yes." Then she realized what he was telling her. "I can do my homework after I eat! I won't get to do *Hello Kitty*, but I won't feel bad anymore. Mrs. Crosby will be happy!"

## Case Study: Noah's Decision

Noah, the short 12-year-old from the beginning of this chapter, was really scared; he was afraid of finally being beaten up by Howard. He was also tired of being scared, and the thought of anyone seeing him like that—cowering, on the verge of tears, trapped in his locker—was too awful to contemplate.

Noah knew that no matter what he did, he would probably get in trouble. His school had a *zero-tolerance* policy for fighting. In fact, another kid in his class was being bullied, and he got expelled just like the bully did—even though he had done nothing but get pushed around. So Noah made his decision; he pulled his elbow back as far as it would go and smashed Howard with his closed fist, as hard as he could. He connected directly with the other boy's nose, which made a sickening cracking noise. Simultaneously, three things happened:

- ✓ Howard stumbled back, with his hands over his face and blood all over. "You broke my nose!" he cried.

- ✓ Noah burst into tears.

- ✓ The vice principal and the sixth-grade girls' volleyball team came running around the corner.

Howard was sent to the nurse, who called his mother. Noah was escorted to the office by Vice Principal Broder, who called *his* mother. She asked him what had happened, and he told her.

After Noah's mother arrived at school, Ms. Broder told her, "This school has a zero-tolerance policy; fighting is grounds for automatic suspension and, without proven extenuation, expulsion.

Your son, as is required by law, will now be suspended until I can contact the superintendent and get a hearing."

Ms. Broder then addressed Noah, "You understand that I have to suspend you for fighting, don't you?"

Noah said, "Yes."

"You've always been an excellent student, but this school has policies that must be followed."

Noah felt like crying again. He just nodded.

Noah felt as if the walls were closing in on him. He never wanted to hit anybody ever again; it was a sickening feeling. He thought he might throw up.

His parents told him that they did not approve of violence, but that they could understand his predicament.

Noah was expelled and transferred to another school. The school board's decision was based on the facts: They had no record of Noah ever complaining about Howard's bullying, but they had an X-ray of Howard's broken nose.

## RESEARCHERS' CONCLUSIONS

The ability to make decisions based on a realistic assessment of all the possible outcomes seems to be both more important and more difficult than it used to be for children; perhaps that's because there are so many environmental factors that can influence them. The good news is that we, as parents, can use our family's homework time to demonstrate the process of choosing the best options—for them. The toughest decisions, of course, are between good and good (like Jonas's) and between bad and bad (like Noah's). All of these children made the hard decisions, took responsibility, and learned from them. That's how learning habits are formed.

# CHAPTER NINE

# Ignoring the Marshmallow: Concentrating on Focus

Concentration and mental toughness
are the margins of victory.
—*Bill Russell, Boston Celtics basketball player, retired*

---

**Powell (age 8)** is one of those kids who's simply all over the place; he has a short attention span, inserts random unrelated comments into conversations, and is always moving and touching everything in range. He's two grades behind in reading and can't sit still in class. He is falling further behind, every day, in school.

**Zoe (age 13)**, previously an honors student, is now failing geometry and science.

**Rob (age 9)** is a good student who suffers from test anxiety. He becomes so anxious that he loses all ability to focus and can't even understand the directions. He freezes and then either gives up entirely or takes wild guesses, simply to get it over with.

---

All of these children are experiencing problems with concentration; they are children whose self-esteem and mental attitude are suffering because of their academic challenges.

During our interviews, many teachers and parents commented on these troubling phenomena: children need more refocusing and encouragement than they did—even five years ago; they seem to have almost no tolerance for frustration and are more generally anxious about their performance.

## LEARNING TO LEARN

Our brains are not a closed system. It isn't true that our cognitive abilities are immutably defined by an IQ test. While it is true that our IQ has a predictive ability of about 50% for academic success, that leaves 50% that is under our control. Thus, 50% of our ability to succeed can be enhanced *by how we choose to expand our capacity to learn.* Our brains can literally *learn to learn.*[1] Brain studies show that humans of all ages can continue to develop neurons (the process of neurogenesis) and both activate and develop brain cells through various kinds of stimulation.[2]

Both physical and mental exercise develop our "brain power," as eight-year-old Powell labels it. "I'm turning on my brain power!" Powell announces. Of course, he usually accesses his "brain power" while playing foosball, where it isn't really necessary. In his therapy group (four eight-year-old boys with the diagnosis of ADHD), we are helping to expand his "brain power" so that he can learn the skill of concentrated focus.

Kids with attention deficits—difficulty focusing on written or auditory material, sitting still for more than a minute or two, retaining information, waiting for their turn to speak, finishing a task, and/or self-regulating—can be helped to train their brains. It takes work, for both the kids and the parents, but the sense of empowerment it brings is immeasurable.

## Case Study: Powell

**Powell (age 8):** When Powell started therapy, he couldn't sit without jiggling and couldn't focus on reading a book with the "beginning reader" label. He was anxious about his grades (1's and 2's on a scale of 5), although he claimed to be "the best" at whatever topic we were discussing. When another boy said that he had a lot of trouble doing his math, Powell asserted, "I'm good at that. I don't have any problems in school." In reference to any kind of academic homework, Powell's usual complaint was, "I don't want to do this; it's stupid." (Translation: "I can't do this because *I'm* stupid, so what's the point of trying?") His mother said they got into "ginormous" struggles about reading; regardless of whatever strategy she employed, Powell absolutely refused to do it. Powell was taking a stimulant medication, but that wasn't all that was needed.

Powell needed to learn three things:

1. To sit and work on a task for a specified period of time without giving up
2. That he was capable of learning
3. To feel proud about *learning to learn*

Powell was a big basketball fan, so we used basketball analogies and stories with him. He understood that his idol, LeBron James, didn't get to be "King James" overnight; that James's mom was young and poor, and that James had to work hard to get to where he is. When I asked Powell how James got to be so good, he said, "He played all the time."

"So, he exercised and trained his muscles? He practiced a lot?" I asked.

"Yeah," Powell nodded.

"Do you think it was easy for him? That he just woke up one morning and somebody from the Miami Heat was knocking on his door?"

Powell laughed. "Nooooo."

I pulled up the ESPN online story "The King James Version" by Chris Broussard and read it to Powell: "LeBron James said, 'You can't be afraid to fail. It's the only way you succeed—you're not gonna succeed all the time, and I know that.'"[3]

"Guess what?" I told him. "The brain is our *thinking muscle*. You can train your brain just like LeBron James trained his body. It's very hard work, and you're not always going to succeed. Are you afraid of hard work?" I asked.

Powell thought for a bit, then answered, "I can do hard work."

We put Powell and the other three boys in the group in "training" to help them concentrate and build their short-term memory skills. Powell just called it "Gettin' that brain power!"

## SELF-MANAGEMENT:
## IGNORING THE MARSHMALLOW

*Circumstances are beyond human control, but our conduct is in our own power.*
—Benjamin Disraeli, former prime minister of the
United Kingdom

Self-management—the ability to control our impulses and delay immediate gratification—plays a key role in both academic and personal success. Walter Mischel, a psychologist at Columbia University, studied delayed gratification—the ability to give up less prized but *instant* rewards in favor of *later* but more prized outcomes. The experimenter seated preschool-age children alone at a table with a marshmallow and, before exiting the room, gave them a choice:

1. Ring a bell to call the researcher back and, when he returns, eat the marshmallow.
2. Don't ring the bell; wait until the researcher came back on his own and be rewarded with not one, but *two marshmallows*.

While some children were unable to wait a full minute (called "low delayers"), others were able to wait up to 20 minutes ("high delayers") by using strategies to distract themselves, like covering their eyes, singing songs, even turning their chair around so they wouldn't be tempted by the marshmallow.[4]

He then repeated the test, this time telling the children to visualize the marshmallows as something that they wouldn't want to eat—like cotton balls. This technique proved very successful. Follow-up studies, conducted years later on the same children, further showed that high delayers achieved greater academic success (for example, higher standardized test scores), better health (such as resistance to substance abuse), and more positive relationships (as measured in lower rates of marital separation and divorce).[5]

This breakthrough research demonstrated not only that willpower can be learned but also that it seems to be "a protective buffer against the development of all kinds of vulnerabilities later in life,"[6] thereby implying that self-control is key to both academic and personal success (see also Chapter Ten).

## Powell's Story, Part II: Self-Control and Focus

When helping young children like Powell develop the learning habit of concentration, start with small increments of time. Powell's mother had him sit at the kitchen table with her for four minutes. During that time, he read aloud to her. She didn't correct any words; the purpose was to have him sit, doing an academic activity, for four minutes. When he did it for the four minutes, he got a treat.

Lack of self-management skills is part and parcel of the problems children face in developing the learning habit of concentrated focus. Using time-limited tasks is reassuring to children; it's easier to concentrate if you know you don't have to do it for very long.

If he complained or started to fidget, she just made the shushing signal (finger in front of lips) and, with a smile, shook her head. She tipped her head, raised her eyebrows, and glanced at the timer on the microwave. She used *non-verbal communication* to signal what she wanted him to do—for example, if he was squirming, she patted the seat of her chair; if he wanted to close the book, she shook her head once and nodded toward the book, signaling him to continue reading.

Self-management is best taught with non-verbal communication. You don't want to start a dialogue, which will only provide a distraction from the task.

Other external distractions need to be eliminated or silenced, such as TV, smartphones, game systems, pets, and other children. This is much tougher in school, where other children are a constant distraction; that's why this skill is an important part of the *homework* that parents can facilitate.

In addition to the treat, Powell also got a compliment, like, "It makes me proud to see you trying." That's a lovely reward for a child who gets a lot of redirection during school.

Powell's mother also used board games to increase her son's ability to stay focused on a task, to wait for his turn, and to control his body (keeping his hands off the board until it was his turn). Candy Land and Chutes and Ladders were the first games she chose. Again, she had simple rules: We take turns, we don't complain or blame or make excuses, and there is no reward for winning. We play for fun.

She set the timer for eight minutes; when it went off, Powell could choose to continue to play, or he could stop. Non-verbal communication was used for redirection. The compliments she gave were always task specific about his effort, such as "Nice job waiting for your turn" or "Good concentration" or "Nice sportsmanship when you got that cupcake."

Self-management skills are most effectively taught in the absence of stressors; hence the "no winners or losers" dictum. Kids who are constantly under stress and get a lot of criticism and correction can develop habits that interfere with their social functioning: seeking to blame others, interrupting, accusing others of cheating, bragging, and making excuses for poor performance are common examples.

By doing their empowering *homework*, parents can have a benign and effective impact on those behaviors.

Even the most self-management-challenged children have periods when they are behaving appropriately; watch for those times and give a compliment. Catching your child doing something *right* is a treat for both of you, and will help ensure that the behavior gets repeated.

When we are called in to consult with teachers, we recommend using stickers to "catch kids doing something right," like waiting to be called on or sitting still. Even middle school kids like stickers; they just have to be cooler. Instant tattoos and glow-in-the-dark stickers are popular with older children. No matter how old we are, each of us appreciates being caught doing something right. Think how good you'd feel if someone in your family said, "It's so nice how you always have good food available for our lunches; it really makes a difference. Thank you!" or "It's amazing that you can work such long hours and still make time to coach my soccer team. Thank you!" or "It makes me feel so happy to look at the bleachers and see you—thanks for coming."

For our therapy groups, we have invented and reinvented a number of games to build the learning habit of concentration. All of these games can be played at home. Board games and games involving sequences of words or numbers are an effective way to increase concentration and memory. In therapy groups, we often use just a few M&M's to reward kids for small steps toward a goal; they're colorful, most kids like them, and they're small enough to use frequently.

For rewards to work, they have to *immediately* follow the event you want to reinforce; they need to be small, so that you can use them frequently.

With the use of games to help him increase his memory and the non-verbal method his mother used to help him sit and focus for gradually increasing lengths of time, Powell developed the habit of concentrated focus. Powell can now sit for 20 minutes to read or do his homework, with minimum fidgeting. As he began to take pride in his efforts, his self-confidence increased. Feeling better about himself allowed Powell to recognize the efforts of others, without feeling threatened or needing to brag.

Set up your child's study area to be distraction free, with no media. The best place is the kitchen or dining room table. You are nearby, but not interacting, during homework time.

Powell now sits at the kitchen table and does his schoolwork and reading as part of his daily routine; he has acquired a learning habit. His ability to concentrate and retain what he is learning has increased exponentially. As he would put it, he's building his brain power!

At the Center, we have found it helpful for parents to have a *baseline*—a specific way to be able to measure their child's behavioral change. Although there is no "test" for either ADHD or Faux-ADHD,[*] there are observable behaviors used in diagnosing these and other conditions. Therefore, we developed this simple list of questions that parents (and/or teachers) can fill out—at the beginning of therapy and at subsequent intervals—to monitor their child's (or student's) progress.

## THE PRESSMAN FOCUS CHECKLIST

On a scale of 1 to 5 (1 is rarely or never; 5 is frequently or always), how frequently does your child do the following:

|  | 1 | 2 | 3 | 4 | 5 |
|---|---|---|---|---|---|
| 1. Sit for a reasonable period of time (more than 10 minutes for children K–3, at least 30 minutes for older children) without fidgeting, getting up and wandering, or checking their phone? | ☐ | ☐ | ☐ | ☐ | ☐ |
| 2. Perform a task requiring three or more steps without forgetting a step? | ☐ | ☐ | ☐ | ☐ | ☐ |
| 3. Self-soothe and return to the task when they become frustrated? | ☐ | ☐ | ☐ | ☐ | ☐ |

---

[*] Faux-ADHD, first reported in the *American Journal of Family Therapy* (June 2011), is a condition that mimics ADHD but is responsive to behavioral intervention, such as a consistent bedtime routine (see Chapter 2). See also pedipsyc.com/abstract _FauxADHD.php for details of our 2011 research study.

|  | 1 | 2 | 3 | 4 | 5 |
|---|---|---|---|---|---|
| 4. Complete a school assignment or a chore without giving excuses (It's boring; I don't understand why I have to do this stupid thing! It's not my turn to do the dishes!)? | ☐ | ☐ | ☐ | ☐ | ☐ |
| 5. Work through a task without creating distractions (such as arguing with a parent, playing with a pet, teasing a sibling, developing a stomachache, demanding a drink or snack)? | ☐ | ☐ | ☐ | ☐ | ☐ |
| 6. Finish a game, when losing, without quitting or crying? | ☐ | ☐ | ☐ | ☐ | ☐ |
| 7. Complete a reading assignment and be able to verbalize what it was about? | ☐ | ☐ | ☐ | ☐ | ☐ |
| 8. Enjoy quiet activity? | ☐ | ☐ | ☐ | ☐ | ☐ |
| 9. Go to bed at a regular time and stay in their own room all night? | ☐ | ☐ | ☐ | ☐ | ☐ |
| 10. Listen to instructions and accurately repeat them back? | ☐ | ☐ | ☐ | ☐ | ☐ |
| 11. Read for pleasure—apart from assigned school reading—every day? | ☐ | ☐ | ☐ | ☐ | ☐ |

**Totals**

The Pressman Focus Checklist is a good resource; see how you answer the questions for your own child. After the baseline is established, it's informative to look at it from time to time and see how your child is doing. It's reasonable to expect that, as children get older, their behaviors (as measured on the checklist) improve.

If they are staying the same or you see a decrement, be sure to take the 21 Family Challenges that seem to be appropriate (see Chapter Eleven).

## Case Study: Zoe

Zoe (age 13) is a seventh grader; she has braces on her teeth and wears glasses, so she thinks she looks "weird." Zoe could be the spokesperson for "dressing well on a limited budget." She always looks adorable, with outfits that match from her headbands (sporting big bows) to her color-coordinated eyeglasses, socks, and sneakers. Zoe's mother is a working single mom, and with two school-age children, her contract paralegal salary doesn't leave a lot for extras.

Zoe's mother brought her into therapy because she was concerned about her daughter's grades. Zoe confessed to her therapist that she'd never really had to work for her grades; school had always been easy. This year was different. Her last progress report showed an F for math/geometry and a D for science. Zoe said, "I hate school! It's too hard!"

When Zoe's mother filled out the Pressman Focus Checklist (see page 213), she answered:

"1" to questions 1, 2, 3, 4, 5, and 9
"2" to question 8
"5" to questions 6 and 7
"3" to questions 10 and 11

Zoe no longer had the ability to sustain focus, and it was affecting her grades.

When Zoe was asked about her bedtime, she said that she had trouble falling asleep, so often didn't turn out her light until midnight or later. Then she didn't want to get up for school; her mom had to come into the room multiple times to rouse her. She was always running late, usually missed the bus, skipped breakfast, and her mother ended up driving her to school. She got no exercise outside of gym class. "I used to run track, but it's *too hard*," Zoe predictably answered.

When queried about what she did in her room from 9:30 on, she said she used to read, but she didn't like going to the library. ("It smells funny and those old ladies look at you weird.") She'd already read the Hunger Games series three times. "My mother won't buy me books anymore," Zoe complained. "She says they're too expensive and I read them too fast." (When I asked her how much she thought books cost, she didn't know.)

What Zoe did, for two or three or even four hours before she fell asleep, was to go on her computer and her smartphone, and pull up Facebook, Instagram, FaceTime, Twitter, Vine, Reddit, and Tumblr while simultaneously watching her TV. ("I can't fall asleep unless the television is on—neither can my mom.") That was in addition to the television and computer time she got before her mother came home (almost three hours of additional screen time), when she was supposed to be doing homework. Talk about multitasking! This child was probably getting an aggregate of eight to nine hours of screen time per day and much more on weekends. *Because of their limited capacity for self-regulation, teens and children are particularly susceptible to Internet addiction and concurrent sleep deprivation—a recipe for disaster.*[7]

Between isolating herself in her room, spending more quality time with media than with humans, avoiding exercise, feeling sleep deprived, and getting poor grades, Zoe was losing both her confidence and her motivation.

Because she'd never *needed* to study, Zoe didn't have any study skills. Her mother had never helped her set up a homework schedule; Zoe always did her homework and got A's. Once an avid reader, Zoe was reading much less. Already shy, spending so much time in her room had eroded her confidence to such an extent that she was afraid to go to the library (those old ladies might look at her weird!). She was sleep deprived and anxious about her grades, so her cognition was impaired.

Her mom was a devoted and caring mother; unfortunately, she subscribed to the idea of indiscriminate praise. Telling a child how smart she is when she's failing two subjects isn't helpful. Furthermore, the corollary to that, "You're such a smart girl; *you just need to work harder*," merely added to Zoe's frustration, anger, and feeling of powerlessness. She didn't need to work harder; she needed to train her brain.

---

Use compliments as a genuine means of rewarding specific behaviors, especially effort. Statements like, "I'm proud of how hard you tried," "You were such a good sport," or "I can really notice your effort" are rewarding, helpful, and make your child feel valued and encouraged.

---

## FOCUS BOOT CAMP*

We told Zoe and her mother that we could *guarantee* that Zoe could raise her math and science grades to B−'s, if they would both agree to abide by nine conditions for six weeks, until the marking period ended. They made a contract and all three of us signed it.

Zoe had equated having trouble in geometry and science with stupidity. She was actually afraid that she had *never been smart*; that she had somehow *conned* her teachers into giving her good grades. She believed that she had essentially been "faking it" for the past six years!

Committing to Focus Boot Camp was a big deal for her. She re-

---

* "*Everybody* knows," according to Zoe, "that boot camp is where you go to train for the army; it's *really hard* and if you don't pass everything, you get thrown out!"

ally hated the terms of the contract, and it took two sessions for her to sign it. Zoe's mother wasn't too thrilled, either, especially the parts about restrictions of media. She was as much a media junkie as her daughter; I had never seen her when she wasn't texting or talking on her phone.

## ZOE'S CONTRACT

1. Zoe will be in a media-free bedroom, lights out, by 10 p.m. Her mother will buy her an inexpensive white noise machine to replace the television.
2. Zoe will order books online from the library and go with her mother to pick them up.
3. Zoe will get 60 minutes total per day for media during the week. That means she has to choose between television, computer, tablet, and smartphone. [Homework assignments requiring the computer are exempt from this rule.] Mom will hold her computer, tablet, and phone; Zoe gets them back at 5 p.m. for an hour; at 6:05 they are locked up. [The extra five minutes are for entering homework, projects, and practices in her phone's calendar.]
4. Zoe will talk to her math and science teachers. She will tell them that she needs extra help and wants to raise her grades. She will stay after school for as long as is necessary and do extra-credit work. [Zoe's goal was to get into the #1 public high school in her state, for which excellent grades, an admissions test, and interviews were required. There was heavy competition for acceptance to the school; a grade of D in any subject was automatically disqualifying. Raising her grades was essential.]
5. Zoe will learn and practice relaxation techniques to self-soothe when she gets frustrated.
6. Zoe will wear a rubber band on each wrist; every time she has a negative or defeatist thought, she will snap the rubber band. [It doesn't do any damage, but it's very focusing.]

7. Zoe will set her alarm and get herself up and out—with breakfast—in time for the bus. Her mother will not drive her to school. In good weather, Zoe will ride her bike.

8. Zoe will sign up for track when the permission slips come out in a week. She will return her signed permission slip to the school.

9. Zoe will spend 70 minutes on homework,* five days a week, at the kitchen table. If she doesn't have homework or gets it done quickly, she will read a book. If she doesn't finish her homework in the allotted time, she stops, anyway. [70 minutes is all she gets, so she needs to *train her brain* to focus during that time; this is boot camp!]

## DESPERATE TIMES CALL FOR DESPERATE MEASURES

The boot camp concept will not work for all children; most kids need to have these steps introduced one by one, over time. Zoe's biggest challenge was that she had not developed the ability to concentrate and be media free. Her mother was not a good role model in this regard, as she was often talking on the phone, texting, or using the TV as background noise. This was really boot camp for both of them. Although Zoe had somewhat given up and was continually sending herself negative messages, she still had motivation: to get into that high school.

Focus Boot Camp was a difficult concept for Zoe's mother to wrap her mind around for another reason. Restricting her daughter so drastically made her feel mean—like a bad mother. It took a bit of explanation for her to understand the difference between enabling and empowering.

---

* Zoe was in the seventh grade; using the 10-minute rule she was assigned 70 minutes for homework.

## SELF-SOOTHING AND RELAXATION

> *The greatest weapon against stress is our ability to choose one thought over another.*
>
> —William James, American philosopher and psychologist

Anxiety is a focus killer. Children who are worried that: they can't understand the assignment, they'll look stupid, they'll get yelled at, they'll do badly and let their team down, they'll embarrass themselves or their parents, will probably be unable to fully concentrate.

Fortunately, there is a technique used to combat anxiety; it's called the relaxation response.[8] Mastery requires only two things:

✓ Practicing breathing techniques, often combined with a device called cueing.

✓ Positive self-talk.

## DEEP BREATHING AND POSITIVE AFFIRMATION

Zoe's contract called for her to "learn and practice relaxation techniques to self-soothe when she gets frustrated."

Deep breathing exercises have been used to aid relaxation and focus from the beginning of recorded history. In China, millions of people practice these methods daily. Children in schools, industrial workers in factories, elders in the parks, and patients in hospitals all apply the preliminary methods faithfully on a daily basis.[9] Here in the United States, one would be hard pressed to find a coach of any professional or collegiate sport who doesn't encourage the use of relaxation techniques to boost their athletes' performance.[10]

According to a report from the National Center for Complementary and Alternative Medicine (NCCAM), a division of the National Institutes of Health:

When you're under stress, your body releases hormones that produce the "fight-or-flight response." Heart rate and breathing rate go up and blood vessels narrow (restricting the flow of blood). This response allows energy to flow to parts of your body that need to take action, for example the muscles and the heart. However useful this response may be in the short term, there is evidence that when your body remains in a stress state for a long time, emotional or physical damage can occur. . . . Stress also has been linked to depression, anxiety, and other mental illnesses.

In contrast to the stress response, the relaxation response slows the heart rate, lowers blood pressure, and decreases oxygen consumption and levels of stress hormones. Because relaxation is the opposite of stress, the theory is that voluntarily creating the relaxation response through regular use of relaxation techniques could counteract the negative effects of stress.[11]

Being able to induce a relaxation response is extraordinarily helpful when doing homework or taking tests; it gives students a sense of power and control in otherwise enervating situations. When we are anxious about something, like taking the SATs, writing up a chemistry lab, reading a paragraph about the Pilgrims and answering questions about it, or taking a timed, online math test, our bodies can react the same way they reacted when a Neanderthal man saw a saber-toothed tiger about to spring. Our nonessential brain functions shut down so that we have the strength and focus to run away or fight. Functions such as short-term memory, encoding, decoding, and ability to perform computational tasks or organize thoughts—*all the skills we need to accomplish academic work*—become unavailable to us.

## BREATHING TECHNIQUES: CALM YOUR BODY

Kids can learn breathing techniques either lying down or sitting in a comfortable position. You will have them close their eyes, place their hands on their bellies,* breathe in deeply through their noses, take the breath all the way down into their bellies, hold it for a count of three, and then blow it out through their mouths. As you can imagine, there is a lot of hilarity when teachers or parents (or therapists) introduce this process. However, if *we* are serious, and keep repeating the instructions in a calm voice while modeling the exercise, eventually the kids will do it.

You first explain that you are going to teach a very cool trick that will let them *calm their bodies* and turn their brains on to *maximum learning*. Tell them they will be breathing in through their noses, taking the air into their bellies, holding it, and then blowing it out through their mouths.

You'll say the following:

> Close your eyes. [You have to close yours, too. You will be doing everything right along with the child/children.] Take a big breath in through your nose—make it as big as you can and push it all the way down into your belly. You can put your hand on your belly and feel it fill up. Now hold your breath for three seconds . . . one, two, three . . . and blow it out through your mouth really hard. Try to get it all out.

You repeat the exercise seven or eight times. The kids may feel a bit light-headed if they are really getting into it; more oxygen is finding its way (more rapidly) to the brain. They may also experience some tingling in the extremities, as oxygen and carbon dioxide

---

* This allows them to feel if their breathing is correct; if it is, they can feel their bellies rise and fall.

are being rapidly exchanged. This will pass—but that's why you do the exercise either lying or sitting down.

Eventually, most kids can do this. After the first few times—when they have mastered the idea of deep belly breaths—you change the instructions to: Breathe in through your nose, like you are smelling a flower . . . hold it for a count of three . . . now breathe out through your mouth, as if you are blowing out a candle.* This has the same calming effect, but is more practical for children to use on a daily basis. In our clinical practice, we ask the children to practice this exercise several times a day—starting with first thing in the morning and ending with last thing at night. If you are teaching this technique at home, try to do it *with* your kids at least twice a day. Over time, children can learn to cue themselves, so that only one or two deep breaths produce the desired degree of muscle relaxation.

Cuing is usually something simple, like touching the index and second fingers to one's temple. It is a signal, combined with one to three deep breaths, for the body to enter a state of relaxation. When teaching cuing, we have the children come up with a positive self-statement—a phrase that makes them feel calm, controlled, and competent. You'll see how Rob did this.

## Case Study: Rob

**Rob (age 9)** had a wonderful fourth-grade teacher, Jack Corey. Mr. Corey had noticed that Rob was struggling with test taking; he knew that Rob was bright, that he worked hard, did all his homework, and had good grades—but he suffered from debilitating test anxiety. No matter how hard he studied or how well he knew the material, he always panicked, froze, and ended up guessing. He failed many of his tests and was frustrated and discouraged. When

---

* These are the breathing instructions used in the Emotional ABC's interactive program, designed to teach emotional literacy skills to children ages four and up.

online, timed tests became part of the curriculum, Rob's anxiety escalated. He couldn't do them.

Mr. Corey had practiced yoga for many years and was teaching Kripalu Yoga at the local YMCA. He explained to Rob and his father how relaxation techniques work; he believed that they could help Rob get a handle on his test anxiety. He recommended Herbert Benson's book on relaxation.[12] Rob's father went straight out and bought the book. He read it and started learning the technique right along with his son.

In a subsequent meeting, Mr. Corey emphasized the importance of Rob's developing a positive self-statement. This would give Rob a feeling of control in a testing situation; he would be able to reassure himself that he had the power to master the test. Rob's self-talk was "I know this. I will do good." (No grammar police, please. It worked for *him*!) He practiced faithfully at home and, with the help of his understanding teacher, used it in the classroom with simulated tests. Ultimately, he was able to use it in real testing situations, with great success. As his confidence increased, his test grades improved dramatically. Rob reported to his teacher that he really liked the "breathing" and it helped him do good—I mean, well.

## ANXIETY AND ITS EFFECT ON FOCUS

Test anxiety is a bigger problem than many parents and teachers realize. Adults can jump to the conclusion that the students didn't study, or didn't study efficiently, or that they were having a bad day. Kids often blame themselves, telling themselves that they just need to try harder or study longer. If students have test anxiety, they can study their heads off and it won't help—too much studying can actually hurt, believe it or not.[13]

The solution lies in their taking control of the test, not letting the test control them. Relaxation is the way this happens: deep breathing, a cue, and a positive message. In a testing situation, the setup is the most important part. When students are handed the test, the strategy is to first turn the paper(s) over to the blank side, do the cuing action (usually touching the temple), take the deep breaths, and say (silently) something like, "I know this. I am the boss of this test. I can do this," then turn the test over and begin. As with all testing strategies, children are taught to answer the questions they know first, rather than spend too much time on ones they don't know; this way they don't miss the opportunity of getting credit for correct answers because they ran out of time. When they start to feel anxious, they turn the paper over and repeat the relaxation exercise. It literally takes seconds, but can make all the difference.

Sometimes children are afraid to do this because "it will waste time" on a timed exam. Have them practice it at home; when they are engaged in the process, time them. They will be shocked to discover that the whole process—turning the paper over, cuing, two or three deep breaths,* saying the message internally, and turning the paper back over—takes less than 15 seconds!

This works great with paper-and-pencil tests, but what about online testing? The principle is the same; the challenge is greater. Children go through the same cuing, breathing, and empowering self-statement ritual. Often, they are able to employ it when they have gotten an answer wrong or between sections. If there is no break at all and kids have just two or three minutes to answer each question, they can still use the technique. When they start to feel anxious or overwhelmed, they give themselves permission to close their eyes and take 10 to 15 seconds to do the relaxation exercise, before reading the next statement, question, or problem. They will be better able to use the remaining time than if they had tried to come up with an answer when their brain was unable to fully focus.

## Case Study: Zoe Redux

Zoe practiced her breathing techniques; she repeated her empowering statement many times a day: "I know more today than I did

---

* With practice, children can learn to induce relaxation with the simultaneous actions of cuing, one deep breath, and their empowering message.

yesterday. I can do this. I trust myself." Zoe became adept at self-soothing. The schoolwork she couldn't complete during the school day was brought home and finished. Her teachers were more than happy to help Zoe, once she convinced them that she was serious. After the third week of Focus Boot Camp, she often had time left over to read her library books. Zoe, her mother, and younger brother started to have reading time together after dinner. It was a quiet activity and encouraged Zoe's cuddling on the sofa with her mother, which hadn't happened in a long time.

Let your children see you read—newspapers, books, or magazines, it doesn't matter. Your children will model what they see you do.

By week five, Zoe was doing much better. She still occasionally whined a bit about the computer restriction, but her mother said she just needed to say "boot camp," and Zoe backed off. In her first track meet (against three other schools), she got a third-place ribbon for the one-mile run. "I don't run the mile; I'm a sprinter," she said. "But when I got there, my coach said I was running the mile because I have long legs and there was no one else. I thought I was gonna die—it was pretty cool!"

Not all kids will respond as rapidly as Zoe did. When her report card came out, she brought it into the office. She was practically vibrating with excitement: she got almost all A's—her science grade was an A– and her math grade was a B+. Zoe was beside herself with pride, "My math teacher says I'll get an A for sure next period if I keep it up!" Of course, being a teenager, her first question was, "Now can I get my computer back?" But she quickly added, "Just joking . . . really!"

## MEDIA CONSUMPTION AND CONCENTRATION

Throughout this chapter, we have inserted many findings from the Learning Habit Study.

However, the bottom line is this: Past a certain point, the more screen time, the worse children do in terms of emotional balance, academic performance, communication, and social skills. The Learning Habit Study is especially valuable because it not only surveyed the *amount* and *type* of media used but it also looked at the *impact of that use on many behaviors.* (In Chapter Three, we presented extensive information about the three different types of media use and provided recommendations concerning best practices.)

A 2010 Iowa State University study assessed more than 1,300 children in grades three through five and 210 college students. They compared students who had screen time of less than two hours a day with those who had two to seven hours of media interaction. They found that students who had more than two hours of screen time had double the attention problems.[14]

This is not new information. Biologist and psychologist Aric Sigman ruffled a few feathers when he suggested that children should be banned *entirely* from computer use until the age of nine, because of their developmental vulnerability. According to Dr. Sigman, a Fellow of the Royal Society of Medicine, computer use retards the development of normal attention span in developing children.[15] Although many scientists took issue with his research, it brought to the forefront the possibility of neurological interference on developing brains through media use.

His research showed a direct conflict between multitasking and a child's ability to sustain attention and concentration. Essentially, children can build on only one of these skills at a time. Parents allow children to use computers at a young age because they think children are learning from them; in actuality, they are *subverting* their ability to learn. These children will not be more intelligent;

they will have a diminished knowledge base and a diminished capacity to concentrate.[16] Fast-forward a few years, and these smartphone and computer wizards may not be able to sit for 30 minutes to complete their homework, as Zoe clearly demonstrated.

## BUILDING FOCUS SKILLS WITH ACADEMIC HOMEWORK

In our clinical practice, we are seeing increasing numbers of children who aren't able to focus for long enough to complete a homework assignment and/or seem to lack the motivation to read a book.

Concentrated focus involves a number of psychological and physiological functions. All of these functions are built into our learning habits. Among them are:

✓ The ability to self-soothe.

✓ The ability to relax.

✓ The ability to function within time limits.

✓ The ability to deal with frustration.

✓ The ability to problem solve.

✓ The ability to set attainable goals.

✓ The ability to understand the relative importance of the task.

✓ The confidence that, if the task presents difficulties that we cannot overcome, we will be able to get help.

Children who exhibit problems with focus, whether or not they have a diagnosis of ADHD and whether or not they are taking stimulant medication, can benefit from learning the habits discussed in this chapter. These habits are essential for children's ability to function with confidence, to complete their education, develop solid social relationships, and pursue a fulfilling career. Kids with attention problems are more likely to have low self-esteem and increased anxiety because of problems in school. As adolescents, they are also more likely to self-medicate with marijuana, alcohol, and other drugs, both for social confidence and to be able to calm themselves.[17]

These kids get a lot of correction, criticism, and messages that they are deficient, defective, or just plain lazy—not because teachers, parents, or coaches are mean, but just because it's the nature of the disorder. The inability to focus on a discrete task for a specified period of time may be difficult, but it can be learned. Developing this learning habit (time-limited concentration) is unbelievably empowering for a child, and savvy parents can make it happen.

# CHAPTER TEN

# True Grit:
# Developing Self-Reliance

Life is not what it's supposed to be.
It's what it is.
The way you cope with it
is what makes the difference.
—*Virginia Satir, American author and psychotherapist*

One of the winners of the 2013 MacArthur Fellowship "genius" grants is a psychologist, Angela Lee Duckworth, who studies "grit and self-control." In an interview in the December 2013 issue of *Monitor on Psychology*, Duckworth defines *grit* as "the disposition to pursue very long-term goals with passion and perseverance, sustained over time. So the emphasis is on stamina. . . . Grit is living life like a marathon, not like a sprint."[1]

## Case Study: Devin and Erin

**Erin** was six years old the first time she picked up a tennis racket. She loved holding the new racket in her hand and playing with the tightly wound strings. Her parents joined a tennis/swim club for the summer and enrolled Erin and her two siblings in lessons.

The first day of tennis lessons, Erin was nervous. Luckily, she and her older sister, Liz, were grouped in the same class. Liz frequently complained about standing outside on the hot concrete, especially during the scorching days of July when the temperatures topped 100 degrees.

Those were the days Liz would beg her parents to let her skip practice, and sometimes her mother would give in to Liz's loud demands. Erin never missed a practice; she couldn't wait to get out on the court. Besides, Ron, the tennis pro, always gave them extra water breaks on those hot days and usually moved them to the shadier court near the trees.

As the summer progressed, Erin's skills began to take shape. She learned her forehand and backhand grip and was practicing her swings. Erin would also watch the adult tournament players. She was amazed at their speed and accuracy. She longed for the day she'd be old enough—and good enough—to compete in tournaments. She continued practicing the following spring, hitting balls against the side of a nearby office building.

By the time June rolled around, Erin couldn't wait to start lessons again. She was pleasantly surprised on her first day of class, by how much better she was than the other students. "Someone's been practicing over the winter!" commented Ron. Erin felt proud; she liked being the best in her class. It made her feel special. She watched as her friends struggled to get their balls over the net, which was no longer a problem for her!

That summer, Erin was frequently grouped with another girl in her class named Devin. Devin was a year younger than Erin, but had the distinct honor of being the "second best player in class." Erin and Devin remained rivals over the course of the next few years. (Liz dropped out of tennis after the first summer.)

When Erin was 12, she started competing in the club tournaments. She was usually paired against an older player, since 12 was the minimum age required to compete. Even though the girls were only a year or two older, their skill dwarfed Erin's. Many times she was unable to return their serves. She felt embarrassed the day her sister, Liz, came to watch her get badly defeated by another player.

None of Erin's friends attended the tennis club, and, by the following summer, she no longer had any interest in going. "Are you sure you don't want to take lessons?" asked Erin's mother. "I'm good. I just want to hang out with my friends. Besides, I'm babysitting a lot this summer," replied Erin.

Erin took a year and a half off. How big a difference could that time make, anyway?

The year Erin took off from tennis, Devin continued. She played that entire summer at the club, and took a few private lessons over the winter. The following summer Devin played at the club and attended a tennis clinic, where she learned how to put backspin on her serve. By the time she completed the clinic, her serve was lethal. Even the tennis pro had difficulty returning it!

Meanwhile, Erin (who had not played in more than a year) heard through the grapevine that some of her friends would be trying out for the high school tennis team in August. She didn't want to be left out, and besides, she'd always liked tennis. She couldn't even remember why she'd quit.

She tried out for the tennis team, and, to her surprise, she qualified for a spot on the varsity team, squeaking into a low-ranked spot playing doubles. That year she played a rival school, and noticed that her old friend Devin was on the team. As a freshman, Devin was seeded #1 on the varsity team.

Erin was shocked. How had Devin become so good overnight?

A few years later, when Erin was packing to go off to college, she saw Devin interviewed on the local news. Devin was ranked the #1 player in the state and had received a college scholarship for tennis.

## RESEARCHERS' CONCLUSIONS

Children and parents go through cycles of interest in activities. What's surprising about this particular story is that there is really nothing unusual about it. In virtually all interviews we conducted for the book about true grit, the stories were similar—and surprisingly unexciting.

In the interviews we conducted, we never found one single story about a boy who was born with the ability to perform physics at the age of three, or a five-year-old girl who could hit a 40-mile-an-hour softball. Those types of stories would have been fascinating, fun to read, and entertaining. They would have helped us feel good about ourselves—by setting an untouchable and unattainable distance between "those people" and ourselves. Then, when we realized that we weren't *that* special, we could give ourselves the excuse to quit.

Children who receive athletic and academic scholarships to college appear to be superstars to many parents and other children. However, if you went back in time and met those children when they were six or ten or even twelve, you probably wouldn't notice anything particularly spectacular, unique, or gifted about them. When a child simply continues to do the same thing, day after day, when they practice, when they refuse to quit, the quality of their work gets better. It's not a superpower, and it's not magic; it's sheer, dogged tenacity. At a certain point in high school, the ones that have stuck with it, put in the effort, and refused to quit (even for one year) will slowly pull in front of the pack.

Erin began to think of herself as *special* at a certain point in time. When she lost that feeling of specialness, she had no reason to continue. In follow-up interviews with both families, we heard the word *special* used, but in drastically different ways. Listen to the words used in the follow-up interviews with Erin's and Devin's parents:

> **Erin's mother:** It was strange the day we heard Devin was the top-seeded player in the state. It really made Erin wish she hadn't quit tennis so easily. I don't think she realized there was anything special about her abilities. Looking back, I wish we'd given her more of an incentive to keep going. Instead, we just let her quit. Maybe . . . I don't know . . . we all could've tried harder. I know what happened with Devin bothers her; I mean—that could have been her.

**Devin's mother:** Devin has always been a really hard worker. When she was younger, we started talking about high school tennis and setting a few goals for her. She really wanted to make the team and asked to take a clinic that summer. Around her sophomore year, my husband and I started noticing that she would probably qualify for a spot on a college team. It was the weirdest feeling, because we'd never thought of Devin as this big athlete. She was just a regular kid who played tennis; there was nothing special about her ability.

## SPECIAL ABILITY

Erin's initial success made her feel special. At the time she decided to quit tennis, a couple of things were happening. Evidently, Erin perceived her success as a reflection of natural ability. When she started losing matches, she began to doubt her ability. The coup de grâce was when her sister came to the match and saw her soundly defeated; she felt ashamed. Had Erin:

- ✓ Equated her success with the *effort* she had put into *practicing*, she might have reacted differently to the losses;

- ✓ Seriously wanted to become an excellent tennis player, she may have decided on that as a long-term goal and dedicated herself to the practice that would allow her to achieve her goal; and

- ✓ Wanted it enough that the cost (not hanging with friends, accepting repeated losses, feeling embarrassed when her sister saw her lose) became irrelevant,

then it might, indeed, have been she who became the state champion. Devin's success came as a surprise, because Erin was still thinking in terms of ability, not effort. Ability alone is no guarantee of success. Erin's mother didn't understand that, either.

The comment by Devin's mother, however, indicates an understanding that her daughter got to be so good *because she kept* playing tennis. She stayed with it for many years, and that was what made the difference. Devin and Erin both had ability; Devin, however, also had *grit*.

## THE KIDS WHO STAY IN COLLEGE

A 2013 article published in the *Journal of Education Psychology* reported on a study of nontraditional predictors of college outcomes. A *key* characteristic of college students who were able to successfully complete their freshman year was described as "general determination . . . a tendency to follow through on obligations and commitments."[2]

Following through—tenacity, determination, willpower, stick-to-itiveness—are what Duckworth and others have labeled *grit*.

## SELF-CONTROL AND DELAY OF GRATIFICATION

*When anyone tells me I can't do anything, I'm just not listening anymore.*
—Florence Griffith Joyner, Olympic gold medalist

Dr. Duckworth also studies self-control; she describes it as "the ability to resist momentary distractions and temptations in order to reach a goal." If you set a goal to exercise or do your homework one night, for example, and end up sitting on the couch and watching TV instead, that's a failure of self-control.[3]

Grit is about pursuing *personal* goals; not about seeking fame or superiority over others. External recognition (compliments or rewards) is not necessary for gritty people to persevere, because it is not their prime motivator.

The ability to focus on a personal goal—be it short-term or long-term—requires children to block distractions, deny themselves immediate enjoyable activities, and complete the task. This kind of dedication takes strength of character, particularly under less-than-optimal circumstances. Children (and adults) who persevere and show this type of dedication deserve to be applauded—although they don't require it—whether they succeed or fail in accomplishing their original goal. The quality we call leadership is very much about strength of character, perseverance, and the ability to put off immediate gratification in service to a goal.

## Case Study: Raymond

**Raymond (age 9):** When we first met Raymond, he was in the third grade and impaired neurologically. He suffered from Tourette syndrome, ADHD, and other learning disabilities, and had been held back in school. He had many tactile and sensory issues, which made everyday activities like getting dressed an ordeal. He was not well coordinated. He couldn't make eye contact with anyone and wouldn't talk unless he was absolutely forced to. His stuttering was painful to witness.

Ray joined a therapy group of four boys, however, who treated him with the kind of respect normally reserved for leaders. The other boys knew how hard it was for Ray to speak, so when he did say something, they listened attentively. When there was a question or a difference of opinion, one of the boys in the group would inevitably ask, "What do you think, Ray?"

He didn't know it yet, but Ray already had the characteristics of a leader.

Several months into therapy, Ray disclosed that his dream was to be a state policeman or federal marshal. The boys were fascinated with his career choice and questioned him endlessly. Ray was able to answer without stuttering, whenever he spoke of being a policeman.

Reading was a challenge for him, so Ray wasn't much of a reader. When we discussed reading as a really important skill, Ray thought for a couple of minutes, then hesitantly asked, "Do comic books count? I like comic books." His dad went out and bought a dozen crime-fighting comics. Ray loved them! His mother asked him to read them aloud to her. He stuttered badly, at first, but once he got involved in the story, he read faster and stuttered less.

We also practiced relaxation techniques with Ray and his friends in group therapy. The boys all took it seriously, right from the start (not that usual, believe me) because they thought the deep breathing exercises might be good for Ray; they were right. Ray participated in every group activity, even storytelling. He knew his friends would be patient, because they respected him, so he was able to relax.

At nine years old, Ray had *grit*. He never gave up, no matter how tough the obstacles—and there were many. Ray was treated poorly by his teachers and their support staff, who thought he just needed to "try harder." His parents eventually had to hire a lawyer to get the school to facilitate an Individualized Education Plan (IEP)—that was blatantly needed. There were days Ray could barely make it off the bus before bursting into tears. He cried occasionally in group sessions, when talking about school; but the worse he was treated, the more determined he became.

One Saturday, Ray practically bounced into group therapy. He was obviously happy about something, but he wouldn't say what. He participated in all the usual activities, then said, "I had a good day in school yesterday," when the boys were telling the "best things" that had happened to them that week. When asked to elaborate, Ray just smiled and said, "It . . . was good."

We found out later that Ray had stood in front of his entire class and given an oral report. His IEP specifically exempted him from this type of activity, but Ray did it anyway. He stuttered and stammered in the beginning, but eventually calmed down and finished his report; the resource teacher had called his mother and described Ray's amazing determination. On the day Ray graduated from his therapy group, there wasn't a dry eye in the room. Lots of boys had come and gone, but Ray was special. Ray was a leader. Quiet, courageous, kind, and self-effacing, Ray never gave up, because Ray had grit.

We still keep in touch with Ray and his family. Despite his neurological limitations, Ray joined the National Guard his junior year of high school, the day after he turned 18; he is paying for college himself. Ray's sergeant told his family he had "officer potential," if he could make it through boot camp. So, the summer between his junior and senior year, while his friends were life-guarding and having fun, Ray suffered through boot camp.

His tics returned in droves, induced by all the stress. He called home a few times, anxious and wanting to quit. His parents urged him to continue. He had a goal, they reminded him, and he'd never given up—ever. They urged him to try his hardest, go the extra mile, and live up to his commitments. "Believe in yourself and your goals," his parents advised.

Ray stayed. He completed boot camp that summer and graduated from high school the next spring. He is now attending college, majoring in sociology with a minor in criminal justice. After college, he will join the National Guard as a military police officer. After that, who knows? The sky's the limit, because Ray's got *true grit*.

### The Three Components of Grit[4]

1. *Belief that you can attain your goal:* This is what allows you to overcome challenges and setbacks, like Raymond's neurological impairments.
2. *Passion about your goal:* This ensures you will remain enthusiastic, committed, and optimistic about your goal over an extended period of time. In Raymond's case, that was virtually his entire life. Valuable goals require work and perseverance; they are not acquired easily.
3. *The ability to recognize the "costs" of attaining your goal and doing it anyway:* People with grit don't worry about failure, lack of approval, or what they're giving up; they're too focused on what they want to achieve. Raymond missed a whole summer vacation and time with his girlfriend, but it was worth it to move closer to his goal.

## Case Study: Gabriella

**Gabriella is the mother of 10 children.** Her family lives in a rambling farmhouse with a wraparound porch—loaded with every type of sports equipment known to man or woman. It may be a bit messy, but it speaks cheerful volumes about the busy, active kids who live there.

Three of Gabby's kids have graduated from college and have excellent jobs. Three are at college now; "just four more to go!" she quipped. They are spread all over the country: California, Colorado, Georgia, and New Mexico. Gabby said that her kids had all been told the same thing before they left for college: "Your dad and I will get you there, and we'll get you home for the summer. But you'll either have to grow your own wings or find out some other way to get home during the school year."

None of her kids have ever missed being home for a holiday.

Gabby and her husband, Will, didn't start out wanting 10 children. "They came at us quickly," said Gabby cheerfully.

"Actually," she continued, "I remember being at the airport with my husband after we had our first child. There was this family with five kids, and I thought it seemed huge! The oldest of the pack was probably leaving for college or Europe and he looked like he was a mess. His hair was all scraggly; his clothes were hanging out of his bag. I thought, 'What kind of a parent would ever let their child leave like that? How do you expect that kid to survive?'"

She was laughing when she reported, "So, there we were at the airport last June, at five in the morning with Hal, he's 18, looking like he'd slept in his clothes, with his overstuffed backpack making him closely resemble the Hunchback of Notre Dame, sending him off to Europe for the summer.

"He'd worked two jobs at school and saved his money to pay for this trip. My husband and I looked at him, and then at each other . . . and just burst out laughing. We laughed until we cried—that kid in the airport from years ago—*was our kid* after all."

She got more serious when she talked about Ethan. "When our

eighth child, Ethan, was born, it was the only time my husband passed out in the delivery room. Ethan's umbilical cord was wrapped around his neck, and he was an awful color blue. He looked dead. When they released the cord, he started screaming—much harder and louder than our other children.

"He was always different; when we sent him to preschool, his teacher said he didn't speak at all—he'd just point. And . . . he was kind of crazy. He'd get this wild-eyed look, and dart around the room. He had no social skills, no idea how to relate to other kids. He'd just scream, for no apparent reason. Getting him dressed was a daily battle. He really didn't like to be held or cuddled and would only tolerate it for brief periods of time. If I wanted to snuggle with my son, I had to wait until he was asleep.

"We were so worried about Ethan; Will and I would be in bed, trying to come up with ways to help our baby, trying to convince ourselves that he was improving, but he really wasn't.

"Then we were referred to a new therapist. He went to Ethan's preschool three times in one week to observe him. He reported that Ethan always sat at the very end of the circle at circle time, never wanted to be too close to any of the other kids, or have anyone between him and the door. The therapist asked if Ethan had been born with the cord around his neck—was he blue?

"Will and I were shocked. I still get goose bumps when I think about it. I said that he had been, and then the therapist asked about other behaviors: Did he complain that his socks were too tight and that the labels on his clothes were intolerable? Did he dislike heavy clothes, like snowsuits? Did he dislike being held or restrained? Had his developmental milestones been later across the board—not just with speech?

"He said that these were common behaviors of children born with nuchal cords. The therapist explained that the moment our son had tried to take his first breath, he had been strangled, virtually to death. 'That was the defining moment in that baby's life,' he explained. My husband started crying.

"'Ethan sits on the end of the circle,' he explained, 'because he needs an escape route. That's also why he can't tolerate tight clothing or enclosed spaces.' The therapist said that he believed that Ethan would be fine; he saw no signs of extreme neurological impairment. It was going to be a long road, however, for Ethan, and Will and I would have to fight discouragement; our job was to make Ethan feel valued and normal, and to create opportunities for growth that still let him know he is safe—that he has an escape route.

"When we got home, my husband turned to me and said, 'I will *never* think about Ethan the same way again.' We just held each other and cried.

"We took that therapist's advice. When we went somewhere where we had to wait in line, we were always at the very front or at the end. In movie theaters, we sat Ethan on the aisle, by the exit. We'd never been as aware of how *crowded* the world is."

Nothing was handed to Gabby's kids, and with 10, she didn't have time to dote on any one child or make large gestures to accommodate any special needs. If the kids wanted something, they were expected to figure out a way to get it.

However, resource constraint didn't mean that Gabby and Will didn't have goals for their children or guide them toward making good choices. Ethan was certainly not the exception. They had several goals for Ethan, but the route to get there was distinctly different for him, and he had to navigate it on his own, with support from his family.

"For Ethan, our goals were different; his first day of kindergarten, my husband and I took him into the classroom. 'Please, God, just let him make a friend, just one friend,' I prayed.

"We live in a small town, and the schools and class sizes are small, so everyone knew Ethan, and he had a reputation for being kind of weird. I can't explain it, but he just pushed people away. His brain had other imperatives for him. It was heartbreaking to see him expending so much effort, with so little gain. But our goal for Ethan was to be able to make connections with other kids. We expected Ethan to make and keep one friend. That was it—eye on the prize.

"Every night at dinner we asked Ethan who he talked to that day. Every day, Ethan went into school and talked more. It took Ethan a year to make a friend, but when it happened, the world opened up for him.

"I swear Ethan was more challenging than all my other children combined. He's away at college right now, and he's great—I mean, he's a *great* kid . . . out of all my children, he probably has the closest friends. *Really* good friends. That's just his personality; when he finally lets you in, it's amazing. It's for life."

*Ethan never gave up.* He kept trying, every single day. The kid has *grit*.

## RESOURCE CONSTRAINT AND GRIT

*Why are young adults so self-centered and always seeking instant gratification? Because older adults, often in positions of power, paint them that way.*

—Raymond Arroyo, author, producer, and news director

### Why Resource-Constrained Children Develop Grit

One of the most fascinating things about *grit* is that it is the only skill set that speaks to a child's *character*. Grit has nothing to do with scoring well on a test, sinking a basket from midcourt, or memorizing a math equation. Yet it is an incredibly accurate predictor of future success. Children who have developed grit have a number of common characteristics, including curiosity, optimism, psychological resourcefulness, and resilience.

When it comes to developing grit, less is more. Fewer things, fewer compliments, and less stress.

Children from resource-constrained families tend to have a number of things in common that help them develop the learning habit of self-reliance (grit). They are given more autonomy and responsibility at a younger age. We're not talking about children simply making their beds before school.

These children are often responsible for chores that are necessary to sustain life. As surprising as this may sound to a helicopter parent, these children not only survive these heavy burdens, but they often thrive on them.

Dayo Olopade is a journalist who has studied innovation and resourcefulness in African children. In her 2012 *New York Times* article "Baby and Child Care, the African Way," she discusses the development of grit in children from various families across the globe.

> [T]he pressure to "just do it," which is unusually present in resource-constrained settings, brings real benefits. It can widen what psychologists call the "window of tolerance" for adversity and improve one's adaptive imagination. Rather like the germs that help build immune systems, autonomy in child rearing can develop resourcefulness. It is also said to help develop a better sense of humor—and of justice.[5]

When we compare the learning habit of self-reliance with the statistics found in our study, it's no wonder that Generation $M^2$ children can look spoiled, entitled, and egocentric.

The Learning Habit Study found that:

✓ More children in elementary school have cell phones than make their beds.

✓ Of 5- to 11-year-old children, 28% to 38% rarely or never do chores.

✓ Of 12- to 18-year-olds, 28% to 40% rarely or never do chores.

Why would these entitled kids work for anything? It's all handed to them on a silver platter! *Grit* is the missing ingredient in the lives of many disenchanted, disconnected, and yet financially advantaged children.

## Case Study: Tom

**Tom, the father of two children,** was raised in a working middle-class family. His father was a police officer, and his mother was a teacher. An honors student, Tom worked two jobs to supplement his scholarship and put himself through college. He is now a high-level executive at a major corporation. He worked tirelessly to obtain his degree, and slowly but surely rose through the ranks of his company. With stock options, Tom now makes more than $300K a year. His is a true success story, and his children have been given every advantage money could provide.

Yet Tom is deeply concerned about them. "They just haven't found their thing yet. I don't get it; both my wife and I were fantastic students. It's not like the kids aren't smart . . . and Trevor [taking a breath], Trevor's been tough. He's . . . I don't know . . . I don't know what's going on with him. My wife took him to a counselor this year. I guess he's got anxiety."

Tom's daughter had an unimpressive academic record through her 12 years of school, but graduated last year. She still lives at home and is currently playing in a band. She's the lead singer and is hoping the band will make her into a rock star.

His son, Trevor, is planning on attending a college in Montana, which he selected because he likes snowboarding.

Tom feels understandably confused, "I thought my job was to provide 'the best' for my children—so they wouldn't have to struggle, like I did. I don't get it; my kids don't struggle—they just . . . wander. They can't really commit to anything."

In all likelihood, Tom will be providing room and board to *both* his daughter and son—rent free, of course—in two years or less, as the odds of Trevor's being able to accomplish the amount of work college requires are not in his favor.

## WHY RESOURCE-CONSTRAINED CHILDREN HAVE GRIT

We can predict that a child who saves money will not likely give up or quit. Children who have more chores, who are expected to lay out their clothes the night before school, make their own bed, and complete tasks have a higher "grit score." Children who don't quit sports and take direction well are more likely to use their words to express their wants and needs. They are also children who talk to their parents about things that bother them. This might explain the connection Olopade made between grit and the ability to laugh at oneself. Children with grit have no sense of entitlement, so don't take things too personally.

### Case Study: Jenna

**In Jenna's house,** you'll notice that her children all have a lot of responsibility. With six children crammed into a small house, you trip if someone leaves their stuff out. "Stuff" equals sports equipment. The family is not poor, but they are not wealthy, either.

They chose to live in a smaller house with fewer "things" because it was in a better school district. There is a rotating schedule detailing which child makes dinner, cleans, and so on. By the age of four—yes, four—her children were expected to make dinner for the family.

Many parents can't imagine letting a four-year-old near the stove. Jenna's children were capable of preparing simple meals; they could read and understand measurements by the age of four.

"People are horrified by that story, like it was child abuse or something. I just shake my head. Please. You want your children to be more independent and less whiney, have more children!" Jenna laughs.

Jenna, her husband, Lucas, and their six children are well known in the town where they currently reside. They are a consistent presence at swim meets, field hockey games, and baseball games. Jenna is unconcerned about what other mothers think of her; she has a system and, thus far, it's working.

"I saw her pull out a massive pot filled with steaming hot water at her kids' practice. Inside the pot were ears of corn. She literally placed the pot on a picnic table, with little kids around, pulled some big tongs, sticks of butter, and a shaker of salt out of her bag and yelled 'dinner.' I was cracking up laughing. I mean, who does that? I'm not passing judgment—look at her kids! They're all terrific!" commented Morgan, whose son is also on the team.

Out of necessity, more than one of Jenna's children had to participate in the same sport in order for her to justify adding it into the carpooling mix. Janie, her youngest daughter, is an outstanding field hockey player.

"Actually, it wasn't Janie who was interested in field hockey; it was Marybeth, her older sister. She begged me to let her play, but the practices were way across town. They know the deal; I'm not driving 30 minutes for one child. . . . So Marybeth taught Janie how to play field hockey.

"The funny part is, Janie's now better than Marybeth."

One year, the third-oldest child, Alex, wanted to play baseball. It was going to throw off the whole schedule, so Alex had to walk to practice. He was six years old, and practice was a quarter mile from his house.

All of Jenna's children play sports. Participation in a sport is not optional, but you don't hear any of Jenna's kids complaining. They joke, but they don't complain.

"My son, Caleb, jokes that all the bikes on our front lawn are bringing down the value of our neighbor's house. They probably are! I don't care. I see these kids whose parents have bought them thousands of dollars' worth of electronics . . . and the kids look miserable. Kids don't need all that stuff; let them find something in themselves, that they can develop, to make them happy."

Caleb, the oldest son, landed a swimming scholarship to a college with a Division 1–ranked swim team. Caleb started swimming classes when he was four. Jenna doesn't recall noticing anything particularly different about Caleb until he was 14.

"He really enjoyed being a part of the high school swim team. His coach pulled me aside and said that if Caleb stuck with it, he could qualify for a scholarship. All my kids know they have to find a way to pay for college. Swimming was Caleb's ticket."

When we interviewed Caleb, he explained his motivation to swim . . . somewhat differently. He described his house as being "really loud." Sometimes, he just needed a break from all the noise and activity of his brother and sisters. When he was at home, he had a lot of chores to do, especially because he was the oldest. His family has only basic cable, so television wasn't a very appealing option. Swim practice was *so much better* than the available alternatives that he kept going. He still had chores to do when he got home, but not as many.

He felt very focused when he was at swim practice, and he liked the way that felt. So he pushed himself harder, and he kept getting better.

Caleb is just of one of many *resource-constrained* children who developed grit and a skill out of necessity.

Jenna's style of parenting is not for everyone, but it does give us pause. Six great kids, one down-to-earth mother, and a whole lot of *grit*.

## GENERATION M²

We would like to believe that parents like Jenna and Gabriella (even though the pot-of-corn incident may have been a bit extreme) who placed "some responsibility on their [children's] shoulders" and produced kids with true grit were the norm. According to our research—and that of many others—they are not. Generation M$^2$ has *more things and fewer skills* than ever before; they are not, on average, being trained to work hard to get the things they want. They have a sense of entitlement that, as clinicians, we have not previously encountered. This sense of entitlement—of being deserving of things without working to earn them—crosses all socioeconomic and parental education boundaries. For many of these kids, *I want* means *I deserve*. This is not the attitude that builds self-reliance, responsibility, or leadership.

## Case Study: Tisa

**Tisa (age 16)** suffered a traumatic brain injury in gym class during her junior year in high school. Her doctors told her she would not be able to graduate with her class or participate in athletics again. She would have to postpone taking the SATs and attending college, perhaps forever. This was devastating for Tisa, who was an honors student and tied with one other girl for class valedictorian. She was also a track star, talented musician, class officer, and all-around popular young lady, who, in one moment, lost everything that mattered to her. She lost her memory, her cognitive skills, her concentration, her sports and extracurricular activities, and her social life.

For months after the accident, Tisa needed 14 to 18 hours of sleep a day. She suffered from horrific headaches that medication could not alleviate. She couldn't concentrate long enough to read or comprehend even a few paragraphs of a book. She watched her friends slip away; not because they didn't care, but because they had busy, active lives.

Tisa battled severe depression; she feared she would never recover her cognitive aptitude—a distinct medical possibility. Then slowly but surely, Tisa exhibited the raw courage, sheer determination, and true grit necessary to make up her classes and take her college SATs—just for the experience. When she got her scores, they were off the charts, probably because of her relaxed state and extremely low expectations! Tisa graduated on time, with her class, and was accepted to her #1 college choice. She received a full scholarship and is studying at a top-tier university with the highest-rated microbiology program in the country. Grit got her there—pure grit.

## RESEARCHERS' CONCLUSIONS

What do the people in our case studies have in common? They all have a clear sense of who they are as people—their priorities, their work ethic, and their goals. They have enough self-esteem to believe that they deserve to reach their goals—so they continue to work, even in the face of severe adversity. They have integrity. They rely on and trust themselves. They are not swayed by peer pressure, and they do not accept other people's assessments of their capabilities or commitments. In short, they have grit.

## OUR CHILDREN'S ROLE MODELS

Ethan, Raymond, and Tisa, in particular, are extraordinary individuals. They are goal-oriented and refuse to be deterred by serious challenges. When told they can't do something, they simply refuse to believe it. These children had empowering parents, but Tisa's "experts" were quite discouraging. It took a lot of grit to achieve what these kids have.

Unfortunately, we live in a world where our children are constantly inundated by images of people who don't have much grit, who are "famous" just for being famous.

An unfortunate side effect of this obsession with fame is that many children grow up believing that if they're not "the best," then what's the point? Why put in the effort? What will they gain? They might as well just quit and move on to the "next thing," which they hope will be easier; if it's not, they'll move on to something else.

## Case Study: Brian

**Brian (age 8)** pulled off his cleats and shin guards and threw them to the ground. "I hate soccer! I'm a crappy player!"

"You're a great player, sweetheart," Brian's mother, Lisa, replied.

"*No, I'm not!*" Brian screamed. "I stink, and I don't want to play anymore. It's a stupid game, and I'd rather run track. I'm the fastest runner in the school."

This was a typical Saturday morning. Brian and two of his friends had signed up for soccer that year, but after a few practices, Brian became frustrated. His mother thought Brian probably didn't have the *natural aptitude* for the sport the other boys seemed to have; Lisa admitted he wasn't very good. "He's kind of clumsy, tripping over his own feet all the time. But if I tell him he's not 'the fastest' or 'the best,' I'm in for hours of tantrums and grief."

The same thing happened with karate the year before. Brian desperately wanted to learn karate, but became bored and quit after a few classes. "He honestly thought he was going to fight like Jackie Chan or Jaden Smith after the first week!" cried Lisa, frustrated. "Then again, the classes were on Mondays and Wednesdays at 4:30, which conflicted with dinner and homework, so it wasn't that much of a loss. He just needs to find his sport. Just because he's not great at one sport, doesn't mean he won't excel at another. Everyone is good at something, right? We just have to find his special thing!"

### RESEARCHERS' CONCLUSIONS

With this kind of parental guidance, it's going to be very difficult for Brian to develop grit. Because the truth is, not all children are gifted athletes—most aren't, actually. That doesn't mean they shouldn't play sports. Athletics teaches children an abundance of good habits: teamwork, goal-setting, persistence, showing up, comfort with social interaction, focus, and the ability to win *and lose* with grace. *These* are the qualities for which children should be praised—not winning or being the best—because *these* are the qualities that build self-reliance.

Losing doesn't make one a loser, but quitting every time things get a little difficult will certainly make one a quitter. Here's what a few professional athletes and Olympic gold medalists have to say about winning, losing, and hard work:

> *There may be people that have more talent than you, but there's no excuse for anyone to work harder than you do.*
> —Derek Jeter, baseball

> *My attitude is that if you push me towards a weakness, I will turn that weakness into a strength.*
> —Michael Jordan, basketball

> *Never underestimate the power of dreams and the influence of the human spirit. We are all the same in this notion: The potential for greatness lives within each of us.*
> —Wilma Rudolph, track and field

> *Winning means you're willing to go longer, work harder, and give more than anyone else.*
> —Vince Lombardi, football

> *To hell with circumstances; I create opportunities.*
> —Bruce Lee, martial arts

Creating grit (the learning habit of self-reliance) requires hard work, determination, and a belief that continued practice is an effective way to build skills—over time. I guess the question is: Are we making grit too hard for our children to learn, by making their lives too easy? In some ways, less might, indeed, be more.

# PART III

///////////////////////////////////////////////////////////////////////////////

## Learning Through Play

# CHAPTER ELEVEN

# Starting Now:
# The 21 Family Challenges

We become what we repeatedly do.
—*Sean Covey, author*

There is so much information in this book—from research, interviews, and clinical case studies—that the thought of trying to assimilate all of it to make changes in the way your family operates might seem too . . . *challenging*. If you look at trying to do all of it at once, it certainly would be! But it is possible, starting today, to begin building learning habits. Your children can become productive, successful learners who have mastered the eight essential skill sets; your entire family can learn to relate better, be more organized, and have fewer arguments and more time to enjoy each other.

We can all get stuck in familiar routines that are nonproductive, simply because they are repeated, day after day. Children are especially vulnerable, because they seek the safety of predictability and repetition; children don't like change! So, after repeatedly doing the same thing, day in and day out, they develop habits that are counterproductive to learning; this book is full of stories describing *those* habits.

Building new lifelong habits can seem like a daunting task, and parents we interviewed during the Learning Habit Studies often felt overwhelmed when it came to making even small changes to their family routines. However, when these same parents and children were invited to try a *challenge* that was in the form of a game, they unanimously agreed. Knowing that the game was time-limited and fun helped them feel excited about trying something new.

That's why we broke down each of the skills outlined throughout the pages of this book into realistic, fun, 24-hour challenges. Children learn through games, and learning should feel fun.

The key to lasting change starts with making a commitment to do something for *one day*. One day leads to another day; days turn into weeks, and weeks into years. These family challenges are designed to be entertaining, a little silly, and to allow both parents and children to acclimate to new activities, at their own pace. They require only a baby step: a 24-hour commitment by families. Complete them all, and your family will have successfully tackled 21 days of learning challenges!

Not all of the challenges will apply to every family. Feel free to start with any challenge, and complete as many or as few as your family feels comfortable doing. Document the experience, and show your children what they accomplished. Start a "Challenge Album" to remind children (and parents) that they are stronger than they ever believed was possible. **Progress at your own pace.** Some families tackle one challenge a week, some progress quickly onto another challenge. Other families only feel comfortable trying one a month. Use each challenge to enhance your parenting skills and create some learning habits for your kids—and, perhaps, for you.

## ABOVE ALL—HAVE FUN

Laugh while you attempt these challenges; they are designed to be challenging (also thought-provoking and highly amusing)—and a great way to involve everyone in the family. The goal is to help families look at their old routines from a new perspective, so that they can evaluate how those routines are working. All families are capable of building new habits. Remember, you and your children are more powerful than you think.

Please introduce these challenges to children as a game. After all, this is how children enjoy learning!

## INCREMENTAL LIFESTYLE CHANGES

Use a family meeting to introduce the idea of 24-hour challenges; let your kids know *why* you think it will be important and good for all of you. After all, you want them to increase their "brain power"—and you believe they can. Have *them* cast the deciding vote on which game to do first; their involvement will get them invested in the challenge. After your family has completed the first challenge, have a follow-up family meeting to discuss how you can incorporate bits and pieces of the routine you just followed into your everyday life. Talk about the experience and have a two-way conversation with your children. Ask yourself, what part of the challenge felt good to me? What specific things were my children and I doing during the challenge that better aligned with my family's core values? Keep the parts that worked. It's these small, consistent, incremental changes that are the cornerstones of learning habits.

## THE 21 FAMILY CHALLENGES

### Challenge #1: Trading Places (Building Grit)

Have a family meeting to discuss this fun 24-hour challenge. Children are challenged to switch places with their parents for one day and do a selection of the household chores. They will take on responsibilities such as laundry, dealing with the trash, preparing dinner, washing dishes and/or loading the dishwasher, straightening up, and so on—with minimal parental involvement, groaning, or other signs of distress. The parents will follow their children's routine for the same time period. If this is a weekday event, the parents will follow the kids' routine after they get home from work. If it's a weekend day, they'll follow it for the day and evening. Be prepared for some craziness!

### INCREMENTAL LIFESTYLE CHANGES
Have a family meeting the next day to discuss the challenge. How did it go? Talk to your children about which chores were the most difficult and which were the easiest. Ask them if they enjoyed any of the chores. Let them know that they are old enough to take on some more responsibilities and ask them to choose a predetermined number (one or two) of the chores to do every day. Have them decide at what point in the day they will do the chore, then put it in your family calendar; also help them enter it into whatever scheduler they use, age dependent. Praise them for following through on the challenge.

## Challenge #2: The Swap Out (Media Skills)

During this 24-hour challenge, each family member is asked to "swap out" 30 minutes of media consumption or media communication for a nonmedia activity. (Examples include board games, cards, playing with friends, sports, reading, face-to-face conversation.)

### INCREMENTAL LIFESTYLE CHANGES
Have a family meeting the next day to discuss the challenge. What activities did family members use in place of consumption/communication media? Discuss what you liked about the challenge and set a goal to swap out 30 minutes a day on a daily basis.

## Challenge #3: Rubber Band Compliments
## (Empowerment Parenting)

**Part One:** During this challenge, developed just for parents, participating adults will wear a rubber band around their wrist. Each time the parent gives *outcome-based praise* to their child (such as "Smart girl," "Great job," "You're so talented!"), they must snap their own rubber band (gently). Then, they will correct themselves and rephrase the praise as an effort-based compliment ("You're working hard," "Nice job staying on task," "Good effort doing those dishes," "All that batting practice really shows"). Your children may need to call some comments to your attention.

**Part Two:** This challenge also gives rubber band snaps for judgmental comments ("If you'd tried a little harder . . ." "You obviously haven't been studying enough, or . . ."). If, instead of praising for effort, you criticize the outcome, give yourself a double snap.

*This challenge is extremely popular with children; they love to see their parents have to snap themselves!* Take the rubber band off when you can go 12 hours without a snap. Make the game even more challenging by having a contest with your partner or spouse.

FYI: If you can't go 12 hours without a snap, do it for another day. You may need to change wrists!

### INCREMENTAL LIFESTYLE CHANGES

What did you learn from wearing the rubber band? How did your child react after 12 hours of effort-based praise? Challenge yourself to keep up the effort-based praise by adding it into your everyday language. Tell stories at dinner about challenges you have overcome; have your children do the same. Ask children what they have *learned* from experiences—rather than praising them for the *outcome*. Talk openly about things that are hard, and about the hard work you put into these tasks.

## Challenge #4: The Stop Station (Media Skills)

During this challenge, your family will agree on a cell phone stop station. All cell phones must be left at the station for 24 hours. The station will be open for only two 15-minute periods throughout the day (for example, 7:00–7:15 a.m. and 7:15–7:30 p.m.). The phone can be used *only* at the stop station during those two 15-minute periods.

### INCREMENTAL LIFESTYLE CHANGES

Have a family meeting the next day to discuss the challenge. Who had the most difficult time with the challenge? Why? What did family members learn from the challenge? Ask everyone if anything else in their day (mood, concentration, focus, energy) felt different without their cell phone.

Use this time to discuss a mutually convenient place where cell phones can be kept while members of the family are in the house. Discuss a reasonable amount of time to use cell phones while at home. Have everyone participate in the conversation, write down the notes, and have the family sign the cell phone contract.

## Challenge #5: Creating Memories (Media Skills)

During this 24-hour family challenge, all members of the family are asked to use media to make something new. Some challenge possibilities could be: uploading a photo and writing a caption under it, typing a letter about family news, making a video, making a digital book, organizing a digital "Challenge Album" and adding music to it (see Chapter Three for more ideas).

### INCREMENTAL LIFESTYLE CHANGES

How can you and your children use media creation rather than media consumption every day? Are your kids using media to learn? Are there 20 or 30 minutes of media consumption you could swap out with a media creation project?

Consider finding a long-term project the family could tackle that requires them to learn a number of office-type production/editorial skills; these will help your children with the kind of projects required in high school and college. Don't be afraid to encourage your children to dream big; they can start, with baby steps, to learn media creation. The best part is that *parents and children are learning these new tools together.*

## Challenge #6: Media Time-Out (Media Skills)

During this extreme 24-hour challenge, your family will go the entire day and night without the use of any consumption, creation, or communication media. This means *totally unplugged—every single one!*

What activities can you and your children plan to do that don't require any media use? Get creative and encourage your children and yourselves to enjoy being fully present.

### INCREMENTAL LIFESTYLE CHANGES

Have a family meeting the next day to discuss the challenge. What was the most difficult part? What parts did you enjoy? Did you notice any mood changes in yourself or in any one else, such as, less anxiety? Use this experience to implement smaller media-free times during the week.

## Challenge #7: The One Step (Goal-Setting Skills)

During this challenge, children are asked to come up with a goal. It can be anything—please don't feel the need to censor. In fact, the wilder it is, the more fun the game is! We've heard:

1. Become a rock star.
2. Learn how to make magic potions (my kindergartner).
3. Be tougher than Bruce Lee.
4. Becoming an astronaut.

Challenge your child to come up with *one step* they can take during the next 24 hours to bring them closer to their goal. It could be learning all the words to a song—and singing it to the family; researching potions at the library or online; learning a move in a martial arts routine—and doing it for the family; getting a book (library or ebook) about space travel.

### INCREMENTAL LIFESTYLE CHANGES

Have a family meeting the next day to discuss the challenge. Is it something they want to continue? What steps can they take every single day to get closer to their goal? Use this time to set and discuss weekly goals for some other areas. Ask children every day if they took any steps to bring them closer to their goal; praise them for thinking in terms of goals.

## Challenge #8: Pin It (Communication Skills)

This challenge requires a stack of safety pins (paper clips will work, too). Have a family meeting and talk to your children about their emotions (moody, frustrated, anxious, angry, shy). Let them know that it's really important to you that they feel comfortable talking about how they feel.

For the next day, any time a member of the family *verbally communicates a feeling* instead of physically displaying it, they get a safety pin. The goal is to make the longest safety pin necklace. Coach your child by practicing Respectful Adult Communication (I feel/I want) with them (see Chapter Seven). Use it for everything: "I feel hungry; I'd like you to pass the cereal, please"; "I feel uncomfortable; I need to use the bathroom." This will get pretty funny, but it will definitely help your kids (and you) become more comfortable with this communication style.

FYI: If you're really modeling it, your necklace could be very long. Make sure you rock that necklace with pride! If you tackle this challenge again and feel "crafty," feel free to add extra "bling" to your paper clips or safety pins with beads or colored paper clips.

## INCREMENTAL LIFESTYLE CHANGES

Have a family meeting the next day to discuss the challenge. Identifying and labeling emotions is an integral part of helping a child learn how to regulate and express them. This is particularly hard for children when they feel frustrated or "less than." You can help your children stay in touch with their feelings by: asking questions about how they feel, when something happens; asking them to tell you "in words" how they are feeling, when their body language tells you that they are experiencing an emotion; offering feedback on how you would have felt if you were in a similar situation (for example, "I would have felt really frustrated if I asked Jenna for the doll five times and she didn't let me play with it. Did you feel frustrated?").*

# Challenge #9: A Penny Earned (Communication Skills)

This challenge is basically the same as the safety pin challenge, except that this version is parents versus children! Put two jars on the kitchen table; label one "parent" and the other "child." Any time parents use Respectful Adult Communication (RAC), put a penny in the parent jar. Any time a child uses RAC, place a penny in the child jar. Remember to clearly explain RAC (I feel/I want) and, especially if your children are younger, all of you contribute to a "feelings list" that you can post before beginning the challenge.

## INCREMENTAL LIFESTYLE CHANGES

Have a family meeting the next day to discuss the challenge. Whose jar had more pennies—kids or adults? Take turns communicating (using RAC, of course!) what you learned and have your children do the same. Continue using I-feel/I-want statements in your everyday life, and watch your children's communication skills improve as they model your conduct.

---

* A good resource for parents to explore is emotionalabcs.com. Their interactive videos and games are fun for children and helpful for parents.

## Challenge #10: Digit Span (Focus Skills)

This is a fun one-on-one 24-hour challenge for a child. In a family meeting, decide on two times to meet with your child: one in the morning, one later in the day. Explain that you have a *special challenge* just for them to help improve their focus and build their "brain power"! Be enthusiastic—it will make your child excited to try their special challenge.

**Part One:** Tell them you are going to read a series of numbers. All they need to do is listen, and repeat the numbers back to you. Start with one number (for example, 6), say it, have them repeat it. Then add a second number (for example, 11); they repeat *both* numbers (6, 11). You keep adding numbers until they miss one or mix up the order. The exercise is to see how many numbers in a row they can remember. For instance, if you said, "6, 11, 3, 1, 9, 14, 2" and they said, "6, 11, 3, 1, 9, 2, 14," you would stop the game, saying, "Nice focusing! I could almost see the wheels turning in that brain!" (or something similar). They would receive a score of 5, because they were able to remember a sequence of five numbers in a row with no mistakes. However many they remember, praise them for concentrating hard.

FYI: Write down the numbers in advance so that *you* remember them. As you read the numbers, pause for a beat (one second) in between each number.

**Part Two** (later that afternoon): Teach your child deep breathing exercises. These are carefully explained in Chapter Nine. Have them practice, lying down with eyes closed. (You lie down, eyes closed, also.) When they seem to be breathing deeply and are fairly relaxed, have them remain lying down, eyes closed, and read aloud another sequence of numbers. See how many numbers they can accurately remember this time. No matter how many they get—the same, more, or even fewer—praise them for doing the exercise.

## INCREMENTAL LIFESTYLE CHANGES

Talk to your children about deep breathing exercises and stress. Encourage them to participate in breathing exercises, at a regular time, for a minute or two every day. This will make it easier for them to do it during stressful times, like exams, school assignments, and standardized testing. Deep breathing oxygenates the body, slows down the heartbeat, decreases anxiety, and increases focus. When you're around, do it with them; it will help you, too.

At another time, substitute words for numbers and go through the same process. It will be interesting for you and your kids to see whether they have an easier time with one or the other.

(Another fun variation is to do the same number or word game with your kids, after they have a brief period of physical exertion. Have them jump rope, do jumping jacks, or just run around for a few minutes—then see how many numbers or words they can remember. Your kids can get some valuable information from these games; there are specific things they can do to help themselves focus better, and for longer periods of time—10 jumping jacks, for instance, may prove to be more helpful as an energy and concentration booster than a snack!)

Here are some additional games to help build concentration and memory:

- ✓ Make trips in the car media free; play games instead. "I'm going on a picnic and I'm taking . . ." with your kids, which can be very silly and fun; they'll like it and they won't be playing videos or texting.

- ✓ Give them challenges that increase observational skills, like "look for a blue house, yellow car, red sign, out-of-state license plate, car with more than two people in it, car with a dog, cemetery, steeple, weathervane, windmill, and police car." Praise them on how well they're noticing things.

✓ Make up some silly stories and write them down. (Or use some stories you already have.) Use lots of descriptions, such as "Molly Bear went out for honey. She wore her red dress and blue sneakers; she found three beehives . . ." (Keep it simple; you want your child to feel good about their remembering and noticing.) Read the story to your child, challenging them to remember the details. Then ask them questions; no matter how they do, praise them for their efforts in building their brain power. You can have your child make up a story for you, too.

## Challenge #11: Reading Challenge (Reading Skills)

Have a family meeting and challenge each member of the family to have an age-appropriate reading goal for 24 hours (for children this should be above and beyond anything required for schoolwork); Mom's or Dad's might be 150 pages of a book, their seven-year-old son's might be three chapters in a chapter book. Family members will be challenged to find time, over the course of the day, to sneak in a few pages of their book (for instance, while waiting in line, when in the car, or at the doctor's office).

In addition, set aside a special time *that day* when all members of the family will read together for a designated period of time, perhaps 20 to 30 minutes after dinner.

### INCREMENTAL LIFESTYLE CHANGES

Discuss the challenge at a family meeting the next day. How did it feel for your whole family to have reading goals? Did everyone achieve the goal? Why or why not? Did making reading a family priority help it to feel more important? Set aside an evening each week for a family reading challenge.

## Challenge #12: Best/Worst (Decision-Making Skills)

Have a family meeting to introduce the theory of the "best things that can happen" versus the "worst things that can happen" and why we need to consider these possibilities when making choices. (If you have a white board, have it accessible.) Then give each family member a piece of paper and have them write a silly situation on it and what the choice would be. Older kids (or parents) can help younger kids to do this; the youngest children often come up with the funniest scenarios. Here's an example:

> *Situation*: Going to a friend's house for dinner and being served fried worms with horseradish sauce
> *Choices*: To eat or not to eat.

Then fold the papers and put them in a bag; each person draws a paper. The challenge is to come up with as many possible consequences—best and worst—as the person can think of. Have someone write them down on the white board or on a big piece of paper. This gets very funny, very fast.

### INCREMENTAL LIFESTYLE CHANGES

This exercise is to introduce the decision-making model, discussed in Chapter Eight. Discuss the challenge at a family meeting the next day. Was this way of thinking new? Had anyone actually done this process before making a decision? Can they see why it's important to consider the worst possible thing that can happen when making choices? Encourage your kids to think in these terms when considering the choices they make—because the worst happens, very often. Incorporate discussions about "a choice I made today" at dinner or family time; ask them how it worked out. Would they make the same choice again? Praise your child for thinking about and talking about the *process* (especially if the worst happened!), not the *outcome* of their choice. If they didn't get the desired outcome, that's a great learning opportunity; again, it's the process that's important.

## Challenge #13: Never Have I Ever (Building Grit)

Have a family meeting and ask each person in the family to come up with a personal 24-hour challenge that encourages them to do something adventurous they haven't done before (or parents have been nervous about letting children do—even though it's age appropriate and not dangerous). Make sure your child has a clear plan and a strong desire to try it.

**For children:** Walking or riding their bike to/from school; using a piece of equipment they haven't used before; having a sleepover; going (for the first time) to a meeting of a club or group; being dropped off at an event or practice or (with a friend) at the mall or the movies, and having you leave and then pick them up later; raising their hand in class to ask a question/volunteer an answer; talking to a new kid; joining a game on the playground; in-line skating; riding a two-wheeler; trying a skateboard.

**For parents:** Taking an exercise class; going to a seminar or lecture; going to a movie you've been dying to see—alone; experimenting with a new food; going roller skating, bowling, or climbing a rock wall; calling someone you've wanted to get to know and making a date to do something with them.

### INCREMENTAL LIFESTYLE CHANGES

Have a family meeting to discuss the challenge. How did your child feel? Would they like to do it again? How did you feel? (Were you embarrassed when you fell on your butt at the roller rink—while all those small children whizzed by? Even so, did you have fun?) Are there more ways you can help build grit and self-reliance into everyday activities? Would your family like to incorporate a weekly challenge into their routine?

## Challenge #14: Stop the Clock
## (Academic Homework Skills/Focusing Skills)

Have a family meeting to introduce the homework challenge. Explain that you are going to try to have the whole family learn to work smarter; that means *really focusing* on just one task and—getting as much of it done as possible—within a limited time.

1. Have each member of the family pick out something they are really excited to read (print book, ebook, magazine, or comic book).
2. Set a timer for 10 minutes. Explain to your child that after spending 10 minutes on homework, they are to stop wherever they are, pick up the book, and read for 10 more minutes.
3. The adults choose an activity too (organizing or paying the bills, making a shopping list, cleaning out a file or drawer). When the timer goes off, they get to read their chosen book.
4. Choose a wise time for this challenge that won't be too stressful for your child (*not* the day before midterms!). Be sure to set a timer so that you can all experience the cutoff time for both activities.

### INCREMENTAL LIFESTYLE CHANGES
Have a family meeting to discuss the challenge. Implement a time-limited homework routine (explained in Chapter Four) into your everyday life to maintain balance and have children become exceptional readers.

## Challenge #15: One-Minute Tasks
## (Focusing Skills/Time Management Skills/
## Academic Homework Skills)

Have a family meeting to introduce the one-minute challenge. Have a stopwatch or timer and ask them to do something fun or silly—that they really enjoy doing—for one minute (make up a dance, make silly faces, act out a charade, draw a masterpiece, sing a song, give a speech on a ridiculous topic—like the best way to cook with gummy worms and mud). The only purpose of this task is to demonstrate how quickly one minute can go by.

Next pick another task that is typically difficult for your child or one that your child might normally complain about (cleaning the bedroom, doing the dishes) and ask your child to *really focus* on that task and see *how much they can get done* in one minute. Have a stopwatch and time them. Stop them at one minute.

### INCREMENTAL LIFESTYLE CHANGES

Was it easier for your child to focus because the task was time-limited? If you had asked your child to complete the entire task for an unlimited amount of time, would you have gotten the same results? Time-limited tasks are extremely helpful for children, because they don't feel interminable. Try adding time limits to other tasks in your children's lives to help them focus—without anxiety—and learn time management skills.

## Challenge #16: Clean Slate (Media Skills)

This challenge is just for adults. We challenge you to take back your phone. If you have a smartphone, delete all kid apps from it.

### INCREMENTAL LIFESTYLE CHANGES

How hard was that challenge for you to complete? Did you really delete *all* your kid apps? Use this experience to talk to your child about cell phone use. Set an appropriate age for them to get their own cell phone—preferably, not until they are 14.

## Challenge #17: Creative Screens (Media Skills)

During this 24-hour challenge, parents and children will swap out as many *consumption media* products on their computers, phones, and tablets as possible with *creative and educational media* replacements.

Examples: Swap a video for a Math Playground app. Swap a link on the computer from Nick Jr. to FunBrain.

### INCREMENTAL LIFESTYLE CHANGES

Do you find it easier to regulate your child's media time now that you have removed many of the consumption media temptations from your household? Have you noticed that your children will play the creative and educational games for only short, reasonable periods of time—and then stop on their own? Incorporate creative media into half of your child's allotted "media time," using gradual substitutions of creative apps that they "beta test" and participate in choosing.

## Challenge #18: Body–Mind Connection (Homework Skills)

Have a family meeting and ask each member of the family to come up with a personal exercise challenge for the next 24 hours— something they are going to do for 45 minutes. It could be a series of combined exercises, like jumping rope, hula hooping, playing tag, dancing, riding bikes, practicing soccer, doing an exercise video; any combination of (sweat-producing) activities works. The focus is simply on an additional vigorous physical activity for 45 minutes.

### INCREMENTAL LIFESTYLE CHANGES

Have a family meeting to discuss how the challenge went. Did every member of the family meet their fitness challenge? Before the challenge, was each member of the family getting at least 30 minutes of exercise every single day? Come up with a plan to incorporate a minimum of 30 minutes of exercise into your family's everyday schedule. Continue to challenge your family until you have reached 60 minutes a day.

## Challenge #19: Counting Sheep
## (Sleep Hygiene—All Skill Sets)

Have a family contest to see who can get 30 extra minutes of sleep tonight—without sleeping later in the morning! Have the children come up with a plan to accomplish this. (Make sure the adults have a plan, too.) It might include setting an earlier bedtime, taking a hot bath or shower an hour before bed, cutting off media use an hour before bed, getting into bed early and reading, or just making the evening calmer.

### INCREMENTAL LIFESTYLE CHANGES
Ask everyone how they felt the next morning. Use this opportunity to evaluate competing devices that impair sleep (TVs, cell phones, computers) in your child's and your bedrooms. Have a family meeting to discuss how important sleep is to our health, and make clear rules about bedtime, as discussed in Chapter Two.

## Challenge #20: Motivating Minds
## (Goal-Setting Skills, Building Grit)

This is a three-part family challenge.

**Part One:** The adults will meet to discuss a task, activity, or commitment that the child may be losing interest in—and about which the parents may have ambivalent feelings.

Examples include:

- ✓ Swim classes that their child isn't really progressing in and complains about a lot (maybe we shouldn't sign them up again?)

- ✓ A school play in which their child has a minor role; they want to drop out (and driving them to rehearsal twice a week is getting to be a pain!)

✓ Sunday school—they can't stand it (and it means getting up an hour earlier on Sunday)

Parents are challenged to come up with a specific goal for their child, which relates directly to the activity. The goal must be reasonable, so that the child will be willing to try it.

**Part Two:** Present this goal as a challenge to your child and make sure you show excitement about it. Make sure that the goal is doable, time-limited, and clear. Your child must agree to the terms of the challenge and to see it through. Draw up an agreement and you all sign it. Here are some examples:

✓ Challenge the child in swim class to work toward one specific thing (such as, swimming a lap using the backstroke—or whatever stroke they have been trying to learn).

✓ Challenge them to work hard on their role; to make those lines/that character unforgettable. Challenge them also to volunteer with something else related to the play (such as making posters, designing the program, helping with the set, or selling tickets).

✓ Challenge them to find out the answers to a specific question at Sunday school, to do some Bible research and ask the *teacher* some questions, or to come up with a short quiz that everyone in the class takes.

Have a small reward (you'll play with them—whatever *they* want to play—for 20 minutes), and give some "You really stuck with it!" compliments if they agree to the challenge and sign the contract. Let them know about the opportunities in Part Three.

**Part Three:** As your child completes the challenge, have them research other activities in which they might prefer to participate. As long as they have honored their commitment (gone to all the swimming lessons you paid for without complaint, finished the play, done their challenge and stuck with Sunday school) they may come up with ideas for other, equally beneficial, activities.

- ✓ The swimmer may want to sign up for basketball; they have to agree to complete the program/classes/season.

- ✓ The actor may prefer to work on the school paper; that commitment must be carried through.

- ✓ The kid who really hates Sunday school may do some research and decide they'd like to commit to volunteering for a specified number of hours: soup kitchens, food banks, daycare centers, nursing homes, libraries—all have need of volunteers.

### INCREMENTAL LIFESTYLE CHANGES

Continue to encourage them to set small goals in their activities; praise their effort in taking small steps toward a goal. It helps them to stay motivated. The overarching goal is to learn to make commitments (goals) and persevere. It has been said that one of the measures of a fully-formed adult is the ability to change one's mind based on new information.[1] That new information is gained by fulfilling one's responsibilities. In this challenge, parents help their children to be creative about carrying out their obligations; that's how you develop gritty kids!

## Challenge #21: Move the Cue (Time Management Skills)

Getting ready for school, dinnertime, homework, and bedtime are just a few of the things parents often need to remind children about. Challenge your children to take control of their entire routine for the next day without any reminders from adults. What alarms or notes will they need to set for themselves so they remember everything? Parents should offer praise to children the next day (nice job remembering to get your backpack, great work going upstairs to bed on your own) as they progress throughout the challenge.

## INCREMENTAL LIFESTYLE CHANGES

Have a family meeting the next day to discuss and award small prizes for participation (stickers, pack of gum). Discuss what you and they liked and disliked about it. Which ones were they unable to do? Which ones were not that hard for them?

Implement a few of the routines that worked well, one at a time, and you'll begin to remove yourself as the cue; you'll be well on the way to building learning habits in your children! (See Chapter Two for the best way to structure new rules and habits.)

# CONCLUDING THE 21 FAMILY CHALLENGES

Family challenges are an invigorating and innovative way to learn more about the habits and routines that families rely on. They also help build family unity and strength. How parents end a challenge is as important as how they begin it. Ending with a calm, happy family meeting and discussing the challenge is extremely important. It gives children the opportunity to verbalize the events that took place. It also gives parents an opportunity to transfer learning from the specific task used in the challenge to more general, everyday tasks.

Always end a challenge with some sort of a reward for the family. This can be spoken praise about the hard work you saw along with another fun activity, such as a trip to the park or a visit to the ice cream parlor. Last, make sure that children *write down something positive* about the experience and post it in an area where the family can see it; young children can draw a picture and a parent can label the picture parts. Feel free to take a picture as a visual reminder and keep it on the refrigerator and/or in a Challenge file (in your photo album) on the computer. Children are highly visual. Taking a few extra minutes to have them create this lasting memory of the experience will help them retain what they just learned and will help parents remember, too!

# ACKNOWLEDGMENTS

## From All of Us

Thanks to our supportive and insightful editor, Marian Lizzi, whose flexibility and unwavering belief in *The Learning Habit* is what brought this book to fruition. We are incredibly grateful for our agent, Helen, who immediately saw the value in this project, held our hands through the entire process, and never (not even for one moment) let go.

A special thank-you to Survey Crafter developer Richard Ward, who exemplifies the learning habit attitude: Give him a challenge, and he enthusiastically does whatever it takes to overcome it. This man's optimism, excitement about the project, "can-do" mind-set, ingenuity, generosity, and tireless effort is what made the online Learning Habit Study a reality and the data meaningful. We couldn't have done it without you, Richard.

An enormous thanks to the WebMD team, who spent hours on the phone with us, brainstorming ideas about how to incorporate the survey to maximize the rate of response from their readers. Ultimately, they drew a staggering number of respondents to the survey, gathering more data than we'd thought possible. Annic Jobin and Tom Carr—we're forever grateful for all your support. A special thank-you to the team at *Huffington Post* and AOL: especially Lisa Belkin, Terri D'Angelo, Farah Miller, Lori Leibovich, Amanda Schumacher, and Arianna Huffington. Thanks to *Parents* magazine: notably, Diane Debrovner and Stephanie Wood. We are grateful for the support of the National PTA, particularly Mary Pat

King and Dr. Renee Jackson. Thanks to Susan Carraretto at the blog *5 Minutes for Mom*.

We are especially thankful to the hundreds of teachers and parents who contributed to the Learning Habit Study research by providing feedback, testing beta models, providing interviews, answering questions, and sharing personal stories with us. Thank you to our research partners: Allison Schettini Evans, PhD, a pediatric neuropsychologist at Brown University's Alpert Medical School; Dr. Judith Owens, MD, MPH, director of sleep medicine at Children's National Medical Center; and the staff at the New England Center for Pediatric Psychology.

Finally, a heartfelt thank-you to every parent who took time out of their busy day to participate in the Learning Habit Study. This book is, truly, for you.

## From Stephanie

Although it might seem impossible to many people to live, work in a clinical practice, and write a book with the same person, my loving partner, Robert Pressman, has made this challenging task easier in myriad ways. While his dedication to his patients and research is unparalleled in my experience, his love and dedication to his family has always been his first priority. Thanks for the love and support, Bobby. You kept us scientifically on target, brought the collaborative team together, wrote up the studies, spent thousands of hours looking at and correlating data and preparing charts—and also did the vacuuming.

Rebecca Jackson—whose original idea was the basis for the entire project—conducted hundreds of interviews for this book as well as being the marketing expert who brought our agent and an impressive array of media partners into the project. Her unique skills as writer, media manager, organizer, and researcher often made her *important* jobs of mother and wife a challenge to fulfill; she did all of them, however, with elegance and grace. Thanks for your irreplaceable presence in this project, Rebecca. You kept us current, learning, and on schedule—and supplied us with wonderful stories.

Donna Musil, lawyer, writer, producer, documentary filmmaker, activist, and friend was my go-to person for advice during the writing of this book. This staggeringly talented woman volunteered to read and edit hundreds of pages of manuscript when I was too tired to have any objectivity. She literally dropped her own projects to help out. Donna, you have helped me and taught me more than you know; no one could have a better—or grittier—friend. Thank you!

Bobby Jackson, Emma Jacque, Gina and Marie Balemian, who were all great sounding boards for ideas and language. Gina—you kept me laughing during some very stressful stages of this enormous project. Laughter *is* the best medicine!

And finally, I am grateful beyond measure to the wonderful parents and children who make my job such a pleasure. So many of you generously participated in our research and allowed your stories to be used in the book; thank you.

## From Rebecca

This project could not have been completed without the love and support of my partner, Robert Jackson. Thank you for keeping our household running, clean laundry in our drawers, food in the refrigerator, and most important, keeping our children entertained during this lengthy process. I couldn't have done it without you. You have redefined what it means to love and support someone. Thank you.

Thank you to my children, Bobby and Hunter, for your patience while I sat for hours and wrote. I love you both more than you will ever know.

Thanks to Jaci Arnone, the incredible mother of my stepson, who has welcomed me with open arms into her son's life, trusted me to co-parent alongside her, and taught me about so many of the important life skills and habits written about in this book.

Thanks to Sarah Jacque, Yasmina Thomas, Hope Hopkins, Alexander Hentz, Bill Cassara from Clarity Media Group, Alyssa Sullivan Goddard, and Berry Brady who all allowed me to bounce ideas off them at a moment's notice.

## From Robert

The exciting, then difficult journey that the three of us undertook to produce *The Learning Habit* had a simple beginning. Rebecca invited Stephanie and me to hear her presentation of what she described as a "really terrific concept." And it was. Armed with a script and even a PowerPoint presentation, Rebecca proposed that we combine our distinctly different talents in the production of books for parents—providing research and clinically based answers to their most pressing parental concerns. Leading experts and statisticians would work together on the studies, which would impact both families and children. We were all affiliated with both entities, so it didn't take much persuasion to convince us of how great her proposal was. I would shepherd the studies, she would coordinate the project, and Stephanie, already a well-known author, would oversee the writing of the book. What a team. Toward the end, Rebecca and Stephanie put in a collective 30-plus hours a day, seven days a week, for six weeks. I marveled at their seemingly endless supply of energy and creativity. When I grow up, I want to be just like them! Thank you, Stephanie and Rebecca.

The research for the principal study run in the fall of 2013 was perfected with the startling degree of involvement of Richard Ward. Richard is the developer of Survey Crafter Professional (SCP), the software used to collect data for the Learning Habit Study research team, its paper, and, finally, for presentation in this book. He cheerfully made modifications in SCP to help the team create an online

110-item science-based survey that could actually be answered in seven minutes. He coordinated every technical aspect of the live online study, which required around-the-clock monitoring. He worked with our statisticians to make sure that the data collection and presentations were done to precision. He spent many evenings and weekend hours working with the authors to deliver contemporary analyses and charts for inclusion in the manuscript. He redefined the term "technical support."

When we started the project, we never dreamed of the vast number of data points that would be gathered . . . millions. The first statistical run generated a nightmare of 10,000 pages of analysis. Several statisticians provided assistance during the course of developing the study, analyzing the results, and preparing material for publication. Most noteworthy, in mining this mountain of data, was Melissa Nemon, PhD. Her patience in dealing with complex concepts and ability to clearly communicate results were extraordinary.

If Melissa was a miner, then Rachel Farr, PhD, was an explorer. Rachel had the uncanny ability to uncover scientific information relevant to the many facets of *The Learing Habit*. In the end, she helped us map a complex array of existing research from the Learning Habit Study, including homework, family routines, sleep, media, mental health, educational performance, and extracurricular activities.

Finally, a note of gratitude for the man who kept the ship technically afloat, Dennis Sousa, our computer tech. Computer technology is wonderful—until it isn't. The most memorable time was when our computer servers delivered notices more feared than the dreaded blue screen: "No Data on Drive." Without fail, whatever the technical challenge, Dennis met it promptly and without drama. Thanks, Dennis.

# REFERENCES

Ackerman, Phillip L., Ruth Kanfer, and Margaret E. Beier. "Trait Complex, Cognitive Ability, and Domain Knowledge Predictors of Baccalaureate Success, STEM Persistence, and Gender Differences." *Journal of Educational Psychology* 105, no. 3 (2013): 911–927. doi: 10.1037/a0032338.

"ADHD and Substance Abuse." WebMD. May 15, 2012. webmd.com/add-adhd/guide/adhd-and-substance-abuse-is-there-a-link.

American Psychiatric Association. *Diagnostic and Statistical Manual of Mental Disorders.* 5th ed. Arlington, VA: American Psychiatric Publishing, 2013.

American Psychological Association. *A Reference for Professionals: Developing Adolescents.* Washington, DC: American Psychological Association, 2002.

American Psychological Association. *Changing Diet and Exercise for Kids: Acting Boldly to Change Diet and Exercise for Kids (A.B.C.D.E.).* apa.org/topics/children/healthy-eating.aspx.

Areepattamannil, Shaljan. "Parenting Practices, Parenting Style, and Children's School Achievement." *Psychological Studies* 55, no. 4 (2010): 283–289. doi: 10.1007/s12646-010-0043-0.

Ashby, F. Gregory, Benjamin O. Turner, and Jon C. Horvitz. "Cortical and Basal Ganglia Contributions to Habit Learning and Automaticity." *Trends in Cognitive Sciences* 14, no. 5 (2010): 208–215. doi: 10.1016/j.tics.2010.02.001.

Aunola, Kaisa, and Jari-Erik Nurmi. "Maternal Affection Moderates the Impact of Psychological Control on a Child's Mathematical Performance." *Developmental Psychology* 40, no. 6 (2004): 965–978. doi: 10.1037/0012-1649.40.6.965.

Baldwin, Doug. "Why vs. How." Stanford: Home of Champions. champions.stanford.edu/voices-of-champions/why-vs-how.

Barber, Brian K. *Intrusive Parenting: How Psychological Control Affects Children and Adolescents.* Washington, DC: American Psychological Association, 2002.

Barboza, David. "Shanghai Schools' Approach Pushes Students to Top of Tests." *New York Times*, December 29, 2010. nytimes.com/2010/12/30/world/asia/30shanghai.html?pagewanted=all&_r=0.

Baumrind, Diana, Robert E. Larzelere, and Elizabeth B. Owens. "Effects of Preschool Parents' Power Assertive Patterns and Practices on Adolescent Development." *Parenting* 10, no. 3 (2010): 157–201. doi: 10.1080/15295190903290790.

Benson, Herbert. *The Relaxation Response.* New York: Morrow, 1975.

Berridge, Kent C., and Morten L. Kringelbach. "Affective Neuroscience of Pleasure: Reward in Humans and Animals." *Psychopharmacology* 199, no. 3 (2008): 457–480. doi: 10.1007/s00213-008-1099-6.

Broussard, Chris. "The King James Version." ESPN. October 15, 2013. espn.go.com/nba/story/_/id/9824909.

Butkus, Heidi. (2004)."Is." In *Sing & Spell the Sight Words*, vol.1. [CD] CA: Heidi-Songs.

Carlson, Cindy, and Sandra L. Christenson. "Evidence-Based Parent and Family Interventions in School Psychology: Overview and Procedures." *School Psychology Quarterly* 20, no. 4 (2005): 345–351. doi: 10.1521/scpq.2005.20.4.345.

Carnevale, Anthony P., Nicole Smith, and Jeff Strohl. *Help Wanted: Projections of Jobs and Education Requirements through 2018*. Washington, DC: Center on Education and the Workforce, Georgetown University, 2010. survey.csuprojects.org/uploads/j-/ul/j-ul01tOShATFY88Kw3B7g/Georgetown-Center-on-Education-and-the-Workforce-jobs-projections.pdf.

Common Core State Standards Initiative. "National Governors Association and State Education Chiefs Launch Common State Academic Standards." corestandards.org/articles/8-national-governors-association-and-state-education-chiefs-launch-common-state-academic-standards.

Dalton, Bridget. "Multimodal Composition and the Common Core State Standards." *The Reading Teacher* 66, no. 4 (2012): 333–339. doi: 10.1002/TRTR.01129.

Deci, Edward L., and Richard M. Ryan. "The 'What' and 'Why' of Goal Pursuits: Human Needs and the Self-Determination of Behavior." *Psychological Inquiry* 11, no. 4 (2000): 227–268. doi: 10.1207/S15327965PLI1104_01.

DeHority, Sam. "Study Suggests Physical Activity Helps Athletes Perform Better on Mental Tests." *Stack*. December 11, 2013. stack.com/2013/12/11/exercise-mental-test.

Dix, Theodore, Amanda D. Stewart, Elizabeth T. Gershoff, and William H. Day. "Autonomy and Children's Reactions to Being Controlled: Evidence That Both Compliance and Defiance May Be Positive Markers in Early Development." *Child Development* 78, no. 4 (2007): 1204–1221. doi: 10.1111/j.1467-8624.2007.01061.x.

Donaldson-Pressman, Stephanie, and Robert M. Pressman. *The Narcissistic Family: Diagnosis and Treatment*. New York: Lexington Books, 1994.

Duckworth, Angela Lee, and Patrick D. Quinn. "Development and Validation of the Short Grit Scale (Grit–S)." *Journal of Personality Assessment* 91, no. 2 (2009): 166–174. doi: 10.1080/00223890802634290.

Duckworth, Angela, and Martin E. P. Seligman. "Self-Discipline Outdoes IQ in Predicting Academic Performance of Adolescents." *Psychological Science* 16, no. 2 (2005): 939–944.

Duhigg, Charles. *The Power of Habit: Why We Do What We Do in Life and Business*. New York: Random House, 2012.

Dumas, Jean E., Jenelle Nissley, Alicia Nordstrom, Emilie Phillips Smith, Ronald J. Prinz, and Douglas W. Levine. "Home Chaos: Sociodemographic, Parenting,

Interactional, and Child Correlates." *Journal of Clinical Child & Adolescent Psychology* 34, no. 1 (2005): 93–104. doi: 10.1207/s15374424jccp3401_9.

Dweck, Carol S. *Mindset: The New Psychology of Success*. New York: Random House, 2006.

Ehrlich, Christian. "Be Careful What You Wish for but Also Why You Wish for It: Goal-Striving Reasons and Subjective Well-Being." *Journal of Positive Psychology* 7, no. 6 (2012): 493–503. doi: 10.1080/17439760.2012.721382.

Evans, Claire. "Student Debt Tops List of Parental Concerns." Beattie Communications. July 23, 2012. beattiegroup.com/prclients/pr-press-releases/2012/july/student-debt-tops-list-of-parental-concerns.aspx.

Feng, Du, Debra B. Reed, M. Christina Esperat, and Mitsue Uchida. "Effects of TV in the Bedroom on Young Hispanic Children." *American Journal of Health Promotion* 25, no. 5 (2011): 310–318. doi: 10.4278/ajhp.080930-QUAN-228.

Froiland, John Mark. "Parental Autonomy Support and Student Learning Goals: A Preliminary Examination of an Intrinsic Motivation Intervention." *Child & Youth Care Forum* 40, no. 2 (2011): 135–149. doi: 10.1007/s10566-010-9126-2.

Gadeyne, Els, Pol Ghesquière, and Patrick Onghena. "Longitudinal Relations Between Parenting and Child Adjustment in Young Children." *Journal of Clinical Child & Adolescent Psychology* 33, no. 2 (2004): 347–358. doi: 10.1207/s15374424jccp3302_16.

Gastel, Willemijn Van, and Robert F. Ferdinand. "Screening Capacity of the Multidimensional Anxiety Scale for Children (MASC) for DSM-IV Anxiety Disorders." *Depression and Anxiety* 25, no. 12 (2008): 1046–1052. doi: 10.1002/da.20452.

Ginott, Haim G. *Between Parent and Teenager*. New York: Macmillan, 1969.

Goleman, Daniel. *Emotional Intelligence: Why It Can Matter More Than IQ*. London: Bloomsbury, 1996.

Gottfried, Adele Eskeles, James S. Fleming, and Allen W. Gottfried. "Continuity of Academic Intrinsic Motivation from Childhood through Late Adolescence: A Longitudinal Study." *Journal of Educational Psychology* 93, no. 1 (2001): 3–13. doi: 10.1037/0022-0663.93.1.3.

Goudreau, Jenna. "The Secret to Being a Power Woman: Play Team Sports." *Forbes*, October 12, 2011. forbes.com/sites/jennagoudreau/2011/10/12/secret-power-woman-play-team-sports-sarah-palin-meg-whitman-indra-nooyi/2.

Graham, Steve, and Karen R. Harris. "Common Core State Standards, Writing, and Students with LD: Recommendations." *Learning Disabilities Research & Practice* 28, no. 1 (2013): 28–37. doi: 10.1111/ldrp.12004.

Greenfield, Karl Taro. "The Homework Wars: How Much Is Too Much?" *Atlantic*, October 2013. theatlantic.com/special-report/homework-debate.

Henry, Julie. "Ban Computers from Schools until Children Reach Age 9, Says Expert." *Telegraph*, June 13, 2010. telegraph.co.uk/education/primaryeducation/7823259/Ban-computers-from-schools-until-children-reach-age-9-says-expert.html.

*Her*. Dir. Spike Jonz. Warner Bros. Pictures, 2014. Film.

Hickman, Gregory P., and Garnet L. Crossland. "The Predictive Nature of Humor, Authoritative Parenting Style, and Academic Achievement on Indices of Initial

Adjustment and Commitment to College among College Freshmen." *Journal of College Student Retention: Research, Theory and Practice* 6, no. 2 (2004): 225–245. doi: 10.2190/UQ1B-0UBD-4AXC-U7WU.

Hilário, Monica R., and R. M. Costa. "High on Habits." *Frontiers in Neuroscience* 2, no. 2 (2008): 208–217. doi: 10.3389/neuro.01.030.2008.

Hilário, Monica R., E. Clouse, H. H. Yin, and R. M. Costa. "Endocannabinoid Signaling Is Critical for Habit Formation." *Frontiers in Integrative Neuroscience* 1 (2007): 6. doi: 10.3389/neuro.07.006.2007.

Holden, George W. "Perspectives on the Effects of Corporal Punishment: Comment on Gershoff (2002)." *Psychological Bulletin* 128, no. 4 (2002): 590–595. doi: 10.1037/0033-2909.128.4.590.

Hulbert, Ann. *Raising America: Experts, Parents, and a Century of Advice About Children.* New York: Alfred A. Knopf, 2003.

Jackson, Christine, Jane D. Brown, and Carol J. Pardun. "A TV in the Bedroom: Implications for Viewing Habits and Risk Behaviors during Early Adolescence." *Journal of Broadcasting and Electronic Media* 52, no. 3 (2008): 349–367. doi: 10.1080/08838150802205421.

Jackson, Rebecca. "How Cell Phone Use Is Destroying Your Kids' Short-Term Memory." *Huffington Post.* September 30, 2013. huffingtonpost.com/rebecca-jackson/how-cell-phone-use-is-destroying-your-kids-short-term-memory_b_4016345.html.

Jackson, Rebecca. "How Changes in Media Habits Could Transform Your Child's Mental Health." *Huffington Post*, October 29, 2013. huffingtonpost.com/rebecca-jackson/how-changes-in-media-habits-could-transform-your-childs-health_b_4054881.html.

Jahnke, Roger. "Breathing Exercises and Self-Healing." Mercola.com. February 20, 2000. articles.mercola.com/sites/articles/archive/2000/02/20/breathing-part-one.aspx.

"Jim Carrey." Feeling Success. feelingsuccess.com/jim-carrey.

Joeckel, Sven, Nicholas D. Bowman, and Leyla Dogruel. "The Influence of Adolescents' Moral Salience on Actions and Entertainment Experience in Interactive Media." *Journal of Children and Media* 7, no. 4 (2013): 480–506. doi: 10.1080/17482798.2013.781513.

Jones, Allison G., and Jacqueline E. King. "The Common Core State Standards: A Vital Tool for Higher Education." *Change: The Magazine of Higher Learning* 44, no. 6 (2012): 37–43. doi: 10.1080/00091383.2012.706529.

Juel, Connie. "Learning to Read and Write: A Longitudinal Study of 54 Children from First Through Fourth Grades." *Journal of Educational Psychology* 80, no. 4 (1988): 437–447. doi: 10.1037/0022-0663.80.4.437.

Kaiser Family Foundation. "Generation M$^2$: Media in the Lives of 8- to 18-Year-Olds." January 20, 2010. kff.org/other/event/generation-m2-media-in-the-lives-of.

Kawabata, Yoshito, Lenneke R.a. Alink, Wan-Ling Tseng, Marinus H. Van Ijzendoorn, and Nicki R. Crick. "Maternal and Paternal Parenting Styles Associated with Relational Aggression in Children and Adolescents: A Conceptual Analysis and

Meta-Analytic Review." *Developmental Review* 31, no. 4 (2011): 240–278. doi: 10.1016/j.dr.2011.08.001.

Kovner, Josh, and Edmund H. Mahony. "Adam Lanza: A 'Quiet, Odd' Loner Living on the Fringes." *Hartford Courant*, December 15, 2012. articles.courant.com/2012 -12-15/news/hc-adam-lanza-newtown-shooting-1216-20121215_1_nancy-lanza -adam-lanza-marsha-lanza.

Kuczynski, Leon. *Handbook of Dynamics in Parent-Child Relations*. Thousand Oaks, CA: Sage Publications, 2003.

Lally, Phillippa, Jane Wardle, and Benjamin Gardner. "Experiences of Habit Formation: A Qualitative Study." *Psychology, Health and Medicine* 16, no. 4 (2011): 484–489. doi: 10.1080/13548506.2011.555774.

Lawrence, Jean. "Train Your Brain with Exercise." WebMD. June 26, 2007. webmd .com/fitness-exercise/features/train-your-brain-with-exercise.

Lazerlere, Robert E., Amanda Sheffield Morris, and Amanda W. Harrist. *Authoritative Parenting: Synthesizing Nurturance and Discipline for Optimal Child Development*. Washington, DC: American Psychological Association, 2013.

Lee, S. J. "Parental Restrictive Mediation of Children's Internet Use: Effective for What and for Whom?" *New Media and Society* 15, no. 4 (2013): 466–481. doi: 10.1177/ 1461444812452412.

Lee, Sook-Jung, and Young-Gil Chae. "Children's Internet Use in a Family Context: Influence on Family Relationships and Parental Mediation." *CyberPsychology and Behavior* 10, no. 5 (2007): 640–644. doi: 10.1089/cpb.2007.9975.

Livingstone, Sonia, and Ellen J. Helsper. "Parental Mediation of Children's Internet Use." *Journal of Broadcasting and Electronic Media* 52, no. 4 (2008): 581–599. doi: 10.1080/08838150802437396.

Maria, Cara Santa. "Insanity: The Real Definition." *Huffington Post*. December 20, 2011. huffingtonpost.com/2011/12/20/insanity-definition_n_1159927.html.

McLuhan, Marshal. *Understanding Media: The Extensions of Man*. New York: McGraw-Hill, 1964.

"McLuhan's Philosophy." Philosophical Society. philosophicalsociety.com/archives/ McLuhan's%20Philosophy.htm.

Mellalieu, Stephen D., and Sheldon Hanton. *Advances in Applied Sport Psychology: A Review*. London: Routledge, 2009.

Milevsky, Avidan, Melissa Schlechter, Sarah Netter, and Danielle Keehn. "Maternal and Paternal Parenting Styles in Adolescents: Associations with Self-Esteem, Depression and Life-Satisfaction." *Journal of Child and Family Studies* 16, no. 1 (2007): 39–47. doi: 10.1007/s10826-006-9066-5.

Mischel, Walter, Ozlem Ayduk, Marc G. Berman, B. J. Casey, Ian Gotlib, John Jonides, Ethan Kross, Theresa Teslovich, Nicole Wilson, Vivian Zayas, and Yuichi Shoda. " 'Willpower' over the Life Span: Decomposing Self-Regulation." *Social Cognitive and Affective Neuroscience* 6, no. 2 (2011): 252–256. doi: 10.1093/scan/ nsq081.

Morris, Amanda Sheffield, Jennifer S. Silk, Laurence Steinberg, Sonya S. Myers, and Lara Rachel Robinson. "The Role of the Family Context in the Development of

Emotion Regulation." *Social Development* 16, no. 2 (2007): 361–388. doi: 10.1111/j.1467-9507.2007.00389.x.

Mullis, I. V. S., M. O. Martin, E. J. Gonzalez, and A. M. Kennedy. *PIRLS 2001 International Report: IEA's Study of Reading Literacy Achievement in Primary School in 35 Countries.* Chestnut Hill, MA: International Study Center, Lynch School of Education, Boston College, 2003.

Mupinga, E. E., M. E. B. Garrison, and S. H. Pierce. "An Exploratory Study of the Relationships between Family Functioning and Parenting Styles: The Perceptions of Mothers of Young Grade School Children." *Family and Consumer Sciences Research Journal* 31, no. 1 (2002): 112–129. doi: 10.1177/1077727X02031001005.

National Center for Complementary and Alternative Medicine (NCCAM). "Relaxation Techniques for Health: An Introduction." NCCAM D461. February 2013. nccam .nih.gov/health/stress/relaxation.htm%E2%80%8E.

National Center for Education Statistics. "Fast Facts: Graduation Rates." nces.ed.gov/ FastFacts/display.asp?id=40.

National Center for Education Statistics. "Table 376. Percentage of First-Time Full-Time Bachelor's Degree-Seeking Students at 4-Year Institutions Who Completed a Bachelor's Degree, by Race/Ethnicity, Time to Completion, Sex, and Control of Institution: Selected Cohort Entry Years, 1996 Through 2005." nces.ed.gov/ programs/digest/d12/tables/dt12_376.asp.

National Institutes of Health. "Information about the Brain." *Biological Sciences Curriculum Study*, NIH Curriculum Supplement Series (Bethesda, MD: National Institutes of Health, 2007–). ncbi.nlm.nih.gov/books/NBK20367.

Nikken, Peter, and Jeroen Jansz. "Developing Scales to Measure Parental Mediation of Young Children's Internet Use." *Learning, Media and Technology* 31, no. 2 (2012): 1–17. doi: 10.1080/17439884.2013.782038.

Nuutinen, Teija, Carola Ray, and Eva Roos. "Do Computer Use, TV Viewing, and the Presence of the Media in the Bedroom Predict School-Aged Children's Sleep Habits in a Longitudinal Study?" *BMC Public Health* 13, no. 1 (2013): 684. doi: 10.1186/1471-2458-13-684.

Olopade, Dayo. "Baby and Child Care, the African Way." *New York Times*, May 23, 2012. latitude.blogs.nytimes.com/2012/05/23/african-hands-off-parenting-breeds -resilience-in-kids/?_php=true&_type=blogs&_r=0.

Parent, André, and Lili-Naz Hazrati. "Functional Anatomy of the Basal Ganglia. I. The Cortico-Basal Ganglia-Thalamo-Cortical Loop." *Brain Research Reviews* 20, no. 1 (1995): 91–127. doi: 10.1016/0165-0173(94)00007-C.

"Parents Give Schools Low Grades for Prevention of Bullying and School Violence." *C. S. Mott Children's Hospital: National Poll on Children's Health* 7, no. 4 (2009). mottnpch.org/reports-surveys/parents-give-schools-low-grades-prevention -bullying-and-school-violence.

Perie, M., W. Grigg, and P. Donahue. *The Nation's Report Card: Reading 2005.* Washington, DC: National Center for Education Statistics, 2005.

Pressman, Robert M., and Steve C. Imber. "Relationship of Children's Daytime Behavior Problems with Bedtime Routines/Practices: A Family Context and the Consideration of Faux-ADHD." *American Journal of Family Therapy* 39, no. 5 (2011): 404–418. doi: 10.1080/01926187.2011.601218.

Pressman, Robert M., Judith Owens, Allison Schettini, Melissa Nemon. "Examining the Interface of Family and Personal Traits, Media, and Academic Imperatives Using the Learning Habit Study." *American Journal of Family Therapy*, in press.

Prochaska, James O., John C. Norcross, and Carlo C. DiClemente. *Changing for Good: The Revolutionary Program That Explains the Six Stages of Change and Teaches You How to Free Yourself from Bad Habits.* New York: William Morrow, 1994.

Reyna, Valerie F. *The Adolescent Brain: Learning, Reasoning, and Decision Making.* Washington, DC: American Psychological Association, 2012.

Robbins, Steven B., Jeff Allen, Alex Casillas, Christina Hamme Peterson, and Huy Le. "Unraveling the Differential Effects of Motivational and Skills, Social, and Self-Management Measures from Traditional Predictors of College Outcomes." *Journal of Educational Psychology* 98, no. 3 (2006): 598–616. doi: 10.1037/0022-0663.98.3.598.

Roberts, Kathryn. "The Linguistic Demands of the Common Core State Standards for Reading and Writing Informational Text in the Primary Grades." *Seminars in Speech and Language* 33, no. 2 (2012): 146–159. doi: 10.1055/s-0032-1310314.

Rostand, Edmond. *Cyrano de Bergerac.* Paris: 1897.

Samtani, Hiten. "Common Core Standards Boon to E-Learning Industry." WNYC. August 3, 2012. wnyc.org/story/302125-common-core-standards-boon-to-e -learning-industry.

Schaffer, M., S. Clark, and E. L. Jeglic. "The Role of Empathy and Parenting Style in the Development of Antisocial Behaviors." *Crime & Delinquency* 55, no. 4 (2009): 586–599. doi: 10.1177/0011128708321359.

Schurgin O'Keeffe, Gwenn, Kathleen Clarke-Pearson, and Council on Communications and Media. "The Impact of Social Media on Children, Adolescents, and Families." *Pediatrics* 127, no. 4 (2011): 800–804. doi: 10.1542/peds.2011-0054.

Shaffer, Suzanne. "Parent vs Students: Biggest College Bound Conflicts." More Than a Test Score. December 22, 2013. morethanatestscore.com/2013/12/22/parent-vs -students-biggest-college-bound-conflicts.

Shek, Daniel T., L. K. Chan, and T. Y. Lee. "Parenting Styles, Parent-Adolescent Conflict, and Psychological Well-Being of Adolescents with Low Academic Achievement in Hong Kong." *International Journal of Adolescent Medicine and Health* 9, no. 4 (1997): 233–248. doi: 10.1515/IJAMH.1997.9.4.233.

Sifferlin, Alexandra. "Study: More Active Teens Get Higher Test Scores." *Time*, October 22, 201. healthland.time.com/2013/10/22/study-more-active-teens-get -higher-test-scores.

Silva, Marc, Erin Dorso, Aisha Azhar, and Kimberly Renk. "The Relationship Among Parenting Styles Experienced during Childhood, Anxiety, Motivation, and Academic Success in College Students." *Journal of College Student Retention: Research, Theory and Practice* 9, no. 2 (2007): 149–167. doi: 10.2190/CS.9.2.b.

Slicker, E. K. "The Relationship of Parenting Style to Older Adolescent Life-skills Development in the United States." *Young* 13, no. 3 (2005): 227–245. doi: 10.1177/1103308805054211.

Steinberg, Laurence. "We Know Some Things: Parent-Adolescent Relationships in Retrospect and Prospect." *Journal of Research on Adolescence* 11, no. 1 (2001): 1–19. doi: 10.1111/1532-7795.00001.

Stöber, Joachim. "Dimensions of Test Anxiety: Relations to Ways of Coping with Pre-Exam Anxiety and Uncertainty." *Anxiety, Stress and Coping* 17, no. 3 (2004): 213–226. doi: 10.1080/10615800412331292615.

Swing, E. L., D. A. Gentile, C. A. Anderson, and D. A. Walsh. "Television and Video Game Exposure and the Development of Attention Problems." *Pediatrics* 126, no. 2 (2010): 214–221. doi: 10.1542/peds.2009-1508.

Tarazi, Bassam. "The Counterintuitive Ingredient to Experiencing Success." Positively Positive. July 30, 2012. positivelypositive.com/2012/07/30/the-counterintuitive -ingredient-to-experiencing-success.

"Too Much Homework Can Cause Stress, Depression and Lower Grades, Studies Suggest." Factual Facts. January 8, 2013. factualfacts.com/science-facts/too -much-homework-can-cause-stress-depression-and-lower-grades-studies -suggest.

Trudeau, François, and Roy J. Shephard. "Physical Education, School Physical Activity, School Sports and Academic Performance." *International Journal of Behavioral Nutrition and Physical Activity* 5, no. 1 (2008): 10. doi: 10.1186/1479-5868-5-10.

Wallace, Kelly. "Forget TV! iPhones and iPads Dazzle Babies." CNN. October 29, 2013. cnn.com/2013/10/29/living/parents-babies-kids-screen-time-guidelines.

Wartella, Ellen, Lee H. June, and Allison G. Caplovitz. "Children and Interactive Media: Research Compendium Update." Children's Digital Media Center, University of Texas at Austin. November 2002. academic.evergreen.edu/curricular/evs/ readings/markleIntro.pdf.

Weinberg, Harvey A. "Raising the ADHD Age Threshold." *The ADHD Report* 19, no. 2 (2011): 1–3. doi: 10.1521/adhd.2011.19.2.1.

Wentworth, Craig. "The Role of Collegiate Sports Participation in Preparing Women for Executive Leadership." EdD dissertation. Athens: University of Georgia, 2009. athenaeum.libs.uga.edu/handle/10724/11744.

Wheatcroft, Rebecca, and Cathy Creswell. "Parents' Cognitions and Expectations About Their Pre-School Children: The Contribution of Parental Anxiety and Child Anxiety." *British Journal of Developmental Psychology* 25, no. 3 (2007): 435–441. doi: 10.1348/026151006X173288.

Winerman, Lea. "What Sets High Achievers Apart?" *Monitor on Psychology* 44, no. 11 (2013): 28. apa.org/monitor/2013/12/high-achievers.aspx.

Xin, Ye. "SASS: Chinese Students Mentally Healthier Than Asian Peers." *People's Daily Online*, April 19, 2011. english.peopledaily.com.cn/90001/90776/90882/ 7355015.html.

Zibreg, Christian. "Mark Zuckerberg Sweats over Facebook Privacy Talk at D8." Geek. June 3, 2010. geek.com/news/mark-zuckerberg-sweats-over-facebook-privacy-talk-at-d8-1260950.

Zygouris-Coe, V., and C. Goodwiler. "Language and Literacy Demands of Content Area Courses in the Era of the Common Core State Standards: Teachers' Perspectives and the Role of the SLP." *Perspectives on School-Based Issues* 14, no. 3 (2013): 61–67. doi: 10.1044/sbi14.3.61.

# NOTES

## INTRODUCTION

1. National Center for Education Statistics, "Fast Facts: Graduation Rates," nces .ed.gov/FastFacts/display.asp?id=40.
2. Ibid., "Table 376. Percentage of First-Time Full-Time Bachelor's Degree-Seeking Students at 4-Year Institutions Who Completed a Bachelor's Degree, by Race/ Ethnicity, Time to Completion, Sex, and Control of Institution: Selected Cohort Entry Years, 1996 Through 2005," nces.ed.gov/programs/digest/d12/tables/ dt12_376.asp.
3. Robert Pressman, Judith Owens, Allison Schettini, and Melissa Nemon, "Examining the Interface of Family and Personal Traits, Media, and Academic Imperatives Using the Learning Habit Study," *American Journal of Family Therapy*, in press.
4. Kaiser Family Foundation, "Generation M$^2$: Media in the Lives of 8- to 18-Year-Olds," January 20, 2010, kff.org/other/event/generation-m2-media-in-the-lives-of.

## CHAPTER ONE: CONNECTING THE DISCONNECT

1. Common Core State Standards Initiative, "National Governors Association and State Education Chiefs Launch Common State Academic Standards," corestandards .org/articles/8-national-governors-association-and-state-education-chiefs-launch -common-state-academic-standards.
2. Suzanne Shaffer, "Parent vs Students: Biggest College Bound Conflicts," More Than a Test Score, December 22, 2013, morethanatestscore.com/2013/12/22/parent-vs -students-biggest-college-bound-conflicts.
3. Claire Evans, "Student Debt Tops List of Parental Concerns," Beattie Communications, July 23, 2012, beattiegroup.com/prclients/pr-press-releases/2012/july/student -debt-tops-list-of-parental-concerns.aspx.
4. "Parents Give Schools Low Grades for Prevention of Bullying and School Violence," *C. S. Mott Children's Hospital: National Poll on Children's Health* 7, no. 4 (2009), mottnpch.org/reports-surveys/parents-give-schools-low-grades-prevention-bullying -and-school-violence.
5. Anthony P. Carnevale, Nicole Smith, and Jeff Strohl, *Help Wanted: Projections of Jobs and Education Requirements through 2018* (Washington, DC: Center on Education and the Workforce, Georgetown University, 2010), p. 3, survey.csuprojects

.org/uploads/j-/ul/j-ul01tOShATFY88Kw3B7g/Georgetown-Center-on-Education
-and-the-Workforce-jobs-projections.pdf.

6. D. Dweck, *Mindset: The New Psychology of Success* (New York, Random House, 2006).

7. D. Goleman, *Emotional Intelligence: Why It Can Matter More Than IQ* (New York, Bantam Books. 2006).

8. Josh Kovner and Edmund H. Mahony, "Adam Lanza: A 'Quiet, Odd' Loner Living on the Fringes," *Hartford Courant*, December 15, 2012, articles.courant.com/2012-12-15/news/hc-adam-lanza-newtown-shooting-1216-20121215_1_nancy-lanza-adam-lanza-marsha-lanza.

## CHAPTER TWO: HOW LEARNING HABITS START

1. Haim G. Ginott, *Between Parent and Teenager* (New York: Scribner, 1969).

2. Rebecca Jackson, "How Cell Phone Use Is Destroying Your Kids' Short-Term Memory," *Huffington Post*, September 30, 2013, huffingtonpost.com/rebecca-jackson/how-cell-phone-use-is-destroying-your-kids-short-term-memory_b_4016345.html.

## CHAPTER THREE: MEDIA MATTERS

1. Hiten Samtani, "Common Core Standards Boon to E-Learning Industry," WNYC, August 3, 2012, wnyc.org/story/302125-common-core-standards-boon-to-e-learning-industry.

2. Robert Pressman, Judith Owens, Allison Schettini, and Melissa Nemon, "Examining the Interface of Family and Personal Traits, Media, and Academic Imperatives Using the Learning Habit Study," *American Journal of Family Therapy*, in press.

3. Kelly Wallace, "Forget TV! iPhones and iPads Dazzle Babies," CNN, October 30, 2013, cnn.com/2013/10/29/living/parents-babies-kids-screen-time-guidelines.

4. Ellen A. Wartella, June H. Lee, and Allison G. Caplovitz, "Children and Interactive Media: Research Compendium Update," Children's Digital Media Center, University of Texas at Austin, November 2002, academic.evergreen.edu/curricular/evs/readings/markleIntro.pdf.

5. Andi Sporkin, "Top-Selling Authors Adopt New York Area Schools, Meet with Local Students," Association of American Publishers, March 10, 2012. publishers.org/press/54.

6. Rebecca Jackson. "How Changes in Media Habits Could Transform Your Child's Mental Health." *Huffington Post*, October 29, 2013. huffingtonpost.com/rebecca-jackson/how-changes-in-media-habits-could-transform-your-childs-health_b_4054881.html.

7. Marshall McLuhan, *Understanding Media: The Extensions of Man* (New York: McGraw-Hill, 1964).

8. "An Overview of McLuhan's Thinking," Philosophical Society. philosophicalsociety.com/archives/McLuhan's%20Philosophy.htm#II. An Overview of McLuhan's Thinking.

9. Rebecca Jackson, "How Cell Phone Use Is Destroying Your Kids' Short-Term Memory," *Huffington Post*, September 30, 2013, huffingtonpost.com/rebecca -jackson/how-cell-phone-use-is-destroying-your-kids-short-term-memory _b_4016345.html.

10. David Callahan, "Online Time Can Hobble Brain's Important Work," KTH, September 20, 2013. kth.se/en/aktuellt/nyheter/online-time-can-hobble-brain-s -important-work-1.415391.

CHAPTER FOUR: THE HOMEWORK HABIT

1. Heidi Butkus. "Is." In *Sing and Spell Sight Words*, vol.1. HeidiSongs. Heidi Butkus, 2004. CD.

2. David Barboza, "Shanghai Schools' Approach Pushes Students to Top of Tests," *New York Times*, December 29, 2010, nytimes.com/2010/12/30/world/asia/ 30shanghai.html?pagewanted=all&_r=0.

3. A. E. Gottfried, J. Fleming, and A. W. Gottfried, "Continuity of Academic Intrinsic Motivation from Childhood through Late Adolescence: A Longitudinal Study," *Journal of Educational Psychology* 93, no. 1 (2001): 3–13.

4. John Mark Froiland, "Parental Autonomy Support and Student Learning Goals: A Preliminary Examination of an Intrinsic Motivation Intervention," *Child & Youth Care Forum* 40, no. 2 (2011): 135–149. doi: 10.1007/s10566-010-9126-2.

5. Ibid.

6. National Governors Association Center for Best Practices and Council of Chief State School Officers, Common Core State Standards for English Language Arts and Literacy in History/Social Studies, Science, and Technical Subjects (Washington, DC: Authors, 2010).

7. Karl Taro Greenfield, "The Homework Wars: How Much Is Too Much?" *Atlantic*, October 2013. theatlantic.com/special-report/homework-debate.

8. Jean Lawrence, "Train Your Brain with Exercise," WebMD, June 26, 2007, webmd .com/fitness-exercise/features/train-your-brain-with-exercise.

9. Jenna Goudreau, "The Secret to Being a Power Woman: Play Team Sports," *Forbes*, October 10, 2011, forbes.com/sites/jennagoudreau/2011/10/12/secret-power -woman-play-team-sports-sarah-palin-meg-whitman-indra-nooyi.

10. Ibid.

11. F. Trudeau and R. Shephard, "Physical Education, School Physical Activity, School Sports and Academic Performance," *International Journal of Behavioral Nutrition and Physical Activity* 5 (2008): 10, ijbnpa.org/content/5/1/10.

12. National Center for Educational Statistics, "Table 376. Percentage of First-Time Full-Time Bachelor's Degree-Seeking Students at 4-Year Institutions Who Completed a Bachelor's Degree, by Race/Ethnicity, Time to Completion, Sex, and Control of Institution: Selected Cohort Entry Years, 1996 Through 2005," nces.ed.gov/ programs/digest/d12/tables/dt12_376.asp.

13. Sam DeHority, "Study Suggests Physical Activity Helps Athletes Perform Better on Mental Tests," *Stack*, December 11, 2013, stack.com/2013/12/11/exercise-mental -test.

14. Alexandra Sifferlin, "Study: More Active Teens Get Higher Test Scores," *Time*, October 22, 2013, healthland.time.com/2013/10/22/study-more-active-teens-get-higher-test-scores.

15. Ibid.

16. Ibid.

17. Ye Xin, "SASS: Chinese Students Mentally Healthier Than Asian Peers," *People's Daily Online*, April 19, 2011, english.peopledaily.com.cn/90001/90776/90882/7355015.html.

18. S. B. Robbins, J. Allen, A. Casillas, et al., "Unraveling the Differential Effects of Motivational and Skills, Social, and Self-Management Measures from Traditional Predictors of College Outcomes, *Journal of Education Psychology* 98, no. 3 (2006): 598–616, doi: 10.1037/0022-0663.98.3.598.

19. Connie Juel, "Learning to Read and Write: A Longitudinal Study of 54 Children from First through Fourth Grades," *Journal of Educational Psychology* 80, no. 4 (1988): 437–447, doi: 10.1037/0022-0663.80.4.437.

20. Ibid.

21. M. Perie, W. Grigg, and P. Donahue, *The Nation's Report Card: Reading 2005*, NCES 2006-451 (Washington, DC: U.S. Government Printing Office, 2005).

22. I. V. S. Mullis, M. O. Martin, E. J. Gonzalez, and A. M. Kennedy, *PIRLS 2001 International Report: IEA's Study of Reading Literacy Achievement in Primary School in 35 Countries* (Chestnut Hill, MA: Boston College, 2003).

## CHAPTER FIVE: TIME FLIES

1. Robert Pressman, Judith Owens, Allison Schettini, and Melissa Nemon, "Examining the Interface of Family and Personal Traits, Media, and Academic Imperatives Using the Learning Habit Study," *American Journal of Family Therapy*, in press.

2. Cara Santa Maria, "Insanity: The Real Definition," *Huffington Post*, updated January 4, 2012, huffingtonpost.com/2011/12/20/insanity-definition_n_1159927.html.

3. S. B. Robbins, J. Allen, A. Casillas, et al., "Unraveling the Differential Effects of Motivational and Skills, Social, and Self-Management Measures from Traditional Predictors of College Outcomes, *Journal of Education Psychology* 98, no. 3 (2006): 598–616, doi: 10.1037/0022-0663.98.3.598.

## CHAPTER SIX: WANTING ISN'T ENOUGH

1. "Jim Carrey." Feeling Success. feelingsuccess.com/jim-carrey.

2. Robert Pressman, Judith Owens, Allison Schettini, and Melissa Nemon, "Examining the Interface of Family and Personal Traits, Media, and Academic Imperatives Using the Learning Habit Study," *American Journal of Family Therapy*, in press.

## CHAPTER SEVEN: MESSAGE SENT = MESSAGE RECEIVED

1. Christian Zibreg, "Mark Zuckerberg Sweats over Facebook Privacy Talk at D8." Geek, June 3, 2010, geek.com/news/mark-zuckerberg-sweats-over-facebook-privacy-talk-at-d8-1260950.

2. Louise Penny, *Bury Your Dead* (New York: St. Martin's Press, 2010).

3. S. Donaldson-Pressman and R. Pressman, *The Narcissistic Family: Diagnosis and Treatment* (San Francisco, CA: Jossey-Bass, 1994).

4. Ibid.

## CHAPTER EIGHT: OPTIONS VERSUS CONSEQUENCES

1. "Michael Jordan—Failure." YouTube. youtube.com/watch?v=GuXZFQKKF7A.

2. Doug Baldwin, "Why vs. How," Stanford: Home of Champions, champions.stanford .edu/voices-of-champions/why-vs-how.

3. S. Donaldson-Pressman and R. Pressman, *The Narcissistic Family: Diagnosis and Treatment* (San Francisco, CA: Jossey-Bass, 1994).

## CHAPTER NINE: IGNORING THE MARSHMALLOW

1. Angela Duckworth and Martin E. P. Seligman, "Self-Discipline Outdoes IQ in Predicting Academic Performance of Adolescents," *Psychological Science* 16, no. 12 (2005): 939–944.

2. National Institutes of Health, "Information about the Brain." *Biological Sciences Curriculum Study*, NIH Curriculum Supplement Series (Bethesda, MD: National Institutes of Health, 2007–), ncbi.nlm.nih.gov/books/NBK20367.

3. Chris Broussard, "The King James Version," ESPN, October 15, 2013, espn.go .com/nba/story/_/id/9824909.

4. Walter Mischel, Ozlem Ayduk, Marc G. Berman, et al. " 'Willpower' over the Life Span: Decomposing Self-Regulation," *Social Cognitive and Affective Neuroscience* 6, no. 2 (2011): 252–256, scan.oxfordjournals.org/content/6/2/252.short.

5. Ibid.

6. Ibid.

7. Gwenn Schurgin O'Keeffe, Kathleen Clarke-Pearson, and Council on Communications and Media, "The Impact of Social Media on Children, Adolescents, and Families," *Pediatrics* 127, no. 4 (2011): 800–804, pediatrics.aappublications.org/ content/127/4/800.full.

8. Herbert Benson and Miriam Z. Klipper, *The Relaxation Response* (New York: HarperCollins, 1975).

9. Roger Jahnke, "Breathing Exercises and Self-Healing," Mercola.com, February 20, 2000, articles.mercola.com/sites/articles/archive/2000/02/20/breathing-part-one .aspx.

10. Stephen Mellalieu and Sheldon Hanton, *Advances in Applied Sport Psychology: A Review* (New York: Routledge, 2008).

11. National Center for Complementary and Alternative Medicine (NCCAM), "Relaxation Techniques for Health: An Introduction," NCCAM D461, February 2013, nccam.nih.gov/health/stress/relaxation.htm%E2%80%8E.

12. Benson, Herbert, *The Relaxation Response* (New York: Morrow, 1975).

13. "Too Much Homework Can Cause Stress, Depression and Lower Grades, Studies Suggest," Factual Facts, January 8, 2013, factualfacts.com/science-facts/too-much -homework-can-cause-stress-depression-and-lower-grades-studies-suggest.

14. E. L. Swing, D. A. Gentile, C. A. Anderson, and D. A. Walsh, "Television and Video Game Exposure and the Development of Attention Problems," *Pediatrics* 126, no. 2 (2010): 214–221, doi:10.1542/peds.2009-1508.

15. Julie Henry, "Ban Computers from Schools until Children Reach Age 9, Says Expert," *Telegraph*, June 13, 2010, telegraph.co.uk/education/primaryeducation/7823259/Ban-computers-from-schools-until-children-reach-age-9-says-expert.html.

16. Ibid.

17. "ADHD and Substance Abuse," WebMD, May 15, 2012, webmd.com/add-adhd/guide/adhd-and-substance-abuse-is-there-a-link.

## CHAPTER TEN: TRUE GRIT

1. Lea Winerman, "What Sets High Achievers Apart?" *Monitor on Psychology* 44, no. 11 (2013): p. 28.

2. Phillip L. Ackerman, Ruth Kanfer, and Margaret E. Beier, "Trait Complex, Cognitive Ability, and Domain Knowledge Predictors of Baccalaureate Success, STEM Persistence, and Gender Differences," *Journal of Educational Psychology* 105, no. 3 (2013): 911–927, doi: 10.1037/a0032338.

3. Winerman, op cit., p. 28.

4. Ibid., p. 30.

5. Dayo Olopade, "Baby and Child Care, the African Way," *New York Times*, May 23, 2012, latitude.blogs.nytimes.com/2012/05/23/african-hands-off-parenting-breeds-resilience-in-kids/?_php=true&_type=blogs&_r=0.

## CHAPTER ELEVEN: STARTING NOW

1. Donaldson-Pressman, op cit.

# INDEX

# ABOUT THE AUTHORS

## Stephanie Donaldson-Pressman

Stephanie Donaldson-Pressman (MSW, LICSW) is a psychotherapist, consultant, and internationally recognized author in the field of family therapy. She is the principal author of *The Narcissistic Family: Diagnosis and Treatment*, one of the bestselling psychiatric texts of all time. A longtime advocate for military personnel and their families, she was featured in the award-winning documentary film *Brats: Our Journey Home* (a Donna Musil film, 2006). Ms. Donaldson-Pressman co-authored *Good Nights Now* and a book for children, *Matilda & Maxwell Good Night*, for Good Parent, Inc.

She maintains a robust private practice and thoroughly enjoys her work with children and families. A former teacher, she has a strong background in education—an advantage when working with parents and children who are experiencing school-related problems. Stephanie is an avid baseball fan who tries to get to the ballpark whenever possible; she still finds time to escape to the beach with a good book and her favorite beach buddies—her three grandchildren.

## Rebecca Jackson

Rebecca Jackson is a neuropsychological assistant, parenting expert, and author. She lives with her family in Rhode Island. Her articles and research have appeared in over 400 publications including *Huffington Post*, *WebMD*, and *Parents Magazine*. An advocate for the

Adopt-a-School program, she has worked on expanding literacy programs throughout the country.

In 2011 she formed the company Good Parent, Inc. to provide scientific research, education, and entertainment to parents, children and educators. She is passionate about improving the lives of families and helping communities, parents, and schools to work together to enhance the long-term quality of our children's lives.

## Robert M. Pressman

Robert is a board-certified family psychologist and a fellow of the American Academy of Couple and Family Psychology. He is a full-time pediatric psychologist practitioner, the research director of New England Center for Pediatric Psychology, and the author of several professional books. Dr. Pressman is an active member of the American Psychological Association, the Society for Family Psychology, the Society for Media Psychology and Technology, the Society for Group Psychology and Group Psychotherapy, and the Society for Clinical Child and Adolescent Psychology. He is attributed with the discovery of Faux-ADHD, a condition that resembles ADHD but is related to non-organic factors.

He and Stephanie reside together happily in New England and are the proud parents of three children and three adorable grandchildren—two teens and one five-year-old. He loves family gatherings, time at the beach, and solitary walks to the river. Martial arts has been an important part of his life for which he continues to train actively.